Disability Discrimination Law

Fourth Edition

By The Same Author

Unfair Dismissal Law

Maternity Rights Law

Taxation of Termination Payments

Disability Discrimination Law

Fourth Edition
2017

by

John Munro Wright,
LL.B (Hons); LL.M.

www.employment-law-expert.co.uk

England, United Kingdom

Published by www.lulu.com

DISABILITY DISCRIMINATION LAW – FOURTH EDITION

This title is published under the employment-law-expert series. First published in 2011 by www.e-authorsdirect.com of Hampshire, England, United Kingdom.
Email: employmentlawexpert@gmail.com
Website: http://www.employment-law-expert.co.uk

Disclaimer

The information contained in this book constitutes information of a general nature and does not constitute legal advice to any particular person in any particular situation. It should not be relied upon as being up to date; the law or policies may have changed since the book was published; and it should not be relied upon as legal or professional advice or as a substitute for it. A suitably qualified professional should be consulted if specific advice or information is required.

Neither the author nor the distributor(s) nor the publisher(s) accept liability or are held responsible for any losses suffered by any person caused either directly or indirectly by reliance on information herewith contained or by acting or not acting on the information contained in the website.

ISBN 978-0-244-91795-1

Formatting by www.bookformatting.co.uk
Book covers design by www.absolutegraphics.co.uk
Printed and bound in the European Community by Lulu Press, Inc.

Contents

To workers everywhere who have disabilities, many of whom are not disabled by their disabilities

INTRODUCTION

At the time of updating this book to a fourth edition, the United Kingdom is engaged in the process of leaving the European Union. When the leaving process is completed, the UK will no longer be a member state of the EU but, instead, will revert to being a sovereign country once again. Upon leaving the EU, most of the existing EU law will remain as part of UK law. However, over the coming years, various parts of EU law which the government deem to be inappropriate or not needed as part of UK law will be repealed and revoked as and when required. As for the leaving process itself, this could be either a lengthy drawn-out process taking more than the two years allowed for under Article 50 of the Treaty of Lisbon or, if the government finds that the European Commission on behalf of the remaining twenty seven member states conduct negotiations unreasonably and obstructively, the UK government may decide to merely repeal the European Communities Act 1972 which would then have the effect of terminating instantly the membership of the UK from the EU and that, in turn, would mean that any part of the leaving negotiations with the EU would not be subject to a review by the Court of Justice of the European Union. As for trade between the UK and the EU, the UK buys far more from the EU than the EU buys from the UK so any tariffs imposed on goods and services would impact detrimentally on the twenty seven remaining EU states, particularly Germany and France, and not on the UK. My own opinion as a lawyer with expertise in European law is that the UK should choose the latter option and effect a quick clean break rather than get mired in a long drawn-out process of negotiations with the EU Commission and the twenty seven remaining EU member states. There are about two hundred countries in the world with whom the UK can trade. In contrast, the EU has just twenty seven member states most of which are failing economically. The EU is currently dominated by Germany because it is the wealthiest member state. The Euro is, in effect, the former German Deutschmark renamed the Euro and, for this reason, it is the Germans who decide and control monetary policy in the EU. This has caused economic and social hardship for those EU member states which find the value of the Euro is too high for their economies yet they cannot improve their competitiveness in relation to international trade by devaluing and achieving an appropriate level for their currencies because they no longer have their own national currencies but have the Euro instead. The departure of the UK from the EU could be a great success; or it could be a great disaster. Only unknown events which have yet to occur over the course of future years will reveal what the fate of the UK will be.

Currently, in 2017 when this fourth edition was published, and over the last few years, the government has been pursuing an economic policy that has impacted adversely on many disabled people in the UK who, because of the effects of their disabilities, are unable to take up paid employment or if they are able to do so work shorter hours than they would prefer and, because of this, rely upon the government for the whole or part of their income. To reduce the cost to the exchequer and, effectively, to taxpayers of which the highest earners pay the majority of income tax, the government has required and looks set to continue to require more working age disabled people to transfer away from State disability benefits onto the lower rated unemployment benefit. To carry out this policy the government are using and are likely to continue to use private companies to assess disabled peoples' fitness to work where the overriding aim that these companies have been instructed to achieve is to assess as many disabled people as possible as being fit to work. One common test that is used is one which tests disabled peoples' ability to walk over a set distance. If they can do that they are assessed as being fit for work, albeit for some amount of paid employment which mean that some or all of their disability benefits, including an entitlement to a government-funded vehicle under the Mobility Scheme is withdrawn. But under the disability legislation the test is not whether or not a disabled person can walk a set distance but, instead, their *ability* to walk a given distance. Many disabled people can walk the required distance set in the test but many can only do so with the greatest difficult and in great pain. People who have disabilities often have good and bad periods where on some days they are reasonably well whereas on other days they can be incapacitated. If they have to attend a government fitness to work assessment on a day when they feel fairly well, they should inform the assessor of that fact and remind the assessor that they, the disabled person, have a disability that is a protected characteristic under the Equality Act 2010 and that they, the disabled person, are a disabled person if the disability has lasted for twelve months or more or is likely to do so or is likely to recur.

When it comes to mental issues, a person suffering from the distressing psychological condition of agoraphobia, although he or she may well be physically healthy, can often not walk unaccompanied along a street because at some stage or stages of the journey he or she will experience a disabling and often incapacitating panic attack or attacks as a result of this mental condition. As a result of EU legislation, disabled people do have an entitlement to a range of legal rights which they can lawfully use to enforce their rights and obtain recompense by way of compensation at an employment tribunal or damages at a civil court if they suffer financial and psychological losses when their rights are breached. But the onus is on them to be proactive and do that. Very few women who are subjected to pregnancy and maternity discrimination choose to enforce the rights given to them by Parliament to regain what they have been deprived of or for recompense. As a result, pregnancy and maternity discrimination against working women remain stubbornly high. Disabled working-age people need to be aware that if they, likewise, choose to forego the legal rights awarded to them then disability discrimination is likely to increase to the chronically high level of pregnancy and maternity discrimination, the latter two being sex discrimination.

On the subject of legal rights and enforcing them at employment tribunals, from the 29 July 2013 the Conservative/Liberal Democrats Coalition government imposed a range of financial charges on claimants who for whatever reason need to make claims against their employers, former employers or would-be employers for recompense for breaches of employment law. The reason put forward by the government for requiring claimants to pay charges is that users of employment tribunals should pay towards the administrative costs and upkeep. Ordinarily, this would be an acceptable reason. But the government has set the range of financial charges, which it calls 'fees,' at an unreasonably high level, so high in fact that the so-called fees are effectively a range of penal taxes. Governments use taxation as a way of raising revenue from activities which are difficult to avoid such as imposing it on motor vehicle fuels or income. It also imposes tax on things it wants to discourage, such as the drinking of alcohol and the smoking of tobacco. It would seem that the reason for making claimants pay what are in effect a range of high taxes in order to make claims to employment tribunals (e.g. £1,200 to make a claim to an employment tribunal for it to hear a claim for unfair dismissal) is to discourage or inhibit those who believe they have had their employment law rights breached.

Prior to the Disability Discrimination Act 1995 receiving Royal Assent on 08 November 1995, the only legislation that provided some help for disabled workers was the Disabled Persons (Employment) Act 1944. This Act came into being towards the end of the Second World War and at the time the legislators probably had in mind that there would be a number of disabled former military service people returning to civilian life who should be given a degree of beneficial treatment when resuming or seeking work. The Act of 1944 introduced a quota system under which employers with twenty or more employees were required to ensure that at least three per cent of their workforce consisted of registered disabled people. This requirement was routinely ignored by both employers and the government, the latter of which rarely enforced it as there were only three prosecutions during that thirty years period to 1974. Fortunately and coincidentally, there was full employment in the UK between 1944 and the mid-1970s which meant that many workers with disabilities were able to find jobs in mainstream employment.

For fifteen years from 1995 to 2010, the Disability Discrimination Act 1995 prohibited unlawful discrimination against disabled workers and other disabled people. Where unlawful discrimination did take place, the Act provided disabled people with a right of access to tribunals and the courts to obtain remedies if they were unlawfully discriminated against because of their disabilities. The Disability Discrimination Act 1995 was introduced by a Conservative government that decided to follow other common-law jurisdiction countries such as Australia, New Zealand and the United States which had introduced disability-related legislation in the early 1990s. Since its inception in 1957, the European Union has pursued a policy which is that disabled workers and female labour should not be regarded as reserve pools of marginalised low paid labour but that both groups, as a fundamental human right, should not only have full access to the employment market but must be able to do so on the same terms as other workers, including receiving equal pay for work of equal value.

On 01 October 2010, the Disability Discrimination Act 1995 was repealed when the Equality Act 2010 came into force on that day. This latter Act replaced all the then existing discrimination legislation and consolidated it into one Act. In addition to the repealed of the Disability Discrimination Act 1995, the new Act repealed and replaced the Equal Pay Act 1970, the Sex Discrimination Act 1975, the Race Relations Act 1976 and much of the Equality Act 2006 as well as the Employment Equality Regulations on religion or belief, sexual orientation and age plus other ancillary legislation. Apart from harmonising and re-stating the provisions of previous anti-discrimination legislation, the Equality Act 2010 now gives a single approach where appropriate and strengthens the law to help achieve equality in the workplace as well as in all other areas of society.

Most of the statements and principles of law which were stated in judgments by employment tribunals, the Employment Appeal Tribunal and the higher courts under the Disability Discrimination Act 1995 are still relevant under the Equality Act 2010 albeit under new section headings and using new statutory wording. Some provisions, like disability-related discrimination under s.3A(1) of the Disability Discrimination Act 1995 that was effectively rendered impotent by the judgment of the House of Lords in the case of London Borough of Lewisham v Malcolm (2008), were not re-enacted in the Equality Act 2010. In addition to that case, this book gives a summary of the other major cases and the principles of law which arose under the Disability Discrimination Act 1995 together with a comparative guide that shows how the provisions of the Equality Act 2010 apply in relation to the former legislation.

The problem with section 3A(1), Disability Discrimination Act 1995 (disability-related discrimination) and the similarly worded section 24(1), which were referred to by the Law Lords in Malcolm (2008), was - in addition to the ambiguous wording of the sections - the requirement to identify 'the others' who were the comparators, and then the complainant had to show that he or she had been subjected to 'less favourable treatment' by the employer. In other words and more specifically, the treatment of the disabled person 'for a reason which relates to the disabled person's disability' had to be compared to the way the employer treated or would have treated its non-disabled workers 'to whom that reason does not or would not apply.' In contrast, the Equality Act 2010 has a new provision being section 15 ('Discrimination arising from disability') under which a person, such as an employer, is regarded as having unlawfully discriminated against a disabled person if (a) the employer treats the worker unfavourably because of something arising in consequence of the worker's disability, and (b) the employer cannot show that the treatment is a proportionate means of achieving a legitimate aim. So, under section 15 of the Equality Act 2010, there is now no requirement to identify comparators which means that instead of a claimant having to show 'less favourable treatment' as was required under ss.3A(1) and 24(1), Disability Discrimination Act 1995, all he or she now need do is show that he or she was treated 'unfavourably' by the employer (because of something arising in consequence of his or her disability); and that the employer cannot show that the treatment is objectively justified (by being a proportionate means of achieving a legitimate aim).

Whereas there were three kinds of unlawful discrimination under the Disability Act 1995 being (i) direct discrimination, (ii) disability-related discrimination and (iii) a failure to take steps to make reasonable adjustments, under the Equality Act 2010 there are two main kinds of unlawful discrimination being (i) direct discrimination, (ii) indirect discrimination as well as six others being, (iii) discrimination arising from disability, (iv) a duty to take steps to make adjustments, (v) associative and perceptive discrimination, (vi) harassment, (vii) victimisation, and (viii) discriminatory advertisements. The Disability Discrimination Act 1995 contained no provision for indirect discrimination because direct discrimination itself was capable of being justified (section 5(3)), and Regulations specified the circumstances in which discriminatory treatment was or was not justified.

Another significant difference between the Equality Act 2010 and the Disability Discrimination Act 1995 is the protection now given by the law in section 4 of the Equality Act 2010 to disabled people and other minority groups of people who are often subjected to unlawful discrimination. Section 4 state the range of 'protected characteristics.' So if a person is subjected to unlawful discrimination because of one or more of these protected characteristics, he or she is entitled to seek a remedy to recover his or her losses, financial or personal, by making a claim to an employment tribunal or the civil courts. Section 4 lists nine protected characteristics and these are: age, disability, gender reassignment, marriage and civil partnership, pregnancy and maternity, race, religion or belief, sex, and sexual orientation. The effect of this provision, in part, is that unlawful discrimination could occur against a worker in a number of ways. The reason it could occur might be because of a protected characteristic he or she has or someone else has. Another reason it could occur might be because he or she is perceived to have a protected characteristic and is discriminated against because of that perceived protected characteristic. Also the reason it could occur might be because he or she associates with another person who has a protected characteristic. So, under the Equality Act 2010, a person could be subjected to unlawful discrimination not just because of his or her protected characteristic, such as his or her sex, sexual orientation, disability, etcetera, but also because he or she is wrongly perceived to be, for example, homosexual and for that reason is discriminated against or because he or she associates with another person who is, to give another example, disabled and, in the latter example, the worker is unlawfully discriminated against by his or her employer for the reason that the employer refuses to make reasonable adjustments to the worker's working time so that he or she can provide care for that disabled person.

Lastly, an interesting set of provisions which are included in the Equality Act 2010 is the Occupational Requirements Exceptions. These provisions lawfully permit an employer to discriminate against or in favour of a person who has a certain protected characteristic. For example, if objectively justified, an employer can require, as a condition of offering employment to a person, that the person must have a certain protected characteristic that is required for the job such as having a particular disability (for example, being deaf in that the job is to teach British Sign Language to other deaf people or being male for the job of Roman Catholic Priest). The Occupational Requirements Exceptions are to be found in Schedule 9, Part 1, of the Equality Act 2010. The Act recognises and accepts – at least for now – that some forms of work such as those within religious organisations (which are in the services sector of the economy) have been and are for doctrinal and traditional reasons reserved solely for those of one gender, namely male (e.g. those in the priesthood of Roman Catholic and Islamic religious organisations). Another religious organisation, being the Church of England, that allows both genders access to roles in its priesthood sought, until recently, to make use of the Occupational Requirements Exceptions by either precluding females from the senior clergy or, if promoting homosexual males to Bishops, required the latter not to be sexually active while holding that office. Whereas the Equality Act 2010, in Schedule 9, Part 1, allows what would normally be unlawful gender discrimination to be lawful in this regard, it does not allow a religious organisation to prohibit a person it employs from practising his or her sexuality as a condition of either being offered work or continuing to work. Arguably, there could be implied from the range of occupational requirements exceptions listed in sub-paragraph 4, which make lawful what would otherwise be unlawful discrimination, being the requirements to be of a particular sex, not to be a transsexual person, not to be married or a civil partner, a requirement as to sexual orientation, that the requirement (i) not to be married or (ii) as to sexual orientation is taken to mean that sexual abstinence is an integral part of the state of being unmarried or being of a certain sexual orientation but, as might be acknowledged, this implication or assertion looks very weak and probably unsustainable in a legal argument in a court of law. Where there is a conflict between the teachings or beliefs of a religion and the law, the latter will prevail. One thing that some people who have a strong religious belief are tempted to do is use their belief in their particular religion to justify what is an act of unlawful discrimination against others who do not follow that religion or any other religion or, if they do have a religious belief, do not follow it to the letter. Essentially, religious beliefs of all kinds are no more than formalised, albeit long-standing, sets of superstitious beliefs which are dignified by tradition and the support of national institutions and governments. When it comes to deciding which should take priority, be it peoples' religious beliefs or the law, then it is and must always be the latter because the latter is based on reason and rationality and has also been decided democratically and reflects the mores and the times in which we live. As Lord Justice Denning, Master of the Rolls and the senior judge of the Court of Appeal, said in 1977: 'Be ye ever so mighty, the law is above you.'

This book is divided into nine main sections. These guide the reader through the substantive law and the principles of law which have originated from the case authorities heard by tribunals and the courts from 1995 into 2017. The last section provides a comparative guide to the provisions of the Disability Discrimination Act 1995 as they relate to the new provisions of the Equality Act 2010.

01 July 2017.

Legislative List

1 UK statutes:

Disability Discrimination Act 1995	1.1, 1.2, 1.3, 1.4, 1.5, 1.6, 1.7, 1.8, 1.9, 2.1, 2.2, 2.3, 2.5, 2.6, 2.7, 2.8, 2.9, 2.10, 3.1, 3.2, 3.3, 3.4, 3.5, 3.6, 3.9, 3.10, 3.11, 3.12, 3.13, 3.14, 4.1, 4.2, 4.3, 4.5, 4.6, 4.7, 5.1, 5.2, 5.3, 5.4, 6.4, 6.1, 6.2, 6.3, 7.1, 7.2, 7.3, 7.5, 7.6, 8.3, 9.1,
s.1, 1(1)	1.2, 1.8, 2.2, 2.3, 2.5, 8.3, 9.1,
s.2	2.6, 8.3, 9.1,
s.3	6.1, 6.3, 8.3,
s.3A(1)(2)(3)(5)(6)	1.2, 1.3, 1.6, 2.1, 2.9, 2.10, 3.1, 3.2, 3.3, 3.4, 3.5, 3.9, 3.10, 3.13, 3.14, 4.1, 4.5, 4.7, 5.1, 5.2, 5.3, 5.4, 6.2, 6.3, 7.3, 9.1,
s.3B	1.4, 9.1,
s.4A(1)	1.2, 1.3, 1.6, 1.7, 3.3, 3.9, 3.10, 3.13, 4.1, 4.2, 4.3, 4.5, 4.6, 4.7, 5.2, 5.4, 6.2, 6.3, 9.1,

Employment Act 2008	7.1,
Employment Rights Act 1996	1.1, 1.10, 4.4, 6.2, 6.3, 7.1, 7.3, 7.4, 7.5, 8.3,
s.57A	6.3,
s.57B	6.3,
s.95(1)(c)	1.7, 6.2,
s.98	1.10, 3.6, 6.3, 7.2,
s.109	7.3,
s.111(2)(b)	4.4,
s.123	7.4,
s.124	7.4,
s.126	7.4, 7.5,
s.127	7.4,
s.127A	7.4,
Employment Tribunals Act 1996	7.1, 7.4,
s.18A and 18B	7.1,
s.18(1)	7.1,
Enterprise and Regulatory Reform Act 2013	7.1,
s.7	7.1,
Schedule 2	7.1,
Equality Act 2006	1.1,
Equality Act 2010	1.1, 1.2, 1.3, 1.4, 1.5, 1.6, 1.9, 1.10, 2.2, 2.3, 2.6, 2.10, 3.1, 3.2, 3.4, 3.5, 3.6, 3.13, 3.14, 4.1, 4.2, 4.6, 5.2, 5.4, 6.4, 6.2, 6.3, 7.1, 7.2, 7.3, 7.5, 7.6, 8.3, 9.1,

s.27	1.4, 6.3, 9.1,
s.39	1.2, 1.4, 3.13, 4.2, 4.6,
s.40	1.4, 9.1,
s.60, 60(2)	1.5,
s.83	1.4, 6.3,
s.109	6.3,
s.110(1)(2)	6.3,
s.112(1)	6.3,
s.119	7.5,
s.119(4)	7.5,
s.120, 120(8)	1.4, 1.5, 6.3, 7.1,
s.121	7.1,
s.123	6.3, 7.1,
s.124	7.5,
s.136	1.9, 3.4,
s.138	7.6,
s.190	2.3,
Part 5	6.3,
Schedule 1	2.2, 2.3, 2.5, 8.3,
Schedules 2, 4, 8, 13, 15 & 21	4.1, 9.1,
Schedule 9, Part 1, para. 1	1.5, 6.4, 9.1,
Human Rights Act 1998	6.4,
Income Tax (Earnings and Pensions) Act 2003	7.5,
s.401	7.5,
Local Government and Housing Act 1989, s.7	6.2,

Prosecution of Offences Act 1985	8.3,
s.6(1)	8.3,
Protection From Harassment Act 1997	8.7,
Race Relations Act 1976	2.9, 3.5, 3.6,
Sex Discrimination Act 1975	2.9, 3.5, 3.6, 7.5,
s.42	7.5,
Trade Union and Labour Relations (Consolidation) Act 1992	7.1,

2 UK statutory instruments:

Disability Discrimination Act 1995 (Amendment) Regulations 2003, SI 2003/1673 (revoked)	1.1, 1.6, 2.3, 3.13, 4.3, 6.2, 7.6,
Disability Discrimination (Employment) Regulations 1996, SI 1996/1456 (revoked)	1.1,
Disability Discrimination (Meaning of Disability) Regulations 1996, SI 1996/1455 (revoked)	1.1, 2.3, 2.7,
Disability Discrimination (Questions and Replies) Order 1996, SI.1996/2793	7.6,
Employment Act 2002 (Dispute Resolution) Regulations 2004	6.3, 7.1,
Employment Equality (Age) Regulations 2006, SI.1031	3.6, 6.4, 7.3,
Employment Equality (Religion or Belief) Regulations 2003, SI.1660	3.6,
Employment Equality (Repeal of Retirement Age Provisions) Regulations 2011	7.3,
Employment Equality (Sexual Orientation) Regulations 2003, SI.1661	3.6,

Employment Tribunals (Early Conciliation: Exemptions and Rules of Procedure) Regulations (draft 2013)	7.1,
Employment Tribunal Rules of Procedure 2004	4.3,
Rule 30(6)(c)	4.3,
Rule 30(6)(d)	4.3,
Rule 30(6)(e)	4.3,
Equality Act 2010 (Commencement No.4, Savings, Consequential, Transitional, Transitory and Incidental Provisions and Revocation) Order 2010, SI.2010/2317 (in force from 01 October 2010)	1.1,
Equality Act 2010 (Disability) Regulations 2010, SI.2010/2128 (in force from 01 October 2010	1.1,
Equality Act 2010 (Guidance on the Definition of Disability) Appointed Day Order 2011, SI.2011/1159	2.3,
The Unfair Dismissal and Statement of Reasons for Dismissal (Variation of Qualifying Period) Order 2012; SI.2012/989	7.3,
Working Time Regulations 1998, SI.1998/1833	8.2,

3 EU legislation:

EC Equal Treatment Framework Directive (No.2000/78/EC)	1.1, 1.6, 2.5, 3.6, 6.3,
European Convention on Human Rights and Fundamental Freedoms	6.4,
European Working Time Directive (No.2003/88)	8.2,

4 Codes of Practice:

ACAS Code of Practice on Disciplinary and Grievance Procedures	6.3, 7.1,
A 'Code of Practice – Employment and Occupation' ('Code of Practice') issued by the Disability Rights Commission. (Neither the Guidance nor the Code of Practice imposes any legal obligations; nonetheless, tribunals are required to take account of any provision contained in them that is relevant to the issue being determined); Code of Practice 25 July 1996	1.1, 6.1, 6.3, 8.3,
Code of Practice on Employment (2011)	3.14,
2011 Guidance issued by the Secretary of State: 'Guidance on matters to be taken into account in determining questions relating to the definition of disability ('the Guidance')	1.1, 1.5, 2.3, 2.5, 3.11, 4.6, 4.7, 5.4, 6.1, 6.3, 8.3,
Guidance 1996	1.8, 6.1,
Guidance 2006	1.8, 6.1,
Equality Act 2010 Guidance issued by the Office for Disability Issues. See: www.odi.gov.uk/equality act. http://odi.dwp.gove.uk/docs/wor/new/ea-guide.pdf.	1.1,
United Nations Convention on the Rights of Persons with Disabilities	2.5.

Case List

Ainsworth and others v Commissioners of Inland Revenue (2005) ICR 1149 (see Stringer and others v HMRC (2009) ECJ, 20.01.09, Cases C-350/06; C-520/06	8.2,
Archibald v Fife Council (2004) ICR 954	1.3, 3.1, 3.13, 4.3, 4.7, 5.4, 6.2, 6.3,
Aylott v Stockton-on-Tees Borough Council [2010] IRLR 994; EWCA Civ 910, CA	2.10, 3.7, 6.3,
Banaszczyk v Bookers Limited (2016) EAT (Case No.0132/15)	2.5, 8.3,
Bank v IBM (UK) Ltd (2003) EAT (Case No.389/03), 09 September 2003	6.3,
Barclays Bank plc v Kapur & others (1991) ICR 208	7.1,
Barlow v Stone (2012) EAT 01 June 2012 (Case No. 0049/12)	6.3,
Basildon & Thurrock NHS Foundation Trust v Weerasinghe (2015) EAT (Case No.0397/14)	3.14, 7.3,
Baynton v Saurus General Engineers Ltd (2000) ICR 375, EAT	3.11,
Beart v HM Prison Service (2003) IRLR 238	4.7,
Bid v KPMG LLP (2009) ET Case No.1300313/09	6.3,

Bowers v William Hill Organisation Ltd (2009) EAT (Case No.0046/09)	6.3,
British Gas plc v Breeze (unreported, 13 September 1988)	6.3,
British Gas Services Ltd v McCaull (2001) IRLR 60	6.3,
BT plc v Pelling (2004) EATS 0093/03 (Scottish EAT)	4.7, 8.3,
Bush v Zurich Financial Services (2004) EAT (Case No.0832/03)	6.3,
Cast v Croydon College (1998) IRLR 318	6.2, 6.3,
Catherall v Michelin Tyres plc (2003) IRLR 61	6.2, 6.3,
Chacón Navas v Eurest Colectividades SA (2006) IRLR 706, Case C-13/05, ECJ	2.5, 6.3, 8.3,
Chagger v Abbey National plc (2010) ICR 397	7.2, 7.5,
Chatwal v Wandsworth Borough Council (2011) EAT (Case No.0487/10)	3.6,
Chez Razpredelenie Bulgaria (2015) CJEU C-83/14	1.3, 1.5,
Chief Constable of Dumfries & Galloway v Adams (2009) EAT, Case No.0046/08, (03.04.09)	2.5,
Chief Constable of West Midlands Police v Gardner (2011) EAT 18 October 2011 (Case No.0174/11)	6.3,
Chief Constable of West Yorkshire Police v Khan (2001) ICR 1065, 1072	6.2,
Child Support Agency v Truman (2009) EAT (Case No.0293/08)	3.9,

Derby Fabrication Ltd V Burton (2001) IRLR 69	6.2, 6.3,
de Souza v Vinci Construction (UK) Ltd (2017) EWCA Civ 879	7.5,
Dundee City Council v Sharp (2011) EAT Edinburgh 11 October 2011 (Case No.0009/11)	1.10,
Dunham v Ashford Windows (2005) IRLR 608, EAT	1.6, 1.9,
DWP v Hall (2005) EAT 31 August 2005	1.9,
Eastern and Coastal Kent PCT v Grey (2009) EAT, 23 January 2009, Case No. 0454/08)	2.8,
East Lindsey District Council v Daubney (1977) IRLR 181 and 184	1.10, 6.3,
EBR Attridge Law LLP (1) (formerly Attridge Law) (2) v Coleman (2009) EAT, 30.10.09, (Case No.0071/09)	6.3,
English v Emery Reimbold and Strick (2002) EWCA Civ 605	6.3,
Environment Agency v Rowan (2008) IRLR 20	4.3, 6.3,
Essex County Council v Jarrett (2015) EAT (Case No.0045/15)	3.1,
Essop and others v Home Office (UK Border Agency) (2017) UKSC 27	1.2,
Eweida v British Airways (2010) EWCA Civ 80	3.6,
Francis v London Borough of Hammersmith & Fulham (2004) EAT (Case No.0942/03)	6.3,
Freer Bouskell v Brewster (2003) EAT (Case No.0377/03)	6.3,

O'Hanlon v HM Commissioners for Revenue and Customs (2006) EAT 04.08.06, (Case No.0109/06); (2007) EWCA Civ 283; (2007) IRLR 404	1.3, 3.1, 5.1, 5.2, 5.3, 6.2, 6.3, 8.1,
Pantry v The Home Office (2004) EAT (Case No.0083/04)	6.2,
Paterson - Chief Constable of Dumfries & Galloway Constabulary v Adams (2009) IRLR 571	2.5,
Paterson v Commissioner of Police of the Metropolis, EAT, 23.07.07 (Case No.0635/06; (2007) ICR 1522	6.3, 8.3,
Paulley v First Group plc (2014) EWCA Civ 1573; (2015) 1 WLR 3384	1.3,
Peacock v CIE International Ltd (2005) ET Case No.1501277/05	1.4, 3.2,
Post Office v Jones (2001) IRLR 384, ICR 805	3.13,
Project Management Institute v Latif (2007) IRLR 579	6.3,
Rainey v Greater Glasgow Health Board (1987) ICR 129, HL	3.11,
Richmond Adult Community College v McDougall (2008) EWCA Civ 4, CA	6.3,
Roberts v North West Ambulance Service (2012) EAT 24 January 2012 (Case No.0085/11)	6.3,
Romec Ltd v Rudham (2007) EAT 13 July 2007 (Case No.0069/11)	4.3,
Rowden v Dutton Gregory (2002) EAT, ICR 971	6.3,
Rugamer v Sony Music Entertainment UK Ltd (2001) ICR 381	2.3,

Saunder v Birmingham City Council (2008) EAT (Case No.0591/07)	6.3,
SCA Packaging Limited v Boyle (2009) House of Lords, 01 July 2009	2.6,
Scottish and Southern Energy plc v Mackay (2007) EAT 30.08.07 (Case No.0075/ 06	4.3,
Secretary of State for the Department for Work and Pensions v Alam (2009) EAT 09.11.09 (Case No.0242/09)	2.8,
Secretary of State for Work and Pensions v Macklin (2008) EAT (Case No.0370/ 07)	3.9, 4.3, 5.3, 6.3,
Secretary of State for Work and Pensions v Wakefield (2010) EAT 26 July 2010 (Case No.0435/09)	4.3, 6.3,
SG Baker Ltd v Haggart (2011) EAT 09 November 2011 (Case No.0007/11)	6.3,
Shaw & Co Solicitors v Atkins (2009) EAT (Case No.0224/08)	6.3,
Simmons v Castle (2012) EWCA Civ 1039	7.5,
Small v Shrewsbury and Telford Hospitals NHS Trust (2017) EWCA Civ 882	7.2, 7.5,
Smith v Churchills Stairlifts plc (2005) EWCA Civ 1220, CA	3.12, 3.13,
Smith Detection–Watford Ltd v Berriman, EAT (Case Nos. 0712/04; 0144/05	4.3,
Sobhi v Commissioner of Police of the Metropolis (2013) EAT (Case No.0518/12)	2.5,
Southampton City College v Randall (2006) IRLR 18, EAT	4.3,
Spencer v 02 UK, ET Case No.1805496/03	8.3,
Spencer v Paragon Wallpapers Ltd (1976) IRLR 373	1.10,

Stockton-on-Tees Borough Council v Aylott (2009) EAT 11 March 2009 (Case No.0401/08)	3.9,
Stringer and others v Her Majesty's Revenue and Customs (2009) ECJ 20.01.09, Cases C-350/06 and C-520/06	8.2,
Surrey Police v Marshall (2002) EAT, IRLR 843	6.3,
Swift v Chief Constable of Wiltshire Constabulary, EAT (Case No.0484/03)	8.3,
Tarbuck v Sainsbury Supermarkets Ltd (2006) IRLR 664, EAT	4.3, 6.3,
The Government Legal Service v Brookes (2017) EAT 28 March 2017 (Case No.0302/16)	4.7,
Tran v Greenwich Vietnam Community (2002) IRLR 735	6.3,
Truman v Bibby Distribution Ltd (2014) ET case 2404176/2014	6.3,
Trustees of Swansea University Pension & Assurance Scheme and another v Williams (2015) EAT (Case No.0415/14)	2.10, 3.14,
Tudor v Spen Corner Veterinary Centre Ltd and another, Case No.2404211/05, 07.04.06	3.4,
Vento v Chief Constable of West Yorkshire (No.2) (2003) ICR 318, CA	7.5,
Vicary v British Telecommunications plc (1999) IRLR 680	6.3,
Webb v EMO Air Cargo (UK) Ltd (No.2) (1995) HL	2.10,
Wilcox v Birmingham CAB Services Ltd (2011) EAT 23 June 2011 (Case No.0293/ 10)	2.8, 6.3,
Wilding v BT (2002) EWCA Civ 349, CA	6.3,

Williams v Ferrosan Ltd (2004) EAT, IRLR 607	7.5,
Williams v J. Walter Thompson Group Ltd (2005) IRLR 376, CA	3.13,
X v Mid Sussex Citizens Advice Bureau and another (2011) EWCA Civ 28, CA	6.3,
Yeboah v Crofton (2002) IRLR 634	6.3.

DISABILITY DISCRIMINATION

Part 1

1.1 The law:

Disability Discrimination (Employment) Regulations 1996, SI 1996/1456 (revoked);
Disability Discrimination (Meaning of Disability) Regulations 1996, SI 1996/1455 (revoked);
Disability Discrimination Act 1995 (Amendment) Regulations 2003, SI 2003/1673 (revoked);
Disability Discrimination Act 1995 (repealed as of 01 October 2010);
Disability Discrimination Act 2005 (repealed as of 01 October 2010);
EC Equal Treatment Framework Directive (No.2000/78/EC);
Employment Rights Act 1996;
Equality Act 2006;
Equality Act 2010 (Commencement No.4, Savings, Consequential, Transitional, Transitory and Incidental Provisions and Revocation) Order 2010, SI.2010/2317 (in force from 01 October 2010);
Equality Act 2010 (Disability) Regulations 2010, SI.2010/2128 (in force from 01 October 2010;
Equality Act 2010 (in force from 01 October 2010);
A 'Code of Practice – Employment and Occupation' ('Code of Practice') issued by the Disability Rights Commission. (Neither the Guidance nor the Code of Practice imposes any legal obligations; nonetheless, tribunals are required to take account of any provision contained in them that is relevant to the issue being determined).
Guidance issued by the Secretary of State: 'Guidance on matters to be taken into account in determining questions relating to the definition of

disability ('the Guidance');
Equality Act 2010 Guidance issued by the Office for Disability Issues. See:
www.odi.gov.uk/equality act. http://odi.dwp.gov.uk/docs/wor/new/ea-guide.pdf.

1.2 Equality Act 2010:

From 01 October 2010, the Equality Act 2010 replaced the Disability Discrimination Act 1995 and the Disability Discrimination Act 2005. The statutory Regulations which accompanied these two Acts are mostly revoked as from 01 October 2010. Note that much of the substantive law stated in the judgments of the case authorities under the Disability Discrimination Act 1995 remains relevant under the disability discrimination provisions of the Equality Act 2010. The notable exception is that 'disability-related discrimination' under s.3A(1), Disability Discrimination Act 1995 no longer exists as a cause of action; instead, a new cause of action is provided by s.15 of the Equality Act 2010 that is 'discrimination arising from disability.'

The old and new section headings are:

Disability Discrimination Act 1995	**Equality Act 2010 provisions**
s.1(1) definition of disability	s.6(1) (and Schedule 1, Part 1)
s.3A(1) disability-related discrimination	no equivalent. But see s.15
s.3A(5) direct discrimination	s.13(1)
s.4A(1) reasonable adjustments	s.20(3), s.4 and s.39(5)
s.18B(2) examples of adjustments	no equivalent.

There is a comparative guide to the provisions of the Disability Discrimination Act 1995 and Equality Act 2010 at 9.1.

There are a number of ways in which employers can break the law – either intentionally or unintentionally, the latter maybe from acting recklessly – by discriminating unlawfully against job applicants or workers for the reason of disability and, conversely, there are a number of claims which job applicants and workers can make for recompense if they are unlawfully discriminated against for the reason of disability, disability being one of the nine protected characteristics under the Equality Act 2010: s.4.

Although it is commonly said that there are four kinds of disability discrimination, there are two main kinds of disability discrimination which may give rise to claims under the Equality Act 2010 and these are: (1) direct discrimination, (2) indirect discrimination (see para.1 Lady Hale in **Essop and others v Home Office (UK Border Agency); Naeem v Secretary of State for Justice (2017)** UKSC 27), and six other kinds of disability discrimination arise out of these two main kinds of disability discrimination, all six of which can occur either directly or indirectly, and either intentionally or unintentionally. The six other forms of disability discrimination, which arise effectively from either direct or indirect disability discrimination, are: (3) discrimination arising from disability; (4) failure to make reasonable adjustments; (5) associative and perceptive discrimination; (6) harassment; (7) victimisation, and (8) discriminatory advertisements.

The Equality Act 2010 came into law on 01 October 2010 and, when doing so, the Disability Discrimination Act 1995 was repealed. One provision in the Disability Discrimination Act 1995 that was not re-enacted in the Equality Act 2010, being disability-related discrimination, effectively ceased to have effect after the judgment of the Appellant Committee of the House of Lords in **Malcolm (2008)**. In its place a new form of indirect disability discrimination was enacted by section 15, Equality Act 2010, called 'Discrimination arising from disability.' Further changes between the two Acts are that under the Equality Act 2010 the effects of the anti-discrimination provisions prohibit 'associative' and 'perceptive' disability discrimination. These changes have come about because the Equality Act 2010 provides protection from discrimination not only for individuals who have 'protected characteristics' (such as having a statutory disability or being of a certain sexual orientation and so on) but also protection from unlawful discrimination for people who may not have a protected characteristic but who are nonetheless unlawfully discriminated against because they associate with a person or persons who do have a protected characteristic (e.g. they might be subjected to discrimination because they are a carer for a disabled person or for a baby or child and, in the latter case, that may constitute unlawful sex discrimination) or they are subject to unlawful discrimination because they are perceived as having a protected characteristic (e.g. being a homosexual or of a particular race or racial origins). So the new provisions provide protection from unlawful discrimination for someone who is subjected to a detriment, including dismissal from his or her job, because he or she (i) associates with another who has a statutory disability or (ii) is perceived to have a statutory disability when he or she does not. Where this occurs, the person who has been unlawfully discriminated against for those reasons can make a claim for recompense for his or her financial and other losses to an employment tribunal if work-related or to a county court if not work-related, if he or she has suffered detriment as a result of being unlawfully discriminated against for the reason of a protected characteristic such as, for example, disability or any of the other eight protected characteristics being: age, gender reassignment, marriage and civil partnership, pregnancy and maternity, race, religion and belief, sex, and sexual orientation..

1.3 Under the Disability Discrimination Act 1995 there were three main kinds of disability discrimination:

(1) Direct disability discrimination.

This occurred where the reason for the less favourable treatment in question was the disabled person's disability, (e.g. an employer had a preconceived prejudicial assumption about blind people and refused to employ such a person for that reason even though the job applicant was the best qualified candidate for the job on offer).

(2) Disability-related discrimination.

This occurred where the reason for the less favourable treatment related to the disability but was not the disability itself (e.g. the dismissal of an employee who was absent from work because of the effects of his or her disability in comparison to a non-disabled employee who was also absent from work but for a non-disability reason.) When Parliament enacted this section it did not intend the courts to treat the absence from work of a disabled employee for a reason that relates to the employee's disability the same as the absence from work of a non-disabled employee for a non-disability reason. Instead, it intended the courts to ask and consider whether the disabled employee's absence from work was caused by the effects of his or her disability and, if so, whether by dismissing the disabled employee for that reason (e.g. a disability-related absence), the employer discriminated against the disabled employee. In **Malcolm (2008)**, however, contrary to the longstanding judgment of the Court of Appeal in **Clark v Novacold (1999)**, the House of Lords held in effect that the absence from work of a disabled employee for a reason that relates to the disabled employee's disability should be judged as no more than an absence from work and nothing more and thus be compared to an absence from work of a non-disabled employee for a non-disability reason. So, if the employer would dismiss the non-disabled employee for that reason then it was lawful and fair to dismiss the disabled employee for the same reason, i.e. ignore the (disability-related) reason for the absence from work. The result of this judgment was that section 3A(1), DDA 1995 became nullified.

(3) A failure to make reasonable adjustments.

This occurred where the employer failed to take steps which are reasonable to take to make a reasonable adjustment(s) when, looked at objectively, the employer could have or should have made such an adjustment(s) to the disabled employee's working environment to avoid a provision, criterion or practice or physical feature or the lack of an auxiliary aid which put the disabled employee at a substantial disadvantage .

Indirect discrimination:

Note that the Disability Discrimination Act 1995 contained no provision for indirect discrimination, because direct discrimination itself was capable of being justified (see s.5(3) of the original section in the Disability Discrimination Act 1995) if, but only if, the reason for it was both material to the circumstances of the particular case and substantial and subsection (3) was subject to subsection (5) which required an employer to comply with the duty to make reasonable adjustments if the duty arose; and Regulations specified the circumstances in which discriminatory treatment was or was not justified.

Under the Equality Act 2010 there are eight main forms of disability discrimination the first five of which are:

(1) Direct disability discrimination, section 13.

This occurs where someone is treated less favourably by reason of a protected characteristic which includes disability. Because the phrase used to describe the treatment in comparison to another or others is 'less favourably, 'the person who has alleged that he or she was unlawfully discriminated against must compared his or her treatment with another being the 'comparator.' A comparator is someone who does not have the protected characteristic of disability and is therefore not disabled either physically or mentally: see s.19(2)(b) and s.20(3), Equality Act 2010. The nature of the comparison between a disabled employee and those not disabled was considered in the leading case of **Archibald v Fife Council**

(2004): see the judgments of Lord Roger at para.42, Lord Hope at para.12, Baroness Hale at para. at para.64. In **Archibald (2004)**, the comparator was an able-bodied person who was not at risk of dismissal because, unlike Mrs Archibald, he or she was able to carry out the duties of the job.

The law: section 13, Equality Act 2010 -

'13 Direct discrimination

(1) A person (A) discriminates against another (B) if, because of a protected characteristic, A treats B less favourably than A treats or would treat others.

(2) … age

(3) If the protected characteristic is disability, and B is not a disabled person, A does not discriminate against B only because A treats or would treat disabled persons more favourably than A treats B.'

(2) Indirect disability discrimination, section 19.

This occurs where the employer applies a provision, criterion or practice, the effect of which is to impact adversely upon a particular group because of their shared characteristic of disability and on the disabled employee who is a member of the particular group.

The law: section 19, Equality Act 2010 -

'19 Indirect discrimination

(1) A person (A) discriminates against another (B) if A applies to B a provision, criterion or practice which is discriminatory in relation to a relevant protected characteristic of B's.

(2) For the purposes of subsection (1), a provision, criterion or practice is discriminatory in relation to a relevant protected characteristic of B's if -

(a) A applies, or would apply, it to persons with whom B does not share the characteristic,

(b) it puts, or would put, persons with whom B shares the characteristic at a particular disadvantage when compared with persons with whom B does not share it,

(c) it puts, or would put, B at that disadvantage, and

(d) A cannot show it to be a proportionate means of achieving a legitimate aim.'

So this statutory tort under s.19 of the Equality Act 2010 is made out where the employer (i) applies a provision, criterion or practice which (ii) impacts adversely upon a particular group because of their shared protected characteristic and (iii) on the disabled employee who has the same protected characteristic and (iv) the employer cannot objectively justify the PCP. But in **Chez Razpredelenie Bulgaria (2015)** CJEU C-83/14, the Court of Justice of the European Union said that all a claimant had to show was that he or she had been subjected to unlawful indirect discrimination by association with a group upon which the PCP adversely impacted but that the claimant did not need to show that he or she was a member of that group. The group in question in **Chez (2015),** that was unlawful discriminated against by the imposition of a PCP, was of Roma ethic origin (Gypsies). Although the claimant was not of Roma ethnicity, she was nonetheless unlawfully discriminated against by her association with the group which arose from her living and working in an area where a community of Roma live.

(3) Discrimination arising from disability, section 15.

This occurs where an employer treats a disabled employee unfavourably because of something arising in consequence of the employee's disability and the employer cannot show that the treatment is a proportionate means of achieving a legitimate aim. As Elias LJ said in **Griffiths v The Secretary of State for Work & Pensions (2015)** EWCA Civ 1265 at para.25, the definition of discrimination arising out of disability does not involve any comparison with a non-disabled person; it refers to unfavourable treatment, not less favourable treatment. The formulation of the duty prior to the Equality Act 2010, being stated in the Disability Discrimination Act 1995, did envisage such a comparison. But in **Lewisham London Borough Council v Malcolm (2008)** UKHL 43, the House of Lords construed the relevant provision then in force (s.3A(1), Disability Discrimination Act 1995) so as to effectively make this form of discrimination (disability-related discrimination) a dead letter, in practice adding nothing to the concept of direct discrimination. The reformulation of the duty in section 15 of the Equality Act 2010 was designed to restore the law as it had been understood prior to **Malcolm (2008)** and thereby give the concept and the protection it affords real substance.

The law: section 15, Equality Act 2010 -

'15 Discrimination arising from disability

(1) A person (A) discriminates against a disabled person (B) if -

(a) A treats B unfavourably because of something arising in consequence of B's disability, and
(b) A cannot show that the treatment is a proportionate means of achieving a legitimate aim.

(2) Subsection (1) does not apply if A shows that A did not know, and could not reasonably have been expected to know, that B had the disability.'

Section 15 is focussed upon making allowances for disability: unfavourable treatment because of something arising in consequence of disability is prohibited conduct unless the treatment is a proportionate means of achieving a legitimate aim. Under EU law, unlawful indirect discrimination is lawful if the provision, criterion or practice that is applied by an employer (or service provider) can be '... objectively and reasonably justified by a legitimate aim and if the means of achieving that aim are both appropriate and necessary.'

(4) Failure to make reasonable adjustments, section 20.

This occurs where an employer applies a provision, criterion or practice which put a disabled employee at a substantial disadvantage in comparison with the employer's employees who are not disabled; and the employer fails to take steps which are reasonable to make adjustments so as to avoid the substantial disadvantage created by the PCP or physical feature or the lack of an auxiliary aid to the disabled employee. Section 20 envisages that there will be a comparison of some kind between the disabled employee and those not disabled as stated by the Law Lords in **Archibald v Fife Council (2004)** ICR 954.

The law: section 20, Equality Act 2010 -

'20 Duty to make adjustments

(1) Where this Act imposes a duty to make reasonable adjustments on a person, this section, sections 21 and 22 and the applicable Schedule apply; and for those purposes, a person on whom the duty is imposed is referred to as A.

(2) The duty comprises the following three requirements.

(3) The first requirement is a requirement, where a provision, criterion or practice of A's puts a disabled person at a substantial disadvantage in relation to a relevant matter in comparison with persons who are not disabled, to take such steps as it is reasonable to have to take to avoid the disadvantage.

(4) The second requirement is a requirement, where a physical feature puts a disabled person at a substantial disadvantage in relation to a relevant matter in comparison with persons who are not disabled, to take such steps as it is reasonable to have to take to avoid the disadvantage.

(5) The third requirement is a requirement, where a disabled person would, but for the provision of an auxiliary aid, be put at a substantial disadvantage in relation to a relevant matter in comparison with persons who are not disabled, to take such steps as it is reasonable to have to take to provide the auxiliary aid.

(6) Where the first or third requirement relates to the provision of information, the steps which it is reasonable for A to have to take include steps for ensuring that in the circumstances concerned the information is provided in an accessible format.

(7) A person (A) who is subject to a duty to make reasonable adjustments is not (subject to express provision to the contrary) entitled to require a disabled person, in relation to whom A is required to comply with the duty, to pay to any extent A's costs of complying with the duty.'

The Code of Practice:

The section 20 duty upon employers to make adjustments which are reasonable in employment matters is referred to in a statutory Code of Practice on Employment that was published by the Equality and Human Rights Commission. It states that courts are obliged to take the Code of Practice into consideration whenever it is relevant: section 15(4). Chapter 6 is concerned with the duty to make reasonable adjustments. Paragraph 6.2 states:

'The duty to make reasonable adjustments is a cornerstone of the Act and requires employers to take positive steps to ensure that disabled people can access and progress in employment. This goes beyond simply avoiding treating disabled workers unfavourably and means taking additional steps to which non-disabled workers are not entitled.'

Paragraphs 6.23 to 6.29 of the Code give guidance as to what is meant by 'reasonable steps' and paragraph 6.28 identifies some of the factors which might be taken into account when deciding whether a step is reasonable. They include the size of the employer; the practicability of the proposed step; the cost of making the adjustment; the extent of the employer's resources; and whether the steps would be effective in preventing the substantial disadvantage. So far as efficacy is concerned, it may be that it is not clear whether the step proposed will be effective or not. It may still be reasonable to take the step notwithstanding that success is not guaranteed; the uncertainty is one of the factors to weigh up when assessing the question of reasonableness: see the observations of Lewison LJ in **Paulley v First Group plc (2014)** EWCA Civ 1573; (2015) 1 WLR 3384, paras.44-45.

In an Employment Appeal Tribunal case, Mr Justice Langstaff, when giving judgment as President of the EAT, observed that when considering the question of reasonable adjustment, it is (i) critical to identify the relevant PCP concerned and (ii) the precise nature of the disadvantage which it creates by comparison with its effect on the non-disabled. The importance of this is that until the disadvantage is properly identified, it is not possible to determine what steps might eliminate it. These observations of the President were approved by Laws LJ giving the judgment of the Court of Appeal in **Newham Sixth Form College v Sanders (2014)** EWCA Civ 734, para.9.

Note: it is an error of law for an employer to put forward the defence that there was no unlawful disability discrimination because the employer treated the disabled and non-disabled employees equally. As Elias LJ stated at para.58 in **Griffiths v The Secretary of State for Work & Pensions (2015)**:

'The fact that they are treated equally and may both be subject to the same disadvantage when absent for the same period of time does not eliminate the disadvantage if the PCP bites harder on the disabled, or a category of them, than it does on the able bodied.'

And he continued by saying:

> ***'... the whole purpose of the section 20 duty is to require the employer to take such steps as may be reasonable, treating the disabled differently than the non-disabled would be treated, in order to remove the disadvantage. The fact that the able-bodied are also to some extent disadvantaged by the rule is irrelevant.'***

On the point referred to in his judgment at para.60 being that '... there are other authorities which show that the section 20 duty is not satisfied by treating all alike, Elias LJ cited **O'Hanlon v HM Commissioners for Revenue and Customs (2007)** as being one such case authority. The material passage to which Elias LJ referred being:

> ***'... there is no basis for saying that the tribunal erred in law in reaching this decision. It is plainly no answer to a claim of this kind to say that the same rules apply to all. The purpose of the provision is that disabled employees may be disadvantaged by common rules. Unlike other forms of discrimination, the employer may be obliged to take positive steps which involve treating the disabled more favourably than others are treated to remove or alleviate the consequences of the disability.'***

With reference to the previous legislation under the Disability Discrimination Act 1995, in **O'Hanlon v HM Commissioners for Revenue and Customs (2007)** EWCA Civ 283; (2007) IRLR 404, **Lord Justice Hooper** cited the EAT by saying: (at paragraph 23) **'I adopt what the EAT said about the three kinds of disability discrimination:**

20. Section 3A identifies three kinds of disability discrimination. First, there is direct discrimination. This is the situation where someone is discriminated against because they are disabled. This particular form of discrimination mirrors that which has long been found in the area of race and sex discrimination. As with other forms of direct discrimination, such discrimination cannot be justified. Here, where all employees are subject to the same rules irrespective of their disability, there can be no basis for a claim of direct disability discrimination and none is alleged.

21. Second, there is disability related discrimination: section 3A(1). This is in some respects similar to indirect

discrimination found in other discriminatory legislation, but there is no requirement here that the discrimination should have a disparate impact on the disabled as a body. It is enough that the employee is treated less favourably for a reason related to his or her particular disability. This form of discrimination can be justified. However, justification can only be established if the employer shows that the reason for the treatment is both material to the circumstance of the particular case and substantial: section 3A(3).

22. Third, there is the failure to make reasonable adjustments form of discrimination in sub-section (2). Here, the employer can be liable for failing to take positive steps to help to overcome the disadvantages resulting from the disability. However, this is only once he has a duty to make such adjustments. That duty arises where the employee is placed at a substantial disadvantage when compared with those who are not disabled.

23. There is a close relationship between these two latter forms of discrimination. Section 3A(6) provides that treatment can only be justified under sub-section (1) if it would have been justified even if the employer had complied with any duty to make reasonable adjustments. It follows that logically it makes sense to consider the question of reasonable adjustment disability discrimination first. That was made clear by Lord Rodger of Earlsferry in the case of *Archibald v Fife Council* [2004] ICR 954 para.32, a case which we consider below.'

At paragraph 92 in **O'Hanlon (2007), Lord Justice Sedley** said:

92 'I agree with the judgment of Hooper LJ and wish to add only the following.

93 The Disability Discrimination Act 1995 in its amended form is not at all easy to follow. This is a particular misfortune in an Act which it ought to be possible for employees and managers to read, understand and implement without legal advice or litigation. It can at least be said with confidence that it creates three kinds of discrimination:

> a. **direct discrimination "on the ground of" a person's disability, which is not open to justification: s.3A(5) and (4);**
> b. **disability-related discrimination, which is open to justification: s.3A(1) and (3);**
> c. **failure to make reasonable adjustments: ss. 4A, 3A(2), 18B.**
>
> **In cases where there is no direct discrimination, it will often be useful to take issue (c) before issue (b). The present case is an example.**
>
> 94 **As to reasonable adjustments, the material provision here is the sick pay scheme. It is said to place Mrs O'Hanlon at a substantial disadvantage in comparison with employees who are not disabled because its effect is that paid sick leave attributable to her disability absorbs the paid sick leave she would otherwise be entitled to for occasional ailments. The employment tribunal accepted this argument and in my view were right to do so. The consequent question, as it has emerged in this court, is whether the employer had made "such adjustments as it [was] reasonable, in all the circumstances of the case, for him to have to make in order to prevent the provision having that effect".**

In **Griffiths v The Secretary of State for Work and Pensions (2015)** EWCA Civ 1265, Elias LJ said at para.73: 'The question whether the proposed steps were reasonable is a matter for the ET and has to be determined objectively: see Churchill Stairlifts paras.44-45 per Maurice Kay LJ.'

Example:

An example of **a failure to make reasonable adjustments** is where an employer employs a blind person and although the employer treats both the disabled employee and its non-disabled employees the same so, as statutory comparators, there is no prima facie unlawful direct discrimination, nonetheless, if the employer applies a provision, criterion or practice (or there is a physical feature of the employer's premises) which places the disabled employee at a substantial disadvantage in comparison with the employer's non-disabled employees and, this is so in all the circumstances of the case, the employer is under a duty to take such steps as it is reasonable for the employer to take to prevent the requirement or feature having that effect on the disabled employee.

So, in the case of a blind person, an example of a requirement that the employer might apply is that its employees check and sign-off in writing certain work documentation. It is a requirement that applies equally to all the employer's employees. A non-disabled employee would be dismissed for a serious breach of this requirement just as a disabled employee would be, so a disabled employee would not be treated less favourably than a non-disabled employee. However, this requirement being a 'provision, criterion or practice,' places the blind employee at a substantial disadvantage compared to the employer's non-disabled employees who can comply. So, under s.4A(1), DDA 1995, the employer was under a duty to **'... take such steps as it is reasonable, in all the circumstances of the case, for him** (the employer) **to have to take in order to prevent the provision, criterion or practice, or feature, having that effect.'** In this example, the employer would discharge its statutory duty by providing the blind employee with a Braille machine or other aids to help the employee check and sign-off written work documentation.

Note: under s.4A, DDA 1995, there was **no duty** on an employer in relation to a disabled person to make adjustments if the employer **did not know, and could not reasonably be expected to have known** that the person has a disability (see s.4A(6), DDA 1995): **Hunter v Timber Components (UK) Ltd (2009)** EAT 17 November 2009 (Case No.0025/09).

This is restated in section 15 of the Equality Act that states:

(2) Subsection (1) does not apply if A shows that A did not know, and could not reasonably have been expected to know, that B had the disability.

(5) Associative and perceptive disability discrimination:

Unlike the Disability Discrimination Act 1995, the Equality Act 2010 provides protection from **associative** and **perceptive** discrimination. The reason for this is that the Equality Act 2010 refers to 'a protected characteristic' and this may be possessed by the claimant or it could be possessed by someone else whom the claimant associates with and, as a result, the claimant is discriminated against indirectly because of that association. Or the claimant does not have a particular protected characteristic but, nonetheless, is unlawfully discriminated against because he or she was perceived to have the protected characteristic. This means that a person who is adversely discriminated against because he or she (i) **associates** with someone who has a protected characteristic such as a disability or (ii) because he or she is **perceived** to have a statutory disability will be able to make a claim to recover his or her financial losses and injury to feelings if, as a result, he or she suffers detriment including dismissal. More specifically, the Equality Act 2010 provides protection from associative or perceptive discrimination, being less favourable treatment because the claimant associates with someone who has or others who have a disability or a wrongful perception that the claimant has a disability. Associative and perceptive discrimination is classed as direct discrimination under s.13 of the Equality Act 2010. See the Explanatory Notes of the Equality Bill Clause 13: Direct discrimination. Case authority: **Chez Razpredelenie Bulgaria (2015)** Court of Justice of the European Union (CJEU) C-83/14, 16 July 2015 (associative race discrimination.)

1.4 In addition to the first five forms of disability discrimination, there are also three other forms:

Three other types of discrimination, which were stated in the Disability Discrimination Act 1995, have now been subsumed into the Equality Act 2010:-

(6) harassment - section 26, Equality Act 2010:

This is where a disabled employee is harassed by someone who engages in unwanted conduct related to a protected characteristic (such as the disabled person's disability or someone else's protected characteristic), and the conduct has the purpose or effect of violating the person's dignity or creating an intimidating, hostile, degrading, humiliating or offensive environment for him or her. The person harassed may possess the protected characteristic that is the subject of the harassment or another person may possess it (e.g. in the latter case derogatory remarks about people who have a disability (e.g. calling them 'bloody malingerers') or one of the other protected characteristic such as sexual orientation (e.g. saying they are 'queer bastards') may have the effect of harassing a person because he or she has a disability or associates with a person who has a disability or is perceived to have a disability) and, because he or she rejects or submits to the harassment, the person engaging in the harassment treats the person less favourably that they would treat the person had he or she not rejected or submitted to the conduct.

Section 26 Harassment -

(1) A person (A) harasses another (B) if

(a) A engages in unwanted conduct related to a relevant protected characteristic,

and

(b) the conduct has the purpose or effect of

(i) violating B's dignity; or

(ii) creating an intimidating, hostile, degrading, humiliating or offensive environment for B: **s.26, Equality Act 2010.**

Subsection (4) of the Equality Act 2010 states that: 'In deciding whether conduct has the effect referred to in subsection (1)(b), each of the following must be taken into account -

(a) perception of B;
(b) the circumstances of the case;
(c) whether it is reasonable for the conduct to have that effect.

Under the Disability Discrimination Act 1995, such conduct was to be regarded as having such an effect and therefore amount to harassment only if: '... having regard to all the circumstances, including in particular the perception of the disabled person, it should reasonably be considered as having that effect:' **s.3B(2).** This provision provides an objective dimension to the test of harassment so that an over-sensitive person who takes offence unreasonably at a perfectly innocent comment is unlikely to succeed with a complaint of harassment. Case authorities: **Peacock v CIE International Ltd;** ET Case No.1501277/05. **Lewis v John Denny Agencies Ltd;** ET Case No.1501368/05;

(7) victimisation - section 27, Equality Act 2010:

This is where an employer victimises a person (whether disabled or not) by subjecting the person to a detriment (being a disadvantage of some kind) because the person has does a protected act or the employer believes that the person has done or may do a protected act.

Section 27 Victimisation -

(1) A person (A) victimises another person (B) if A subjects B to a detriment because -

(a) B does a protected act, or
(b) A believes that B has done, or may do, a protected act.

(2) Each of the following is a protected act

(a) bringing proceedings under this Act;
(b) giving evidence or information in connection with proceedings under this Act;
(c) doing any other thing for the purposes of or in connection with this Act;
(d) making an allegation (whether or not express) that the employer or another person has contravened this Act.

(3) Giving false evidence or information, or making a false allegation, is not a protected act if the evidence or information is given, or the allegation is made, in bad faith.
(4) This section applies only where the person subjected to a detriment is an individual.
(5) The reference to contravening this Act includes a reference to committing a breach of an equality clause or rule.

(8) discriminatory advertisements - sections 39(1)(3); 40; 83(4):

This occurs where an employer invites applications for a relevant appointment or benefit and might reasonably be understood as indicating an intention to determine the application in a manner that discriminates against a disabled person or, alternatively, a reluctance to make a reasonable adjustment for an applicant. A job applicant will have no right to take legal action in respect of discriminatory advertisements. This type of claim is enforceable only by the Disability Rights Commission (that has now been subsumed into the Equality and Human Rights Commission).

1.5 Pre-employment health enquiries, section 60, Equality Act 2010:

Such enquiries by employers about the health and disabilities of job applicants are thought to be one of the main reasons why people with disabilities often fail to be invited to interviews and to be offered employment. As a result, to address this problem, a new section was introduced into the Equality Act 2010 at the Commons Report stage. This section was then substantially amended at the Lords' Committee stage prior to being included in the Act.

Section 60 states that an employer must not ask about a job applicant's health (and that includes any disability the applicant may have) before offering him or her work or, where the employer is not in a position to offer work immediately, before including the applicant in a pool of persons to whom he intends to offer work in the future. Only the Equality and Human Rights Commission has the power to enforce this provision as an unlawful act: Part 1 of the Equality Act 2006; s.120(8), Equality Act 2010.

Under s.60, an employer does not commit an act of disability discrimination merely by asking a job applicant about his or her health. But the employer's conduct in reliance on information given in response may lead an employment tribunal to conclude that the employer has committed an unlawful discriminatory act. In such circumstances, where a claimant can show a prima facie case of discrimination, the burden of proof will shift to the employer who is required to show that it did not act in an unlawfully discriminatory way: s.136. (**Igen Ltd v Wong (2005)** IRLR 258, Court of Appeal). See: last paragraph, 1.7; and paragraphs 12 and 13, 1.9.

Note that if an employer did ask the job applicant if he or she had a disability and the job applicant said 'yes,' then the employer, having knowledge of the job applicant's disability, would need to observe a raft of duties and obligations under the Equality Act 2010.

The Act does not impose a complete ban on pre-employment health enquiries. Significantly, s.60 does not apply to the asking of questions which are necessary to establish whether the job applicant will be able to comply with a requirement to undergo an assessment (such as an interview or selection test); whether a duty to make reasonable adjustments will arise in connection with any such assessment; or whether the applicant will be able to carry out a function that is intrinsic to the work concerned. In addition, an employer is also entitled to ask questions necessary to monitor diversity in the range of job applicants; to enable it to take positive action; or to establish whether the applicant has a particular disability, where having that disability is an occupational requirement: s.60(5). (See too Schedule 9, Part 1, para.1).

Under a direct disability discrimination provision of the Equality Act 2010, it is not unlawful discrimination to treat a disabled person more favourably than a person who is not disabled: s.13(3). An example of a situation where this provision may be relevant is where an employer makes reasonable adjustments to the times that a disabled employee starts and leaves work to enable him or her to mitigate the difficulties he or she might encounter during rush-hour travel. Another employee who does not have a disability would not be able to assert that he or she has suffered less favourable treatment by not being allowed to start and finish work at the same times as the disabled employee.

1.6 Disability discrimination law prior to the Equality Act 2010:

Those who have a good knowledge of the Disability Discrimination Act 1995 are greatly advantaged when advising about or making or defending a claim for disability discrimination because much of the previous law has been subsumed into the Equality Act 2010 and many of the case authorities which were decided under the previous legislation are still valid case authorities. The previous law was that for the period from the 1st October 2004 to the 01 October 2010, the Disability Discrimination Act 1995 (DDA 1995) was amended by the Disability Discrimination Act 1995 (Amendment) Regulations 2003 SI 2003/1673. These amending statutory regulations implemented the disability part of the EC Equal Treatment Framework Directive (No.2000/78/EC) that requires Member States to introduce laws prohibiting discrimination on the grounds of religion or belief, sexual orientation, age and disability. On December 2005, the Disability Discrimination Act 2005 came into force and removed from the 1995 Act the requirement that a mental illness be clinically well-recognised in order to amount to a disability. This meant that employees suffering from mental illnesses were (and still are), when providing evidential proof of the effects of their disability, to be treated the same as those with physical impairments and the same as those with other mental impairments, which are not mental illnesses, such as learning difficulties. See: **Dunham v Ashford Windows (2005)** IRLR 608, EAT.

The Disability Discrimination Act 1995 (Amendment) Regulations 2003 changed the law that existed before 01 October 2010 by: -

- removing the exemption for small employers. Before 1st October 2004, employers with 15 or fewer employees had an exemption from the employment provisions of the DDA 1995 by virtue of s.7 DDA 1995. The Regulations removed the small employer exemption so that the DDA 1995 applied to all employers (except the armed forces) regardless of the number of employees they employed: Reg.7;
- extending the DDA 1995 to all employers (except the armed forces). Previously excluded occupations such as police, firefighters, barristers, Scottish advocates as well as partners in firms, now came within the provisions of the Act: Regs. 6, 8, 24 and 25;
- prohibiting discrimination by qualifications bodies: Reg.13. A 'qualifications body' is defined as 'an authority or body that can confer, renew or extend a professional or trade qualification.' Such bodies do not include bodies responsible for schools or further and higher education institutions because discrimination by such bodies was already covered by Part IV of the DDA 1995 that relates to discrimination in the provision of education. Prior to the 1st October 2004, examination boards were outside Part IV of the DDA 1995 but were included when the Disability Discrimination Act 1995 (Amendment) Regulations 2003 was enacted;
- changing the section headings of the Act. Examples were: s.5(1) (less favourably treatment for a reason related to disability) became s.3A(1); s.5(2) (the failure to make reasonable adjustments per old s.6 (now s.4A(1)) became s.3A(2); s.6(3) (examples of steps which an employer may need to take in relation to a disabled person in order to comply with a duty to make reasonable adjustments) became s.18B(2); and s.6(4) (determining whether it is reasonable for a person to have to take a particular step in order to comply with a duty to make reasonable adjustments) became s.18B(1): DDA 1995 as amended by the Disability Discrimination Act 1995 (Amendment) Regulations 2003;
- introducing a new definition of discrimination. After 1st October 2004, there were three kinds of disability

discrimination under the DDA 1995 which were amended under the Equality Act 2010 by the repealed of s.3A(1), DDA 1995 that was s.5(1) of the original DDA 1995 being 'disability-related discrimination' and, in its place, the enactment of s.15, Equality Act 2010 being 'discrimination arising from disability' and also the enactment of s.19 being 'indirect discrimination;'

1.7 Changes to the Disability Discrimination Act 1995 from 01 October 2004:

Note 1: from the 1st October 2004, the DDA 1995 was amended in that, where a disabled person's employment came to an end, it was unlawful for his or her former employer to: -

- discriminate against him or her by subjecting him or her to a detriment; or
- subject him or her to harassment - providing that the discrimination or harassment arises out of the employment that has come to an end and is closely connected to it: Reg.15.

The explanatory memorandum to the Regulations states that the intention of introducing a free-standing definition of harassment that does not require the need for a comparator is that, for example:

> **'...it will be unlawful for a disabled former employee to be discriminated against at an internal appeal hearing following their dismissal, or in relation to the provision of references, or in access to company sports or social facilities offered to other ex-employees.'**

The correct comparator is with a former employee. Therefore, if a disabled ex-employee claims that he or she has been placed at a substantial disadvantage, he or she must show a disadvantage relative to a non-disabled ex-employee and not a current employee. A former employer may subject an ex-employee to an act of discrimination some months or even some years after he or she has left the employment. If this happens, the ex-employee must bring a claim within the usual three months' statutory time limit of the alleged act of discrimination occurring. Ex-employees who left employment before 1st October 2004 are covered by the new provision in just the same way as those who leave employment after that date.

Note 2: from 1st October 2004, the pre-1st October 2004 duty upon employers under the old s.6(1)(a)(b) and s.6(2)(a)(b) DDA 1995 (s.4A(1)(2)), the first being - to make reasonable adjustments where any arrangements made by or on behalf of the employer or physical features of premises occupied by the employer place a disabled person at a disadvantage in comparison with a non-disabled person; and the second being - the duty under s.6(2)(a)(b) to make adjustments in relation to 'arrangements' applies only to arrangements made for determining to whom employment should be offered, and any term, condition or arrangement on which employment, promotion, a transfer, training or any other benefit is offered or afforded - were both extended by the new Regulations in that the pre-1st October 2004 statutory definition 'arrangements' now had a wider meaning encompassing any 'provision, criterion or practice:' Reg.5;

Note 3: from 1st October 2004, the reasonable adjustment duty applied to all stages of the employment process. Prior to 1st October 2004, the DDA 1995 limited the old s.6 duty in that it did not apply to cases of discrimination by dismissal or by subjecting an employee to a detriment. After 1st October 2004, this limitation was removed and the duty also applied after employment had ended;

Note 4: from 1st October 2004, the employers' justification defence (the old s.5(4)) for failing to make reasonable adjustment was removed by the Regulations. The Government accepted the Disability Rights Task Force recommendation that the justification defence was unacceptable and that '… employers should focus on what adjustments were needed and whether they were reasonable;'

Note 5: from 1st October 2004, 'dismissal' includes constructive dismissal. A constructive dismissal occurs when an employee terminates the contract '… in circumstances such that he is entitled to terminate it with or without notice by reason of the conduct of the employer:' Reg.5;

Note 6: from 1st October 2004, discriminatory job advertisements will be unlawful where they indicate an intention to discriminate against a disabled person or a reluctance to make a reasonable adjustment for a job applicant: Reg.15. Only the Disability Rights Commission may take enforcement action against those who place discriminatory advertisements.

Note 7: from 1st October 2004, the burden of proof changed in that once a complainant made out a prima facie case of discrimination or harassment, the tribunal 'shall' find for the complainant unless the employer can prove that he did not commit the act in question: Reg.9. Previously, if the employer could not prove that he did not discriminate against the complainant, the tribunal could draw an inference of discrimination and uphold the claim. Under the new Regulation, where the onus is not discharged, the tribunal must uphold the claim. See 1.9; **Igen Ltd v Wong (2005)** IRLR 258, CA; (and the statutory provision s.136, Equality Act 2010.)

1.8 Guidance to the definition of disability from 01 May 2006:

The Disability Rights Commission published a revised 'Guidance on matters to be taken into account in determining questions relating to the definition of disability.' This new guidance, that came into force on 01 May 2006 and applied to acts of discrimination occurring on or after that date, replaced the 1996 version. The then new guidance took account of the changes introduced by the DDA 2005 on 05 December 2005. These changes included the removal of the requirement that a mental illness be 'clinically well-recognised' as well as a specific provision stating that progressive illnesses such as cancer, HIV infection and multiple sclerosis are disabilities under the Act from the point of diagnosis.

The EAT took into account the new Guidance when it held that an ET had erred in finding that it had to disregard a claimant's 'coping strategies' when determining whether his impaired vision had a substantial adverse effect on his day-to-day activities within the meaning of s.1(1), DDA 1995 because the finding by the ET was in clear contradiction of the new Guidance. The new Guidance specifically recognised that 'coping strategies' can prevent or mitigate adverse effects of a disability. The result is that a person is not disabled for the purposes of the DDA 1995: **Commissioner of Police of the Metropolis v Virdi (2006)** EAT (Case No.0338/06.)

The meaning of 'discrimination' in the employment context under the Disability Discrimination Act 1995 is where a job applicant or employee or former employee is treated less favourably than another for a reason that relates to or is connected with that person's disability and, importantly, is not justified.

For disability-related discrimination claims under the DDA 1995, the relevant comparators were (but no longer are because this cause of action is now repealed along with the Act of 1995) persons to whom the reason for the disabled employee's treatment (e.g. long-term disability-related absence from work) does not apply. The Court of Appeal, in **Clark v Novacold (1999)** found that the correct comparator was someone to whom C's reason for dismissal did not apply - i.e. the correct comparator being an employee who had not been absent from work. On the basis of the correct comparison, it was clear that C had been less favourably treated for a reason related to his disability.

1.9 Disability Discrimination Act 2005:

This Act, that amended and made significant changes to the Disability Discrimination Act 1995, was in force from 05 December 2005 to 30 September 2010 when, upon the coming into force of the Equality Act 2010 on 01 October 2010 that repealed the Acts of 1995 and 2005, most of the provisions of the Disability Discrimination Act 2005 and the Disability Discrimination Act 1995 were subsumed into the Equality Act 2010. Note that the public sector duty applied from 04 December 2006. Among the significant changes made by the 2005 Act was that it widened the definition of 'disability' and it also placed a new positive duty on public bodies to promote equality of opportunity for disabled people. Prior to the enactment of the Act of 2005, the Government published a draft Disability Discrimination Bill in response to recommendations made by the Disability Rights Task Force in a series of reports it issued during 2000/01. Note that until the Equality Act 2010 came into effect on 01 October 2010, the DDA 1995 remained the main Act for employment purposes.

The Disability Discrimination Act 2005:

- amended by strengthening the statutory provisions in s.16B, DDA 1995 relating to discriminatory job advertisements so as to make liable a third party that published a discriminatory advertisement as well as the person who placed the advertisement. This meant, for example, a newspaper or magazine that published an advertisement that discriminated against disabled persons regarding applications for employment, promotion, transfer or other relevant benefit on behalf of another, say an employer, would be liable as would the employer who placed it. A defence was available to a publisher which was: (1) if the publisher can prove that, in publishing the advertisement, it relied on a statement made by the person or organisation that placed the advertisement that the publication of the advertisement would not be unlawful and, (2) it was reasonable for the publisher to rely upon the statement;
- placed a new positive duty that consisted of a general and specific duty on public authorities that required them, when exercising their functions, to have regard to the need to eliminate unlawful discrimination against disabled persons as

well as to eliminate harassment. The then new positive statutory duty would also include: promoting positive attitudes towards disabled people; encouraging disabled people to participate in public life; promoting equality of opportunity between disabled people and others; taking steps to take account of disabled persons' disabilities, even where that involves treating disabled persons more favourably than other persons s.49A(1), DDA;

- provided that all appropriate functions of public authorities which were not already covered by the DDA 1995 were brought within its scope;
- provided that people with illnesses such as HIV, multiple sclerosis and major cancers were to be regarded, from the point of diagnosis, as disabled for the purposes of the DDA 1995: para. 6A of Schedule 1 of the DDA 2005. A claimant with a physical illness in a case such as **Mowat-Brown v University of Surrey (2002)** IRLR 235 was now to be regarded as having a disability as defined by the disability provisions of the DDA. The Act removed the requirement in the Act of 1995 (Sch.1(1)) that a mental impairment must be 'clinically well-recognised' in order that the effects of the disability are covered by the Act. A claimant with a mental illness in a case such as **Morgan v Staffordshire University (2002)** IRLR 190 was now to be regarded as having a disability as defined by the disability provisions of the DDA; (learning difficulties: a case arising from the judgment in **Morgan (2002)** is that of **Dunham v Ashford Windows (2005)** EAT 13 June 2005 (Case No.0915/04); (2005) IRLR 608, EAT - see 1.3. The decision in **Dunham (2005)** is that: an employee with 'generalised borderline moderate learning difficulties' can, using the fourth route as stated by Mr. Justice Lindsay in **Morgan v Staffordshire University (2002)** EAT, IRLR 190, make a claim under the DDA 1995 that he was discriminated against on the ground of disability by being dismissed and by the employer failing to make reasonable adjustments to accommodate his difficulties and, in making his claim, the evidence of a suitably qualified psychologist, rather than a medical doctor, was sufficient);
- extended section 56 of the DDA 1995 so that the questionnaire procedure now covered claims under Part 3 of the Act (goods, facilities and services) as well as Part 2 as previously;
- extended section 64A so that a chief officer for police was

now vicariously liable for acts of discrimination committed by police officers in the course of their employment where these are unlawful under Part 3;

- stated that the previous exemption from sections 19-21 in Part 3 of the DDA 1995 for transport services extended only to transport vehicles themselves rather than, for example, the provision of timetables;
- stated that certain aspects of Part 3 now applied so that landlords and others who manage rented premises have a duty to make reasonable adjustments;
- required private clubs with 25 or more members to comply with the relevant provisions of Part 3 of the DDA 1995.

Burden of proof and liability - note that (1) regarding discrimination on the ground of disability (or any other reason), a claimant must establish facts from which it may be presumed that discrimination has taken place. If the claimant is able to do that, the burden of proof passes to the employer who must then establish that there has been no discrimination: **Igen Ltd v Wong (2005)** IRLR 258, Court of Appeal; (2) it is a precondition of liability that there is evidence that shows that the employer knew of or should have known of the employee's disability at the time when the alleged act of discrimination took place: **Naicker v Lanarkshire Primary Care NHS Trust (2005)** EAT 18 May 2005; **DWP v Hall (2005)** EAT 31 August 2005; **London Borough of Lewisham v Malcolm (2008)** UKHL 43.

When applying the 'reverse burden of proof' in discrimination cases, a tribunal is not obliged to rigidly follow the two-stage test from **Igen v Wong (2005)** IRLR 258, CA. If it makes positive findings that the acts complained of were motivated by something other than the proscribed factor, then the burden of proof has been discharged: **Gay v Sophos plc (2011)** EAT 16 September 2011 (Case No.0452/10).

'Reverse burden of proof' is now contained in s.136, Equality Act 2010.

For further information on disability issues see:
www.disability .gov .uk

1.10 Long-term illness – dismissal for that reason:

When an employee has a period of long-term sickness, during which he or she is absent from work for that reason, this does not necessarily mean that the illness from which the employee is suffering comes within the statutory definition of a disability within the meaning of the Equality Act

2010. Where an employee has been off work because of long-term sickness, his or her employer may decide to dismiss the employee for the reason of capability (i.e. incapability) that is a potentially fair reason for dismissing under s.98(2), Employment Rights Act 1996. This happened to an employee who had 35 years service with Dundee City Council.

Employment tribunal:

The employee made a claim of unfair dismissal to an employment tribunal. The ET upheld the claim but his employer, Dundee City Council, made an appeal against that decision to the Employment Appeal Tribunal sitting in Edinburgh.

Employment Appeal Tribunal:

The EAT allowed the appeal and remitted the claimant's claim to a fresh tribunal.

The facts:

The claimant, who had been employed by the respondent for 35 years, was dismissed on capability grounds. He had received counselling and was receiving the correct medical treatment. The employer referred him to an independent occupational health service. At a meeting, the claimant was advised that he was at risk of dismissal on capability grounds but the claimant said that he was no better and was not ready to come back to work. The claimant was dismissed after 12 months off sick. His internal appeal failed and he took his claim of unfair dismissal to an employment tribunal. The tribunal upheld his claim, saying that the respondent had made assumptions instead of making straightforward enquiries to ascertain all the relevant facts. The respondent also did not take into account the claimant's length of service.

The EAT upheld the employer's appeal, ruling that the employment tribunal had set the bar too high in concluding that the fact that there was a further enquiry that could have been made by the respondent rendered the dismissal unfair. Further, the tribunal was plainly influenced in its decision on whether or not there had been a reasonable investigation by the fact that the claimant was a long serving employee which was not relevant to that issue.

The central question for the EAT was whether or not the employer had acted reasonably by dismissing the employee for what was a potentially fair statutory reason? An employee dismissed because of his or her long-term sickness absence could be dismissed either for the reason of capability under s.98(2)(a), ERA 1996 or for 'some other substantial reason' under s.98(1)(b), ERA 1996.

The employment tribunal was held by the Employment Appeal Tribunal to have erred by '...***erroneously requiring that employers follow a particular procedure re further medical enquiries before determining on dismissal'*** and by ***'...wrongly taking account of length of service when considering reasonableness of investigation.'*** Accordingly, the EAT remitted the claim to be heard by a fresh tribunal ***'... to consider, on facts already found, whether or not the Respondent could reasonably have been expected to wait longer.'***

Lady Smith, presiding at the EAT in Edinburgh, at para.19 of the judgment, reviewed the case authorities in this area of the law:

'Put shortly, an employment tribunal has to consider whether the employer's conclusion that their employee was not fit to return to work was one which he was reasonably entitled to reach and if so, whether or not the decision to dismiss was, in all the circumstances, reasonable. In cases where dismissal follows a period of long term ill health, it will usually be the case that at the time of the decision to dismiss, there is no real issue as to whether or not the claimant is unfit as at that date. Rather, the issue becomes whether or not it is reasonable for the employer to decide, in effect, that matters have gone on long enough and the stage has been reached at which he can reasonably decide that the time has come to take the employee 'off his books'. The observations of LJ Mance, as he then was, in [2004] EWCA Civ 939 are relevant:

> **"43 ... I turn to the law which can be taken quite shortly as it was not essentially in dispute. The basic test for incapacity arising from ill–health is "whether, in all the circumstances, the employer can be expected to wait any longer and, if so, how much longer." <u>See Spencer v Paragon Wallpapers Ltd [1976] IRLR 373</u>, paragraph 14. The basic question which the Employment Tribunal had to address was whether the Trust's conclusion that there was incapacity, and its decision to dismiss on that ground on 28th June was within the range of reasonable responses which an employer in the circumstances could adopt."'**

At para.20, Lady Smith continued: 'In cases of ill health, the employer requires to assess the implications of that ill health so far as the employee's ability to return to work is concerned. He will, obviously, need to speak to the employee and, usually, also consider medical evidence – hence the views expressed by Phillips J, as he then was, sitting in this tribunal, in the case of **East Lindsey District Council v Daubney [1977]** EAT/7/77/2004; IRLR 181; 184:

> **"18. Unless there are wholly exceptional circumstances, before an employee is dismissed on the ground of ill health it is necessary that he should be consulted and the matter discussed with him, and that in one way or another steps should be taken by the employer to discover the true medical position. We do not propose to lay down detailed principles to be applied in such cases, for what will be necessary in one case may not be appropriate in another. But if in every case employers take such steps as are sensible according the circumstances to consult the employee and to discuss the matter with him and to inform themselves upon the true medical position, it will be found in practice that all that is necessary has been done.'"**

At para.21, Lady Smith continued by saying:

'It is also worth noting that in the **East Lindsey District Council** case, the industrial tribunal had been very critical of the employer's failure to obtain more medical evidence before the decision to dismiss but as explained by Phillips J, this tribunal considered that the tribunal were asking too much of the Council:

"...it seems to us on the whole that the Industrial Tribunal required overmuch of the District Council when saying that they should have demanded a detailed medical report, and should have questioned Dr Haigh about it.'"

At para. 28, Lady Smith said:

'... there is no absolute rule that, in the case of sickness absence, dismissal will be unfair unless the employer has sought and obtained all "relevant" facts. That begs the question of what, in any particular case, is relevant and that is something as to which reasonable employers might reasonably differ. Further, the overall fairness of a decision to dismiss is not determined by reference to whether or not there was something else that an employer might have done that might have produced a different result and to approach matters as if there was such a rule involves the risk of too high a hurdle being set for the employer to overcome.'

Lady Smith continued at para.31 by saying: '… the Claimant's length of service was not relevant to the assessment of the Claimant's state of health. The reasonableness of an employer's investigation in an ill health case is not to be judged by reference to the employee's length of service. An employer is not obliged to carry out a more detailed investigation in the case of a long serving employee nor is he entitled to carry out only a casual investigation in the case of an employee whose length of service is short. An employee of only, say, two years standing would, in the Claimant's position have been entitled to the same level of investigation as in the Claimant's case and the Claimant was not entitled to extra investigation by reason of his 35 years' service. The Tribunal were wrong to conclude as, at paragraph 82 they did, that the length of the Claimant's service meant that further investigation was required.'

Giving the decision of the EAT at para.38, Lady Smith said: 'We accept that both grounds of appeal are well founded for the reasons we have explained above. The Employment Tribunal set the bar too high in concluding that the fact that there was a further enquiry which could have been made by the Respondent (with, on the evidence, nothing to point to any more accurate an indication of the likely date of the Claimant's return to fitness for work being able to be made by OHSAS or the Claimant's GP) rendered the dismissal unfair. By adopting a technical and over analytical approach the Tribunal failed to stand back and ask whether the Respondent had consulted with the employee (to which the answer was 'yes, repeatedly'), had carried out a reasonable investigation and had a reached a reasonable view on the issue of whether or not it was reasonable for them to wait longer before deciding whether or not to dismiss. Further, they were plainly influenced in their decision on whether or not there had been a reasonable investigation by the fact that the Claimant was a long serving employee which, as we have explained, was not relevant to that issue. Their decision that the Claimant was unfairly dismissed cannot, accordingly, stand:' **Dundee City Council v Sharp (2011)** EAT Edinburgh 11 October 2011 (Case No.0009/11).

Another case where a long-serving employee of twenty years was dismissed after a period of long-term sickness of 14 months, although in this case the employee had a statutory disability, was **O'Brien v Bolton St Catherine's Academy (2017)** EWCA Civ 145; 15 March 2017, Court of Appeal. The claimant was head of ICT at an academy and she was assaulted by one of the pupils at the school. Instead of excluding pupils who had assaulted staff, the academy had introduced a new policy whereby such pupils were not excluded. After some further incidents she went off sick, the initial diagnose being stress at work and she was later diagnosed as suffering from anxiety, depression, post-traumatic stress disorder. On the point of her employer having a policy of not excluding disruptive and violent pupils, the employer would have been in breach of its statutory duty by failing to provide a safe working environment for its staff. Under the common law, the employer would have been in breach of its common law duty, the breach of which could have given rise to a claim for negligence there being:

(1) foreseeability of loss or damage to the claimant;
(2) legal proximity in that there was a close and direct relationship between the two parties as employer and employee;
(3) and a court may consider it fair, just and reasonable to impose liability on the employer towards the employee.

After the employee had been absent from work for over a year the employer dismissed her summarily for medical incapacity, the dismissal being upheld after an internal appeal. In response she sought to recover her financial and other losses by making claims to an ET for unfair dismissal contrary to s.98, ERA 1996 and unfavourable treatment (being dismissal) arising from her disability contrary to s.15, Equality Act 2010.

The ET held that her employer had dismissed her unfairly under both s.98, ERA 1996 and under s.15, Equality Act 2010. Her employer appealed to the EAT and the EAT upheld the academy's appeal and remitted the case to be re-heard by a differently constituted ET. She appealed to the Court of Appeal that then restored the judgment of the ET. On the point about the claimant's s.15, Equality Act 2010 claim, the CA said that the section states:

"A person (A) discriminates against a disabled person (B) if -

(a) A treats B unfavourably because of something arising in consequence of B's disability, and
(b) A cannot show that the treatment is a proportionate means of achieving a legitimate aim."

So, when considering s.15 of the Equality Act 2010, an employment tribunal has to ask itself (1) whether the employer treated the claimant unfavourably '... because of something arising in consequence of the claimant's disability?' (Being her long-term ill health absence from work). And, (2), whether the employer can objectively justify the unfavourable treatment? (Dismissing her).

Under s.98 of the Employment Rights Act 1996, the employment tribunal has to ask itself a different question which is: did the employer dismiss the claimant reasonably (s.98(4), ERA 1996) and for a potentially fair statutory reason (s.98(2)(a), ERA 1996) in response to what the employee had done, namely, she had been absent from work long-term because of sickness and, when dismissing her it did so summarily even though she had shown her employer at the appeal hearing that she was almost fit enough to return to work?

The reason her employer gave for dismissing her was the reason of capability under s.98(2)(a) of the Employment Rights Act 1996, capability being a potentially fair statutory reason for so doing. Where an employer dismisses an employee for one of the five statutorily potentially fair reasons it must do so reasonably, i.e. within the range of reasonable responses of a reasonable employer. In contrast, where an employer dismisses an employee who has a disability, s.15 of the Equality Act 2010 requires the employer to show that the treatment (in O'Brien's case being the dismissal) '... is a proportionate means of achieving a legitimate aim.'

The Court of Appeal concluded that there was not much difference between the test under s.98, ERA 1996 (a requirement to dismiss reasonably, etcetera) and the test under s.15, Equality Act 2010 (a requirement to objectively justify the treatment). In actual fact, of course, there is. Unless, that is, it is possible to conclude that 'reasonableness' is more or less the same as 'objective justification.' Importantly, the two tests under the two Acts are different; and the right questions have to be asked to get the right answers.

Under EU anti-discrimination law, the 'provision, criterion or practice' (PCP) applied in this case by the employer was that the employee return to work without any further delay. To determine whether that PCP was objectively justified and therefore lawful it is necessary to ask: was the employer's PCP '... objectively and reasonably justified by a legitimate aim (being to get its employee back to work in the interests of the academy although the ET said the aim was: 'the efficient running of the school, the reduction of costs and the need to provide a good standard of teaching') ... and if the means of achieving that aim are appropriate and necessary?'

The reason why the ET and the Court of Appeal both held that the employee had been unfairly dismissed under s.98, ERA 1996 and discriminated against under s.15, Equality Act 2010 was because at the appeal hearing against her dismissal conducted by her employer the claimant, who at that time had been absent from work for 14 months and which was likely to continue for another three months, produced a 'Fit Note' from her GP and a report from an associate psychologist which stated that the claimant had undergone sufficient treatment to feel fully recovered. Nonetheless, her employer dismissed her appeal and confirmed the decision to dismiss her. From reading the case, it seem that the employer had made up its mind that it wanted to terminate her contract of employment and, in this regard, decided to ignore the last minute medical evidence produced by the claimant and it was not prepared to wait a further three months for the claimant to complete her treatment and return to work. This was a clear breach of the disability discrimination provision of the Equality Act 2010 and, because there was a failure by the employer to consider s.15, Equality Act 2010 by considering objective justification, the dismissal was a breach of the unfair dismissal provision of the Employment Rights Act 1996. Because her dismissal constituted an act of unlawful disability discrimination, any compensation awarded to her at the remedy hearing to which the Court of Appeal remitted her claim would be uncapped unlike an award for ordinary unfair dismissal: **O'Brien v Bolton St Catherine's Academy (2017)** EWCA Civ 145 Court of Appeal, 15 March 2017.

Part 2

2.1 Meaning of 'discrimination:'

The Disability Discrimination Act 1995 (now repealed) stated: 3A Meaning of "discrimination"

1. For the purposes of this Part, a person discriminates against a disabled person if –

    (a) for a reason which relates to the disabled person's disability, he treats him less favourably than he treats or would treat others to whom that reason does not or would not apply, and
    (b) he cannot show that the treatment in question is justified.

2. For the purposes of this Part, a person also discriminates against a disabled person if he fails to comply with a duty to make reasonable adjustments imposed on him in relation to the disabled person.
3. Treatment is justified for the purposes of subsection (1) (b) if, but only if, the reason for it is both material to the circumstances of the particular case and substantial.
4. But treatment of a disabled person cannot be justified under subsection (3) if it amounts to direct discrimination falling within subsection (5).
5. A person directly discriminates against a disabled person if, on the ground of the disabled person's disability, he treats the disabled person less favourably than he treats or would treat a person not having that particular disability whose relevant circumstances, including his abilities, are the same as, or not materially different from, those of the disabled person.
6. If, in a case falling within subsection (1), a person is under a

> duty to make reasonable adjustments in relation to a disabled person but fails to comply with that duty, his treatment of that person cannot be justified under subsection (3) unless it would have been justified even if he had complied with that duty.

2.2 Disability Discrimination Act 1995 – having a disability may not necessarily disable the person:

The fact that an employee has a disability does not, by itself, mean that a disabled employee has an automatic right to make a claim against his or her employer under the now repealed Disability Discrimination Act 1995 or under the Equality Act 2010 that replaced the former Act if discriminated against by the employer for a reason related to or arising from his or her disability. Before making a claim to an employment tribunal to recover financial losses caused by an act of unlawful disability discrimination by an employer or potential employer, the employee or job applicant with a disability must show that his or her disability is a statutory disability that comes within the definition of the Act. The definition of 'disability' was contained in s.1 of the Disability Discrimination Act 1995 and is now stated in s.6 of the Equality Act 2010. In addition, the previous guidance on determining whether a claimant has a disability that was stated in Schedule 1 of the DDA 1995 is largely retained in Schedule 1 of the Equality Act 2010.

2.3 Statutory definition of 'disability:'

The Disability Discrimination Act 1995 (DDA 1995) defined 'disability' as per s1(1): 'Subject to the provisions of Schedule 1, a person has a disability for the purposes of this Act if he has a physical or mental impairment which has a substantial and long-term adverse effect on his ability to carry out normal day-to-day activities.'

This definition was supplemented by: Schedules 1 and 2 of the Act; the Disability Discrimination (Meaning of Disability) Regulations 1996 SI 1996/1455; the Disability Discrimination Act 1995 (Amendment) Regulations 2003 SI 2003/1673; a Code of Practice; and the 'Guidance on matters to be taken into account in determining questions relating to the definition of disability.'

For employment purposes, the relevant sections and schedules of the Disability Discrimination Act 1995 were contained in Part 1 (Disability); Part 11 (Discrimination by employers); Part V11 (Supplemental); Part V111 (Miscellaneous); and Schedules (1-3). An A4 size copy of the

Disability Discrimination Act 1995 could be obtained from HMSO bookshops and the Parliamentary bookshop.

Note that new guidance was issued to take account of the coming into effect of the Equality Act 2010 and the subsequent repeal of the Disability Discrimination Act 1995. The guidance is:

Equality Act 2010 (Guidance on the Definition of Disability) Appointed Day Order 2011, SI.2011/1159.

This Order appoints 1st May 2011 as the day for the coming into force of the Guidance on matters to be taken into account in determining questions relating to the definition of disability issued by the Secretary of State on 7th April 2011 under paragraph 14(3) of Schedule 1 to the Equality Act 2010 ("the 2010 Act").

The Guidance provides practical guidance on matters to be taken into account when considering whether a person is a disabled person for the purposes of the 2010 Act and replaces guidance on the same matters (ISBN 978-0-11-703686-4) which was issued by the Secretary of State under the now repealed Disability Discrimination Act 1995 on 29th March 2006.

Paragraph 12(1) of Schedule 1 to the 2010 Act requires an adjudicating body to take account of such guidance as it thinks is relevant.

The Equality Act repealed the Disability Discrimination Act 1995. The provisions of the Disability Discrimination Act 1995 were substantially re-enacted by the Equality Act 2010. The Guidance reflects that paragraph 4 of Schedule 1 (classification of normal day to day activities by reference to a list of capacities) to the Disability Discrimination Act 1995 was not re-enacted in the 2010 Act. The Guidance also reflects developments in relevant case law since the guidance (ISBN 978-0-11-703686-4) issued by the Secretary of State under the now repealed Disability Discrimination Act 1995 on 29th March 2006.

Article 3 of this Order makes transitional provision in relation to proceedings arising from a complaint to an adjudicating body, whenever presented, under Part 9 of the 2010 Act concerning an alleged act of discrimination or harassment committed before 1st May 2011 or an alleged course of conduct amounting to discrimination or harassment that was commenced before 1st May 2011. The Guidance is not to have effect for the purposes of paragraph 12(1) of Schedule 1 to the 2010 Act in relation to such proceedings. The Guidance issued by the Secretary of State (ISBN 978-0-11-703686-4) under section 3 of the Disability Discrimination Act 1995 on 29th March 2006 is to continue to have effect in relation to such proceedings. Section 3(3) of the Disability Discrimination Act 1995 requires an adjudicating body to take into account any guidance which appears to it to be relevant.

A copy of the Guidance may be downloaded free of charge from the websites of the Equalities and Human Rights Commission (http://www.equalityhumanrights.com/), the Government Equalities Office (http://equalities.gov.uk/) and the Office for Disability Issues (http://odi.dwp.gov.uk/).

Made: 26 April 2011. Coming into force: 1st May 2011.

Equality Act 2010 - definition of disability:

s.6 Disability

1. A person (P) has a disability if -

    (a) P has a physical or mental impairment, and
    (b) the impairment has a substantial and long term adverse effect on P's ability to carry out normal day-to-day activities.

2. A reference to a disabled person is a reference to a person who has a disability.
3. In relation to the protected characteristic of disability –

    (a) a reference to a person who has a protected characteristic is a reference to a person who has a particular disability;
    (b) a reference to persons who share a protected characteristic is a reference to persons who have the same disability.

4. This Act (except Part 12 and section 190) applies in relation to a person who has had a disability as it applies in relation to a person who has the disability; accordingly (except in that Part and that section) -

    (a) a reference (however expressed) to a person who has a disability includes a reference to a person who has had the disability; and
    (b) a reference (however expressed) to a person who does not have a disability includes a reference to a person

who has not had the disability

6. Schedule 1 (disability: supplementary provision) has effect.

All the descriptive words contained in the legal definition of s.1(1) DDA 1995 (as restated in the relevant provisions (s.6(1) and Schedule 1, Part 1 and Part 2) of the Equality Act 2010) have an important and a specific meaning:

'physical or mental impairment' means an impairment that affects the body or the mind or both (i.e. 'impairment' means damage, defect, disease or disorder of the body or of the mind that amount to a 'disability' in that the person so affected is disabled to some degree by the impairment). There is no statutory definition of what constitutes a physical or mental impairment. However, in **Rugamer v Sony Music Entertainment UK Ltd (2002)** ICR 381 and **McNicol v Balfour Beatty Rail Maintenance Ltd (2001)** IRLR 644, the EAT suggested a common law definition being: 'some damage, defect, disorder or disease compared with a person having a full set of physical and mental equipment in normal condition;'

'substantial' means a substantial effect that is more than 'minor' or 'trivial' per the 'Guidance' ('Guidance on matters to be taken into account in determining questions relating to the definition of disability,' issued by the Secretary of State) and the 'Code of Practice' ('Code of Practice for the elimination of discrimination in the field of employment against disabled persons or persons who have had a disability');

'long-term' means that the effect of an impairment is such that it (a) has lasted at least 12 months or (b) is likely to last 12 months or (c) is likely to last for the rest of the life of the person affected: per para 2(1) of Schedule 1, DDA 1995 or (d) is likely to recur: para 2(2);

'adverse effect' means great difficulty in doing normal day-to-day activities (or everyday activities). In **Goodwin v The Patent Office (1999)** IRLR 4, the EAT said that: 'In order to constitute an adverse effect, it is not the doing of the acts which is the focus of attention but rather the ability to do (or not to do) the acts.' The EAT continued: 'Thus, for example, a person may be able to cook, but only with the greatest difficulty;'

'normal day-to-day activities' mean just that, i.e. normal daily activities which DO NOT include work of any particular form because no particular form of work is 'normal' for most people: paragraph C3 of the Guidance.

Excluded conditions:

The Equality Act 2010 prohibits unlawful discrimination against people with the protected characteristics which are listed in s.4 of the Equality Act 2010. Only those people who are defined as disabled in accordance with s.6 of the Act and the associated Schedules and Regulations made under that section will be entitled to the protection that the Act provides.

For policy reasons, people who have certain disabilities are excluded from the protection and remedy provisions of the Equality Act 2010 where they are discriminated against because of these certain disabilities. The policy reasons are similar to the concept of the deserving and undeserving poor in that while some people with certain disabilities are given both protection and a remedy if discriminated against because of their disabilities, other people with other equally disabling disabilities are not.

Paragraph A8 of the Guidance issued by the Office for Disability Issues states: 'It is not necessary to consider how an impairment is caused, even if the cause is a consequence of a condition which is excluded. For example, liver disease as a result of alcohol dependency would count as an impairment, although an addiction to alcohol itself is expressly excluded from the scope of the definition of disability in the Act. What is important to consider is the effect of an impairment not its cause – provided that it is not an excluded condition. See also paragraph A12 (exclusions from the definition).'

Excluded disabilities (or 'conditions' as the Guidance prefers to describe them) are those arising mainly from the mental disability of depression. Many people think that depression consists of no more than a person sat alone in a darkened room feeling low, very isolated and anti-social. But the majority of people who suffer from depression look and act almost normal apart from a slight or obvious quirkiness of character or personality. Many who suffer from depression do not even realise or acknowledge that they have this disability. The reason for this is that depression, as an illness and as a disability, is not ordinarily recognised as such. Essentially, it is the many manifestations of depression – i.e. the way the illness affects people – which show how serious and debilitating it can be.

The cause of depression is deceptively easy to diagnose but, because of this very reason, it is also one of the most difficult disability to treat or cure. Depression in many cases is caused as a result of a person living an extremely unsatisfactory life from which he or she has no realistic escape. Packing things in a bag, leaving the family home, giving up the job and then wandering the streets is not a viable alternative which is why some seek the ultimate escape by killing themselves. However, over a period of time life can change and difficulties can disappear and, as they do, so can depression.

Like all disabilities, there is a scale of effects from mild and annoying to seriously disabling and even life-threatening. Depression is one such disability. On a mild level, people suffering from depression can be bad-tempered, short-tempered or suffer from mild anxiety for no obvious reason. Going up the scale, people can suffer from the range of phobias such as agoraphobia, claustrophobia (e.g. when 'trapped' in an aircraft or lift), social phobias or panic attacks. More seriously still, depression may manifest itself in so-called eating disorders such as anorexia, bulimia or eating excessively and compulsory until clinical obesity occurs. Other manifestations of depression, can take the form of 'conditions' which are expressly listed as being excluded from protection under the Equality Act 2010 in the statutory Guidance at paragraph A12 issued by the Office for Disability Issues and these are:

- 'addiction to, or dependency on, alcohol, nicotine, or other substance (other than in consequence of the substance being medically prescribed);
- the condition known as seasonal allergic rhinitis (e.g. hayfever), except where it aggravates the effect of another condition;
- tendency to set fires;
- tendency to steal;
- tendency to physical or sexual abuse of other persons;
- exhibitionism; and
- voyeurism.'

Other conditions which could be added to the list are an obsessive interest in sex, particularly in bizarre or proscribed sexual activity such as paedophilia and also promiscuous homosexual and heterosexual encounters. What seems to be happening here is that those afflicted in this way seek to displace their depressive thoughts and behaviour with other equally strong ones and thereby gain some relief from the condition albeit a very unsatisfactory form of relief.

The Guidance adds that: 'The exclusions apply where the tendency to set fires, tendency to steal, tendency to physical or sexual abuse of other persons, exhibitionism, or voyeurism constitutes an impairment in themselves. The exclusions also apply where these tendencies arise as a consequence of, or a manifestation of, an impairment that constitutes a disability for the purposes of the Act.'

Thus there is a recognition by the government that these conditions can be the manifestation of disability but, for probably understandable policy reasons being that people so afflicted with the manifestation of these disabilities could, if given protection and a remedy under the Act, seek to be excused for their anti-social behaviour and, further, use their disability as a licence to continue doing what are often criminal acts. So, for these reasons of policy, such conditions or manifestations of disability are excluded from the protection and remedy provisions of the Equality Act 2010 as they were excluded previously from the Disability Discrimination Act 1995.

2.4 What is the role and function of an employment tribunal?

What the general function of an employment tribunal is or should be, and whether it should have a more inquisitorial role in disability discrimination cases, was made clear by the Court of Appeal in **McNicol (2002)** ICR 1498 where, at paragraph 26, Mummery LJ set out the position thus:

> ***'As to the function of the tribunal, it was submitted that it should adopt an inquisitorial and more proactive role in disability discrimination cases, as they can be complex and involve applicants whose impairment leads them to minimise or to offer inaccurate diagnoses of their conditions and of the effects of their impairment. I do not think that it would be helpful to describe the role of the employment tribunal as "inquisitorial" or as "proactive." Its role is to adjudicate on disputes between the parties on issues of fact and law. I agree with the guidance recently given by Lindsay J in Morgan v Staffordshire University (2002) ICR 475, 483, para 20. The onus is on the applicant to prove the impairment on the conventional balance of probabilities. In many cases there will be no issue about impairment. If there is an issue on impairment, evidence will be needed to prove impairment. Some will be difficult borderline cases. It is not, however, the duty of the tribunal to obtain evidence or to ensure that adequate medical evidence is obtained by the parties. That is a matter for the parties and their advisers. Sensible and sensitive use of the tribunal's flexible and informal procedure and its case management powers enable it to do***

justice on this issue by reminding the parties at the directions hearing of the need in most cases for qualified and informed medical evidence, bearing in mind that an unrepresented person may need some explanation about what is involved and what is required also bearing in mind the cost of obtaining such…'

2.5 Disability - case authorities on 'normal day-to-day activities:'

On this point, i.e. 'normal day-to-day activities,' Lady Smith who presided at the Scottish Employment Appeal Tribunal in the case of a probationer police constable who suffered ME and for whom the employment tribunal found in his favour being that he did have a statutory disability, analysed in relation to the law whether work of a particular form can be a normal day-to-day activity. By way of comparison, walking, climbing stairs, driving and undressing can all be described as being 'normal day-by-day activities' in terms of s.1, DDA 1995. But activities such as those of a skilled employee operating his or her skilled tools, although normal daily activities for him or her, are not 'normal day-to-day activities,' so held the EAT. Addressing this point, Lady Smith said:

> ***'When assessing, for the purposes of section 1 of the DDA, whether a person is limited in their normal day-to-day activities, it is relevant to consider whether they are limited in an activity which is to be found across a range of employment situations. It is plainly not meant to refer to the special skill case. It does though, in our view, enable a Tribunal to take account of an adverse effect that is attributable to a work activity that is normal in the sense that it is to be found in a range of different work situations. We do not, in particular, accept that "normal day-to-day activities" requires to be construed so as to exclude any feature of those activities that exists because the person is at work. To put it another way, something that a person does only at work may be classed as normal if it is common to different types of employment:'*** **Chief Constable of Dumfries & Galloway v Adams** (2009) EAT, Case No.0046/08, (03 April 2009).

In **Banaszczyk v Bookers Limited (2016)** EAT (Case No.0132/15) judgment 01 February 2016 the judge said at para.22 -

'22. The **Equality Directive** itself did not lay down any

definition of disability. The European Court of Justice has done so most recently in **Ring**, revisiting **Chacón Navas** in the light of the EU's approval of the United Nations Convention on the Rights of Persons with Disabilities. The Convention was adopted by the United Nations in 2006 and ratified by the EU in 2009. In **Ring** the European Court of Justice said:

"37. The UN Convention, which was ratified by the European Union by decision of 26 November 2009, in other words after the judgment in Chacón Navas had been delivered, acknowledges in recital (e) that 'disability is an evolving concept and that disability results from the interaction between persons with impairments and attitudinal and environmental barriers that hinders their full and effective participation in society on an equal basis with others'. Thus the second paragraph of Article 1 of the convention states that persons with disabilities include 'those who have long-term physical, mental, intellectual or sensory impairments which in interaction with various barriers may hinder their full and effective participation in society on an equal basis with others'.
38. Having regard to the considerations set out in paragraphs 28-32 above, the concept of 'disability' must be understood as referring to a limitation which results in particular from physical, mental or psychological impairments which in interaction with various barriers may hinder the full and effective participation of the person concerned in professional life on an equal basis with other workers."

23. Later the European Court confirmed that the definition does not imply complete exclusion from work or professional life. It must be understood as referring to a hindrance to the exercise of a professional activity not to the impossibility of exercising such an activity: see paragraphs 42 to 43. The European Court also confirmed that the definition applies only where a physical, mental or psychological impairment is long-term: see paragraph 32.

26. Schedule 1 to the **Equality Act** sets out supplementary provisions concerning the determination of disability. It does not contain any provision as to what may amount to "normal day-to-day activities". However, section 6(5) (together with part 2 of Schedule 1) provides that a Minister

of the Crown may issue guidance about matters to be taken into account in deciding any question for the purposes of section 6(1).

27. In 2011 there was issued "Guidance on matters to be taken into account in determining questions relating to the definition of disability". The **Guidance** does not purport to be an authoritative statement of the law. But Employment Tribunals are required to take into account any aspect of the **Guidance** which appears to be relevant: see Schedule 1, paragraph 12 of the **Equality Act**.

28. Section D of the **Guidance**, which is concerned with the meaning of "normal day-to-day activities". The Employment Judge cited from paragraph D4:

"The term 'normal day-to-day activities' is not intended to include activities which are normal only for a particular person, or a small group of people. In deciding whether an activity is a normal day-to-day activity, account should be taken of how far it is carried out by people on a daily or frequent basis. In this context, 'normal' should be given its ordinary, everyday meaning.

34. In **Paterson – Chief Constable of Dumfries & Galloway Constabulary v Adams (2009)** IRLR 571 the Claimant suffered from dyslexia. This condition had not prevented him from passing a number of examinations and rising to the post of Chief Inspector. His case was that he required adjustments to the processes for determining whether he might be promoted to Superintendent. The Employment Tribunal held that the taking of promotion examinations or assessments was not a normal day-to-day activity. The Employment Appeal Tribunal allowed the appeal.

35 On the question of day-to-day activity the Employment Appeal Tribunal held that carrying out an assessment or examination is properly to be described as a normal day-to-day activity. The Employment Appeal Tribunal said:

"66. ... We would have reached that conclusion simply taking domestic law on its own without any reference to the decision in Chacón. In our view carrying out an assessment or examination is properly to be described as a normal day-to-day activity. Moreover, as we have said, in our view the act of reading and

comprehension is itself a normal day-to-day activity. In any event, whatever ambiguity there may be about that, in our view the decision of the Court of Justice in Chacón Navas is decisive of this case.

67. We must read section 1 of the 1995 Act in a way which gives effect to European Community law. We think it can be readily done, simply by giving a meaning to day-to-day activities which encompasses the activities which are relevant to participation in professional life. Appropriate measures must be taken to enable a worker to advance in his or her employment. Since the effect of the disability may adversely affect promotion prospects, then it must be said to hinder participation in professional life."

36 On the question whether the impairment had a substantial effect on the Claimant's ability to carry out the normal day-to-day activity, the Employment Appeal Tribunal said:

"68. … In our judgment, the only proper basis, as the Guidance makes clear, is to compare the effect on the individual of the disability, and this involves considering how he in fact carries out the activity compared with how he would do if not suffering the impairment. If that difference is more than the kind of difference one might expect taking a cross-section of the population, then the effects are substantial."

37 The focus is therefore upon the impact of the impairment on the individual. The question is not whether the individual is disadvantaged compared with the population as a whole. The Employment Appeal Tribunal explained why this was so in paragraph 70 of its Judgment:

"70. … The purpose of the legislation, at least in part, is to assist those who are disabled to overcome the disadvantages which stem from a physical or mental impairment… Take someone who has all the skills to be a highly successful accountant, but lacks manual dexterity. This may require that he or she should be given longer to do the relevant examinations. It would surely be no answer and would be wholly inconsistent with the purposes of the legislation, simply to say that that individual was not disadvantaged when compared with the population at large and therefore no obligation to make the adjustment arose…"

38 This approach was applied in **Adams** (police work on night shifts a normal day-to-day activity) and **Sobhi v Commissioner of Police of the Metropolis (2013)** EAT (Case No.0518/12) (completion of an application to become a police officer, including a security questionnaire, a normal day-to-day activity):' **Banaszczyk v Bookers Limited (2016)** EAT 01 February 2016 (Case No.0132/15).

2.6 Past disabilities – the law:

The DDA 1995 Part 1 (disability) and Part 11 (employment) and Part 111 (goods, facilities and services) applied in relation to a person who has had a disability as they applied in relation to a person who has that disability: s.2(1) DDA 1995.

'Where an impairment ceases to have substantial adverse effects on a person's ability to carry out normal day-to-day activities, it is to be treated as continuing to have that effect if that effect is likely to recur:' paragraph 2(2) Schedule 1 of the DDA 1995;

And, as above, but ending '... continuing to have that effect if that effect recurs:' paragraph 5(2), Schedule 2 of the DDA 1995.

Equality Act 2010: past disabilities – a person who has had a disability:

s.6 Disability –

s.6(4) This Act (except Part 12 [transport] and section 190 [improvements to dwelling houses] applies in relation to a person who has had a disability as it applies in relation to a person who has the disability; accordingly (except in that Part and that section)...

A tribunal must disregard the effect of any measures (such as medical treatment) being undertaken by the person concerned in determining whether the impairment has created an adverse effect on the applicant's ability to carry out normal day-to-day activities: Paragraph 6(1) of Schedule 1 of the DDA 1995.

The House of Lords held that the word 'likely' in section 1 and in Schedule 1 of the DDA 1995, means 'could well happen' and not 'more probable than not:' **SCA Packaging Limited v Boyle (2009)** House of Lords, 01 July 2009. Specifically, Baroness Hale held that the previous use of a '... more probable than not' test should no longer be followed.

The outcome and conclusion of the above case of **SCA Packaging Limited v Boyle (2009)** is that in April 2010, the claimant, Mrs Boyle, who brought claims against SCA Packaging Limited alleging discrimination on grounds of sex, victimisation and unfair selection for redundancy as well as disability, agreed a settlement between the parties that was made without admission of liability of £125,000.

2.7 Disability – impairment and the likelihood of recurrence:

The correct approach to the issue of impairment and the likelihood of recurrence: in December 2005, the Disability Discrimination Act 2005 removed from the 1995 Act the requirement that a mental illness be clinically well-recognised in order to amount to a disability. On that point and the circumstances in which an impairment should be treated as likely to recur, an appeal heard by the Employment Appeal Tribunal on 15 June 2010 gave two examples which clarified the meaning of: **'Where an impairment ceases to have substantial adverse effects on a person's ability to carry out normal day-to-day activities, it is to be treated as continuing to have that effect if that effect is likely to recur.'** The EAT also clarified whether or not such an impairment is to be treated as having a substantial adverse effect on a claimant's ability to carry out normal day-to-day activities, which was material both to the question of whether he or she had an impairment at a given time and to the potential application of para. 2 (2) of Schedule 1 of the Act. The judgment of the Employment Appeal Tribunal was given by its President, Underhill J. -

8. 'The definition in section 1 is expressed to be "subject to Schedule 1". That Schedule contains a number of glosses or qualifications affecting particular elements in the definition. Those which are material for present purposes are as follows:

(1) Para. 1 relates to the term "impairment". In the Schedule as originally enacted, sub-para. (1) provided that:

"Mental impairment" includes an impairment resulting from or consisting of a mental illness only if the illness is a clinically well-recognised illness.

However, that provision was repealed, with effect from 5 December 2005, by the Disability Discrimination Act 2005. In the result, therefore, there is now no statutory gloss on the meaning of "impairment", either generally or in the case of a mental illness. Sub-paras. (2) and (3) empower the Secretary of State to make regulations requiring "prescribed conditions" either to be or not to be treated as

amounting to impairments. The Disability Discrimination (Meaning of Disability) Regulations 1996 were made under those powers and exclude various conditions, e.g. certain addictions and personality disorders.

45. ***The second general point that we need to make about depression as a disability concerns the question of recurrence We proceed by considering two extreme examples. Take first the case of a woman who suffers a depressive illness in her early 20s. The illness lasts for over a year and has a serious impact on her ability to carry out normal day-to-day activities. But she makes a complete recovery and is thereafter symptom-free for thirty years, at which point she suffers a second depressive illness. It appears to be the case that statistically the fact of the earlier illness means that she was more likely than a person without such a history to suffer a further episode of depression. Nevertheless it does not seem to us that for that reason alone she can be said during the intervening thirty years to be suffering from a mental impairment (presumably to be characterised as "vulnerability to depression" or something of that kind): rather the model is of someone who has suffered two distinct illnesses, or impairments, at different points in her life. Our second example is of a woman who over, say, a five-year period suffers several short episodes of depression which have a substantial adverse impact on her ability to carry out normal day-to-day activities but who between those episodes is symptom-free and does not require treatment. In such a case it may be appropriate, though the question is one on which medical evidence would be required, to regard her as suffering from a mental impairment throughout the period in question, i.e. even between episodes: the model would be not of a number of discrete illnesses but of a single condition producing recurrent symptomatic episodes. In the former case, the issue of whether the second illness amounted to a disability would fall to be answered simply by reference to the degree and duration of the adverse effects of that illness. But in the latter, the woman could, if the medical evidence supported the diagnosis of a condition producing recurrent symptomatic episodes, properly claim to be disabled***

> ***throughout the period: even if each individual episode were too short for its adverse effects (including "deduced effects") to be regarded as "long-term" she could invoke para. 2 (2) of Schedule 1 (provided she could show that the effects were "likely" to recur):'* J v DLA Piper UK LLP (2010)** EAT 15 June 2010 (Case No.0263/09).

See **Swift v Chief Constable of Wiltshire Constabulary (2004)** at 8.3.

2.8 Employer's knowledge of an employee's disability was and is relevant:

An employer could not claim that it did not know about a person's disability if its agent or employee (e.g. an occupational health officer, personnel officer or line manager) knew in that capacity of the disability: paragraph 4.62 of the Code of Practice. In these circumstances, such knowledge was imputed to the employer.

But where an employer did know of an employee's disability, could the employer claim an exemption from liability for disability discrimination under what was s.6 and became s.4A, DDA 1995? Under the Disability Discrimination Act 1995, an employer had a defence to the allegation that it failed to make reasonable adjustments for one of its employees if it did not know that the employee has a disability: s.4A(6), DDA 1995. Section 4A(6)(b), DDA 1995 stated that the duty to make reasonable adjustments did not arise '**... where the employer does not know and could not reasonably be expected to know... that the person has a disability and is likely to be affected in the way mentioned in subsection (1)...**' that is to say, placed at a substantial disadvantage. Case example: **Wilcox v Birmingham CAB Services Ltd (2011)** EAT 23 June 2011 (Case No.0293/10). Held by the employment tribunal and upheld by the EAT: respondent had no knowledge of the claimant's disability to attract liability under s.4A, DDA 1995.

In a claim where s.4A(3) of the DDA 1995 was relevant, the claimant suffered from dyslexia and was therefore 'disabled' as defined in the DDA 1995. The employment tribunal at first instance held that the respondent employer was **not** exempt in respect of s.4A(3), DDA 1995 and, therefore, had committed an unlawful act of disability discrimination against the claimant under the Act.

The Employment Appeal Tribunal, however, held that the ET had erred as it ought to have considered (but did not consider properly) the requirements of s.4A(3)(b) of the Act which meant that an employer was exempt from the duty to make adjustments if **each** of four matters could be satisfied and they are that the employer:-

(a) does not know that the disabled person has a disability;
(b) does not know that the disabled person is likely to be at a substantial disadvantage compared with persons who are not disabled;
(c) could not reasonably be expected to know that the disabled person had a disability; and
(d) could not reasonably be expected to know that the disabled person is likely to be placed at a substantial disadvantage in comparison with persons who are not disabled.

The presiding judge, Silber J. stressed that the word 'and' rather than the word 'or' demonstrated that these matters are **cumulative**. That is to say, they are not alternatives. All four matters must be established for an employer to rely on the subsection.

The facts were that the claimant had applied for a promotion within her employer's organisation. On her application form, one question that required to be answered was whether the candidate suffered from a disability. In response, the claimant replied in the negative as to whether any special arrangements were required for her to attend the interview. She did, however, select from a number of drop-down answers as to her disability 'learning difficulty/disability' in order to describe her disability. She also applied for a guaranteed interview (if necessary) under the 'Positive about Disability' scheme. The members of the interview panel were not told of the claimant's disability and remained unaware of it. But the person who arranged and supervised the interviewing process did know of the claimant's disability. The interview did not go well for the claimant because of a problem with the projector that was to be used for a presentation by her during the interview. Instead, she had to use the screen of a laptop as a substitute. As a result of the low marks she was awarded for her interview, during which she had felt disadvantaged by her disability for which her employer had made no reasonable adjustments, she made a claim for unlawful disability discrimination under s.4A(1), Disability Discrimination Act 1995 (Duty of employer to make adjustments). Overturning the decision of the employment tribunal that the claimant had been discriminated against by the employer for the reason of disability, the Employment Appeal Tribunal allowed the appeal by the respondent employer to the extent that the case was remitted to a fresh tribunal to properly apply the test to see whether, on the evidence, the 'provision, criterion or practice' applied by the employer exempted it from the duty to make reasonable adjustments: **Eastern and Coastal Kent PCT v Grey (2009)** EAT, 23 January 2009, (Case No.0454/08).

A provision to this effect is now stated by s.15(2) of the Equality Act 2010:

Section 15 Discrimination arising from disability…

Subsection (1) does not apply if A shows that A did not know, and could not reasonably have been expected to know, that B had the disability.'

But the exemption from the duty to make reasonable adjustments was construed more generously in the employer's favour in a later EAT case wherein it was held that an employer may rely on s.4A(6), DDA 1995, to defeat an employee's claim of failure to make reasonable adjustments if the employer **knew or ought to have known** about the employee's disability **but did not know and could not be expected to have known about its particular effect**: **Secretary of State for the Department for Work and Pensions v Alam (2009)** EAT 09.November 2009 (Case No.0242/09).

With regard to the EAT cases of **Grey (2009)** and **Alam (2010)**, some commentators believe that these two cases have conflicting approaches to the question of whether or not an employer can or should be able to rely on the 'ignorance defence' in response to a claim by a claimant that the employer failed to make reasonable adjustments under what was s.4A(6) of the Disability Discrimination Act 1995 and is now s.20 of the Equality Act 2010. However, while hearing the appeal in the case of **Wilcox v Birmingham CAB Services Ltd (2011)**, the President of the Employment Appeal Tribunal, Mr. Justice Underhill, took the opportunity to state the correct approach to the 'ignorance defence' in s.4A(6), DDA 1995 (that is now s.20, Equality Act 2010). He believed that, contrary to what has been said about these two cases, there is no conflict between the two authorities if they are properly understood. He said that what the EAT was saying in both cases is that no duty to make adjustments arises unless the employer knows (actually or constructively) **both** that the employee is disabled **and** that the employer's practices, or a physical feature of the workplace, place that employee at a disadvantage compared with others who are not disabled. He added that Lady Smith in **Alam (2010)** had correctly identified that, as a matter of logic, the second element of the 'ignorance defence' – i.e. knowledge of the disadvantage – cannot come into play unless there is first knowledge of the disability: **Wilcox v Birmingham CAB Services Ltd (2011)** EAT 23 June 2011 (Case

No.0293/10). (Note that there were two requirements in s.4A(6)(b) linked by the word 'and').

In the Employment Appeal Tribunal, Lady Smith presiding, it was held that in respect of s.4A, DDA 1995, there is no duty on an employer in relation to a disabled person to make adjustments if the employer does not know, and could not reasonably be expected to know that the person has a disability per s.4A(6), DDA 1995: **Hunter v Timber Components (UK) Ltd (2009)** EAT 17 November 2009 (Case No.0025/09).

2.9 Comparators under the Disability Discrimination Act 1995:

Unlike the Sex Discrimination Act 1975 and the Race Relations Act 1976, the comparison that was to be made under the DDA 1995 was not a like-for-like comparison. The judgment of the Court of Appeal in **Novacold (1999)** was that the comparator need not be in the same or similar circumstances as the disabled complainant. So, for example, in a case like **Novacold (1999)** where the employee was dismissed for sickness absence arising from his or her disability, the comparator would be a person who had not been absent from work (and so would not have been dismissed), whereas in a later disability discrimination case, being **Malcolm (2008)** heard by the House of Lords, the correct comparator was held to be a non-disabled person who had also been absent and who would, accordingly, have been treated in the same way as the disabled claimant.

In **Novacold (1999)**, the Court of Appeal held that s.5 (that became s.3A(1)), DDA 1995 did not require a comparison with different persons in the same or not materially different circumstances. **The focus in the DDA 1995 was narrower: (i) it was on the 'reason' for the treatment of the disabled employee; (ii) and the comparison to be made was with the treatment of '... others to whom that reason does not or would not apply.'** The 'others' with whom comparison was to be made were not specifically required to be in the same or not materially different circumstances: they only have to be persons '... to whom that reason does not or would not apply.' To put it another way, the relevant comparators were simply persons to whom the reason for the disabled employee's treatment – his or her disability – did not or would not apply.

Novacold (1999) was **overruled** (after being regarded as the correct law for nine years) in relation to comparators by the House of Lords in (Mayor and Burgesses of the) **London Borough of Lewisham v Malcolm (2008)** UKHL 43; the Law Lords held that the correct comparators for the purposes of s.3A(1) are: **employees without a disability whose conduct was the same as that of the disabled employee and that conduct was the reason the employer took action**.

2.10 Background to Novacold (1999) and Malcolm (2008):

The Appellant Committee of the House of Lords gave its judgment in the disability discrimination case of **London Borough of Lewisham v Malcolm (2008)** IRLR 700 after the Green Paper on the Equality Bill was published. Although **Malcolm (2008)** was a housing case and, for that reason, was brought under Part 111 of the Disability Discrimination Act 1995, soon afterwards the Employment Appeal Tribunal and the Court of Appeal confirmed that the **Malcolm (2008)** judgment applied equally to employment disability discrimination claims: **Aylott v Stockton on Tees Borough Council (2010)** IRLR 994, CA.

The judgment of the House of Lords was that the appropriate comparator in cases of disability-related discrimination is a non-disabled person who is otherwise in the same circumstances as the disabled claimant. This decision effectively reduced to a nullity the protection given to disabled job applicants and workers in Part 11, s.3A(1) of the Disability Discrimination Act 1995. For the previous nine years, since the decision of the Court of Appeal in **Clark v TDG Ltd t/a Novacold (1999)** ICR 951, the law had been that the comparator need not be in the same or similar circumstances as the disabled complainant.

This meant, for example, in a case like **Novacold (1999)** where the employee had been dismissed for sickness absence arising from a disability, the **Novacold (1999)** comparator would be a person who had not been absent from work (and, therefore, would not have been dismissed), whereas the **Malcolm (2008)** comparator would be a non-disabled person who had also been absent and would, accordingly, have been treated in the same way as the disabled claimant. The effect of **Malcolm (2008)** – as shown by later cases - was to make disability-related discrimination virtually impossible to prove.

When the Equality Act 2010 came into effect on 01 October 2010, the Disability Discrimination Act 1995 was repealed and the disability-related discrimination provision contained in s.3A(1) of the latter Act was not restated in the Equality Act 2010. Instead, a new form of comparable disability discrimination was provided for in the Equality Act 2010 being s.15 that is 'Discrimination arising from disability.' This new provision provides a better degree of protection for disabled job applicants or workers than that provided for by s.3A of the Disability Discrimination Act 1995 after the judgment in **Malcolm (2008)** when, on 01 October 2010, the Equality Act 2010 came into force. The reason that s.15 of the Equality Act 2010 provides a better degree of protection is that, unlike s.3A(1) of the DDA 1995 that required the complainant to show that he or she had been treated **less favourably** by the employer than the employer treated others, the claimant need only show that he or she was treated **unfavourably** (because of something arising in consequence of his or her disability) – in other words, no comparator is required and this change between what was stated in s.3A(1) of the DDA 1995 and what is stated in s.15 of the Equality Act 2010 removes the main problem that arose in **Malcolm (2008)** which were the questions: Who is the comparator? Was the complainant treated less favourably than the comparator? As the European Court of Justice held in pregnancy and maternity leave discrimination cases, notably that of **Webb v EMO Air Cargo (UK) Ltd (No.2) (1995)** HL, for some forms of unlawful discrimination it is not appropriate to try and make a comparison with others who do not have what is now known as a particular protected characteristic, such as attempting to compare the treatment of a man absent from work because of illness with that of a female absent from work because of pregnancy or maternity because pregnancy and maternity are uniquely female conditions. The same now applies to (i) comparing a person absent from work because of disability with (ii) the absent from work of a non-disabled person because of a non-disability reason. Under s.15, an employer is given the opportunity to defend its decision to treat a disabled employee unfavourably if the employer can show that the treatment '... is a proportionate means of achieving a legitimate aim: s.15(1)(b).

The meaning under the Equality Act 2010 of 'less favourable,' 'unfavourably' and 'detriment': -

Langstaff, P., President of the Employment Appeal Tribunal, explained the meaning and use in employment law of the terms 'less favourable,' 'unfavourably,' and 'detriment' in the case of **Trustees of Swansea University Pension & Assurance Scheme and another v Williams (2015)** EAT (Case No.0415/14) judgment 21 July 2015, by saying: (1) the word 'detriment' does not mean the same as 'unfavourably' ('detriment' means a disadvantage of some kind); (2) that where an employee is treated 'unfavourably,' and subsequently bring a claim for compensation to recover losses caused by the alleged unlawful discrimination, the employee does not need to show that he or she was treated adversely (i.e. subjected to unlawful discrimination) in comparison to an actual or hypothetical comparator of the opposite sex; (3) but if an employee is subjected to 'less favourable' treatment by his or her employer then, if the employee makes a claim for being subjected to unlawful discrimination, he or she would need to show that an actual or hypothetical comparator of the opposite sex would not have been unlawfully discriminated against in the way that the employer discriminated against him or her: -

"Unfavourably"

27. As to the reasoning by reference to other possible discrimination claims, the meaning of the word "unfavourably" cannot, in my view, be equated with the concept of "detriment" used elsewhere in the **Equality Act 2010**. The word "unfavourably" is deliberately chosen. So, too, the choice not to use the word "detriment" must be assumed to be deliberate: the draftsman would have been well aware of the use of the word "detriment" elsewhere within the **Equality Act**, and avoided it. Nor, as the parties were agreed, does the word "unfavourably" require a comparison with an identifiable comparator, whether actual or hypothetical, as would the description "less favourable". "Less" invites evidence to be provided in proof of "less than whom?"; "un." is by contrast to be measured against an objective sense of that which is adverse as compared with that which is beneficial.

28. Section 15 as such was introduced into the **Equality Act 2010** for the first time. The word "unfavourably" is used elsewhere in the Act in respect of provisions which have a longer pedigree. Thus in Section 18, a person is held to discriminate against a woman if in a protected period in relation to a pregnancy of hers that person treats her unfavourably because of the pregnancy or because of illness suffered by her as a result of it (Section 18(2): see also Sections 18(3) and (4)). In this use it has the sense of placing a hurdle in front of, or creating a particular difficulty for, or disadvantaging a person because of something which arises in consequence of their disability. Since the word "unfavourable" is the same word in section 15 as it is in section 18, in the same part of the same Act, it is likely that the draftsman had in mind that it would mean much the same in both.

29. I accept Mr O'Dair's submission that it is for a Tribunal to recognise when an individual has been treated unfavourably. It is impossible to be prescriptive of every circumstance in which that might occur. But it is, I think, not only possible but necessary to identify sufficiently those features which will be relevant in the assessment which this recognition necessarily involves. In my judgment, treatment which is advantageous cannot be said to be "unfavourable"

merely because it is thought it could have been more advantageous, or, put the other way round, because it is insufficiently advantageous. The determination of that which is unfavourable involves an assessment in which a broad view is to be taken and which is to be judged by broad experience of life. Persons may be said to have been treated unfavourably if they are not in as good a position as others generally would be. Sometimes this may be obvious: as for example, where a person may suffer a life event which would generally be regarded as adverse – taking the **Malcolm** case as an example, eviction; or being surcharged; being required to work harder, longer, or for less. A person who is asked, on pain of discipline, to perform at a rate which he cannot achieve because of his disability would be treated unfavourably if he were then to be subjected to that discipline, or threatened with it: this would not be directly because of his disability, but because of that which arose from it – his inability to perform work at the same speed or with the same efficiency. In a case such as this the contrast with the **Malcolm** approach is clear – for in **Malcolm**, the question would be whether an able bodied worker in the same position without the disability, who did not complete work at the rate or to the standard required would be subject to discipline. This approach is both consistent with and reflective of the sense in which "unfavourably" is applied in a case coming within section 18.

Part 3

3.1 Direct discrimination – definition:

section 13 of the Equality Act 2010 -

(1) A person (A) discriminates against another (B) if, because of a protected characteristic, A treats B less favourably than A treats or would treat others.

Two things can be said about section 13. The first is that the section refers to 'a protected characteristic' which means that the claimant may have the protected characteristic or another person has the protected characteristic. If the latter is the case, the reason that the claimant can make a claim for compensation is because he or she suffered financial loss and/or injury to feelings because he or she was adversely affected by unlawful discrimination caused to that other person or being associated with that other person. That unlawful discrimination may have occurred because of distress suffered by the claimant when the other person was harassed because of that person's protected characteristic, e.g. the claimant may work in the same workplace as the person who was harassed there and the harassing of the other person caused distress to the claimant or the claimant may have been victimised after he or she objected to the harassment of the other person. Or the claimant may have suffered financial loss or injury to feelings caused by being associated with another who has a protected characteristic (such as disability, age, etc) e.g. the claimant may be and still is the carer for a disabled person or a young person or an old person and the claimant was unlawfully discriminated against by his or her employer because of his or her caring responsibilities which meant that he or she could not work the hours or the shifts demanded by the employer and so was subjected to a detriment of some kind.

The second thing to say about section 13 is that because this section uses the term 'less favourably,' the claimant must show that he or she was treated 'less favourably' than a comparator. The question that then arises is: who is the comparator? That question used to be answered by the previous and now repealed law. But the previous law was narrower by referring not to 'a protected characteristic' but to 'the disabled person's disability.' The rest of this section addresses the question: who is the comparator? See immediately below and also 3.6 in particular per Elias LJ.

Less favourable treatment and the correct comparators:

In the appeal case of **Essex County Council v Jarrett (2015)** heard by the EAT on 3 & 4 November 2015, the President of the EAT, Mr Justice Langstaff clarified the law as to (i) the meaning of less favourable treatment and (ii) the correct comparators. This was a race discrimination case but for the purpose of disability discrimination, the word 'race' can be replaced by the word 'disability.' At para.10, Langstaff P referred to the employment tribunal, that had heard the case at first instance, saying it was '... purportedly addressing direct discrimination under the **Equality Act 2010** ("EqA"), under the terms of section 13 of the Act. Section 13(1) provides:

> **"(1) A person (A) discriminates against another (B) if, because of a protected characteristic, A treats B less favourably than A treats or would treat others."**

11. What this calls for is well established. It has, first, to be shown that there was less favourable treatment. That is not "unfavourable" treatment. Treatment may be unacceptable, inappropriate, bullying or irrational, but it may nonetheless be no less favourable than that given to others, the "others" in the context of a claim for race discrimination being those of a race other than that of the Claimant. This is so well established in case law that neither counsel thought it necessary to refer us to any particular authority upon the point, but if one were needed, reference might be had to **Glasgow City Council v Zafar** (1998) ICR 120, a decision of the House of Lords to that effect. Establishing "less favourable" treatment calls for a comparison. The comparison may or may not show that people of the same racial characteristic have been treated equally as badly as each other, but that those who are not of that characteristic have not, or it may show that there is no significant difference in the treatment of a person of one race when compared to that of another. Bad treatment is not necessarily less favourable treatment: it is less favourable

treatment, not merely bad treatment, which is a necessary step in establishing a claim for direct discrimination. Indeed treatment which is not "bad" at all may nonetheless be "less favourable" if better treatment is given to others.

12. There may be cases, of which this is not one, where no comparison with others is needed because it is plain that there has been detrimental treatment on the ground of race because of the particular criterion by which it is applied to an individual. An example, not in the field of race but that of sex, was that of the granting to female pensioners the right to enter a swimming pool free of charge at the age of 60 whereas male pensioners had to be aged 65 to qualify for free entry. There the very criterion (being in receipt of an old age pension) contained the discrimination and no further comparison was required. By contrast, in a case such as this, section 23 of the **Equality Act 2010** comes into play. That is headed "Comparison by reference to circumstances". It provides:

"(1) On a comparison of cases for the purposes of section 13, 14 or 19 there must be no material difference between the circumstances relating to each case."

13. The comparator considered may be an actual comparator or an hypothetical one: the phrase is "treats or would treat" others. In this case, the Claimant had submitted further information in relation to her claim in which by individual reference to the several allegations she made she put the names of comparators: either actual comparators to whom she was referring or hypothetical ones. There are some boxes where no comparator is named, but otherwise a number of persons whose identities were clearly spelt out:' **Essex County Council v Jarrett (2015)** EAT 03 & 04 November 2015 (Case No.0045/15).

From **1st October 2004**, under the previous law, the Regulations defined **'direct' discrimination** as –

'A person directly discriminates against a disabled person if, on the ground of the disabled person's disability, he treats the disabled person less favourably that he treats or would treat a person not having that particular disability whose relevant circumstances, including his abilities, are the same as, or not materially different from, those of the disabled person:' Reg. 4.

The difference in the definition of 'direct discrimination' compared to 'disability-related discrimination' was that the former occurred when the ***reason*** for the less favourable treatment in question was the disabled person's disability. In contrast, 'disability-related discrimination' occurred when the reason ***relates*** to the disability but is not the disability itself. The Disability Rights Commission gave an example in its employment code:

'An employer seeking a shop assistant turns down a disabled applicant with a severe facial disfigurement solely on the ground that other employees would be uncomfortable working alongside him. This would amount to direct discrimination and would be unlawful. The appropriate comparator is a person who does not have such a disfigurement but who does have the same abilities to do the job. Such a person would not have been rejected in the same way.'

Direct discrimination may occur where, for example, the employer acts on assumptions, which are often erroneous, about a person's disability. This is particular true in mental impairment cases, as mental illness still carries with it a stigma that may lead to inappropriate and, indeed, unlawful responses.

3.2 Direct disability discrimination:

(1) **Direct disability discrimination** as it applied under the Disability Discrimination Act 1995 – this was less favourable treatment on the grounds of disability than that of a real or hypothetical comparator whose relevant circumstances, including abilities, were the same as or not materially different from those of the disabled person: s.3A(5) of the DDA 1995 as amended by the Regulations. Put another way, **direct discrimination** under the DDA 1995 occurred when a person discriminated against a disabled person if, on the ground of that person's disability, he treated him or her less favourably than he treated (or would treat) a person not having ***that*** particular disability: **s.3A(5).** Example: an employer refuses to give the job of shop assistant to a woman who has a facial disfigurement even though she is the best qualified of the job applicants.

This type of less favourable treatment is analogous to **direct discrimination** in sex and race discrimination claims. The law did not make provision for direct discrimination under s.3A(5) to be justified: **s.3A(4).** Cases which involve direct discrimination are those where the treatment was because of the person's disability; or the disability itself was a significant factor in the treatment or where generalised and/or stereotypical assumptions were made about the disabled person. In direct discrimination claims, a real or hypothetical comparator is required in the same way as in claims of direct sex or race discrimination. See a relevant case example below as well as others.

The law prohibiting direct disability discrimination is now stated by s.13(1) and (3) of the Equality Act 2010. This statutory tort is committed when, say, an employer treats another, such as a disabled job applicant or worker, less favourably because of the job applicant's or worker's disability than the employer would treat others who do not have a disability.

The statutory tort can occur under the Equality Act 2010 where a worker is treated less favourably not, for example, because the worker has a statutory disability but because the person for whom he or she acts as a carer is disabled (i.e. has a protected characteristic) and requires care that, in turn, means that the worker/carer cannot work the hours or shifts that the employer requires and the employer subjects the worker/carer to a detriment for that reason. This is unlawful discrimination by association. A similar form of unlawful discrimination is by perception. This can occur where a worker is discriminated against by the employer because the worker is perceived to be disabled because of the worker's sexual orientation which might imply that he or she is infected with HIV and that the worker's work performance will be affected or he or she poses a health risk to his or her colleagues and for one or other of those reasons subjects the worker to detriment such as not promoting the worker or the employer simply thinks that the worker's continued employment is undesirable or may be limited for that perceived health reason.

Immediately below are some case authorities which arose under the Disability Discrimination Act 1995 and which show how the law was applied by the tribunals and courts. Although the Disability Discrimination Act 1995 and the Disability Discrimination Act 2005 were repealed on the coming into force of the Equality Act 2010 on 01 October

2010, much of the substantive law stated in the disability discrimination cases immediately below and in other disability discrimination cases remains just as relevant under the Equality Act 2010 as under the previous disability discrimination Acts, apart from different section headings and the repeal of 'disability-related discrimination' and the enactment in its place of 'discrimination arising from disability.'

3.3 Direct discrimination case authorities:

High Quality Lifestyles Ltd v Watts (2006) IRLR 850, EAT
Facts – W, the claimant, was a care worker for a company that provided care services to people with learning disabilities and autistic spectrum disorders. W informed his employer that he was HIV-positive. Accordingly, the employer carried out a risk assessment. The assessor noted that HQL Ltd's employees frequently sustained bites and injuries from those for whom they provided a care service. As these injuries often resulted in broken skin, the view of the assessor was that there was a high risk of the transmission of HIV and other infectious diseases. This view was contrary to that of the guidance at the time from the Department of Health – **HIV infected Health Care Workers: guidance on management and patient notification** – that stated that the risk of transmission was 'theoretical.' The guidance added that infected care workers should not be prevented from working with patients simply because there was a risk of sustaining a broken skin injury. However, after accepting uncritically the assessor's risk assessment, W's employer told him that his continued employment was 'untenable' and, after suspending him, dismissed him.
Employment tribunal: as a result of being dismissed, W brought three claims against HQL Ltd. These were: (1) disability-related discrimination contrary to **s.3A(1), DDA 1995** in respect of his suspension and dismissal as well as the disclosure of confidential information to third-parties; (2) direct disability discrimination contrary to **s.3A(5), DDA 1995** in respect of his dismissal; and (3) disability discrimination by virtue of his employer's failure to comply with its s.4A(1) duty to make reasonable adjustments contrary to **s.3A(2), DDA 1995**.

The ET upheld all of W's claims. In particular, the ET held that his dismissal was direct disability discrimination and compared his treatment to that which would have been received by a person in the same position as W **but without HIV**. Thus, the ET held, the employer had treated W less favourably than it would have treated a comparator.
Employment Appeal Tribunal: making an appeal against the decision of the ET, the employer contended that according to **s.3A(5), DDA 1995**

(direct disability discrimination), the ET was required to consider the 'relevant circumstances' of the case which meant that it should have identified a comparator in exactly the same position as W, i.e. an employee who also had a communicable life-threatening disease.

Giving its judgment, the EAT stated that there were a number of errors in the ET's conclusion that W's dismissal amounted to direct disability discrimination. Firstly, for the purposes of **s.3A(5)** a comparator is a person whose 'relevant circumstances, including his abilities' are the same as 'or not materially different' to those of the claimant. Secondly, that the word 'including' meant that the 'relevant circumstances' to be imputed to a comparator are wider than just his or her abilities. Thirdly, although the ET had correctly assumed that the comparator had the same abilities, skills and experience as W, the ET had failed to impute to the comparator an attribute (whether caused by a medical condition or otherwise) that carried the same risk of causing illness or injury to others as W's condition. Lastly, the EAT said that only by imputing relevant characteristics to the comparator could the ET consider whether such a person would also have been dismissed by HQL Ltd. If the ET answered this question in the affirmative, the logical conclusion would be that W had not been treated less favourably on the ground of his disability.

On this point, the EAT illustrated why a proper comparative stage is so important by giving the example of a surgeon with hepatitis and a dentist with tuberculosis where both have been suspended due to the risk of transmitting their respective diseases. If neither had their diseases, neither would pose any risk of transmitting the diseases to their patients. Therefore, neither would have been suspended. Thus, a causal link could be established between their diseases and their less favourable treatment. If the judgment of the ET was allowed to stand, direct discrimination would be established. But the EAT said that this would be an error of law for the reason that if the evidence showed that both medical practitioners would have been suspended, then neither could say that suspension amounted to less favourable treatment. In other words, if an employer dismissed or would dismiss a comparator with a similar disability as that of the claimant then there is no direct disability discrimination because the essential element required to be shown by **s.3A(5)**, namely 'less favourable treatment,' would be missing.

So, to use the above example, it would be an act of unlawful disability discrimination against one of the employees if the employer, who employed both the surgeon and the dentist, dismissed one but not the other when both had a potentially transmittable disease that could be passed to their patients. The employer in HQL Ltd successfully rebutted the direct disability discrimination claim but lost (i) the disability-related claim under s.3A and (ii) the failure to make reasonable adjustments claim under s.4A and was therefore liable to compensate the employee for these alternative disability claims.

The problem with s.3A(5), DDA 1995 was that the law allowed employers to directly discriminate against a disabled employee by using a comparator who was also disabled but who did not have the 'particular disability' that the claimant has.

3.4 Direct discrimination – burden of proof:

An example that shows how the burden of proof works in a case of **direct discrimination on the grounds of disability** is: **Tudor v Spen Corner Veterinary Centre Ltd and another (2006)** Case No. 2404211/05, 07 April 2006 – the majority of claims for disability discrimination were made under section 3A(1), Disability Discrimination Act 1995, that is less favourable treatment for a reason that ***relates*** to the claimant's disability (see below) - but in **Tudor (2006)**, the claimant made a claim for **direct disability discrimination** in respect of a breach of section 3A(5) of the 1995 Act.

Facts: the claimant (T) had been employed by the first respondent (S Ltd) as a veterinary nursing assistant and receptionist. The second respondent (ST) was a veterinary surgeon employed by S Ltd and its sole director. T suffered a stroke in May 2005. While still in hospital in June of that year, she was told that she had gone blind. She was also told that it was impossible to say if or when her sight might return. T's mother told ST about her daughter's condition. Shortly afterwards, ST informed T that she was being dismissed and that her employment would terminate in July 2005. Accordingly, T made a claim to an employment tribunal that she has been unlawfully directly discriminated against on the grounds of her disability.

Employment Tribunal hearing: the ET held that ST had made generalised and stereotypical assumptions about T as well as about the duration of her disability and its effects. The tribunal further found that these assumptions had been reached without meeting with T or seeking her input or making any reference to medical reports. **These findings were enough to raise a prima facie case of discrimination and so shift the burden of proof onto S Ltd and ST to show that no discrimination had occurred**. Using a hypothetical comparator, that was an employee with a broken leg who did not know when she would be able to return to work, the tribunal found that, in respect of such an individual, ST would not have made stereotypical assumptions nor rushed to a decision without a proper consideration of the circumstances. S Ltd and ST were, therefore, found to have directly discriminated against T on the grounds of her disability. ('Reverse burden of proof' is now contained in s.136, Equality Act 2010.)

Tudor (2006) can be contrasted with the previous case of direct disability discrimination about an employee with HIV whom the employer dismissed after it had received a risk assessment report from an assessor who considered that there was a high risk of transmission to residents of a care home for those with autism and other learning difficulties. In upholding the employer's appeal against a finding of direct disability discrimination by the employment tribunal, the Employment Appeal Tribunal held that the proper (hypothetical) comparator for a direct discrimination claim was a person who had an attribute (whether caused by a medical condition or otherwise), that carried the same risk of causing illness or injury to others as the respondent employee's condition. When hearing direct disability discrimination claims, an employment tribunal should consider whether the employer would have dismissed such a person: **High Quality Lifestyles Ltd v Watts,** EAT 13 January 2006 (Case No. 0671/05).

Regarding **direct discrimination** - care must be taken not to confuse a person's disability and the consequences of that disability. For example, an employer may refuse to employ a woman with epilepsy because it has reliable information that she cannot drive safely. The reason for the refusal to employ was because of her driving capability, not because of her disability. This means that the reason the employer treated her the way it did would not amount to direct discrimination. By contrast, an example of an act of direct discrimination would be a refusal of access by the employer's sports and social club simply on the basis that the club does not allow disabled members, without considering whether the employee might benefit from membership, even though he or she could access the club with a reasonable adjustment.

3.5 Disability-related discrimination case authorities:

(2) **Disability-related discrimination** – this is where an employer, for a reason relating to the disabled person's disability, treats that disabled person **less favourably** than he treats or would treat others to whom that reason does not or would not apply, and the employer cannot show the treatment was justified: was s.5(1) and then became 3A(1) of the DDA 1995 as amended by the Regulations. This form of discrimination is also known as 'disability-related discrimination,' the term used by the Disability Rights Commission in its statutory Code of Practice. Leading case authority: (**Mayor and Burgesses of the) London Borough of Lewisham v Malcolm (2008)** UKHL 43, HL.

This category of discrimination consists of less favourable treatment that does not amount to direct discrimination. Prior to the House of Lords' judgment in **London Borough of Lewisham v Malcolm (2008)**, the comparators were those as defined in **Clark v TDG Ltd t/a Novacold (1999)** IRLR 318. In **Novacold (1999)**, the Court of Appeal held that the less favourable treatment does not turn on a like-for-like comparison of the disabled person and of others in similar circumstances. Therefore, it was not appropriate to make comparisons of the cases in the same way as the Sex Discrimination Act and the Race Relations Act. **Instead, the comparison is to be made with others to whom the reason for the treatment does not apply, even if their circumstances are different from the disabled person.** For example, to dismiss a person who is absent from work for a long time because of a reason which relates to the disabled employee's disability is less favourable treatment when compared with the non-dismissal of a non-disabled worker who is still performing his or her work: **Clark v TDG Ltd t/a Novacold (1999)** 318. **Note: Clark v TDG Ltd t/a Novacold (1999) 318 was overruled by the House of Lords on 25 June 2008. Their Lordships, on a majority of four to one (Baroness Hale dissenting), held that the comparators as stated in Novacold (1999) were wrong and that the correct comparators for the purposes of s.3A(1) (i.e. to compare a disabled person's treatment with others) were:**

- **(i) employees who were not disabled and -**
- **(ii) whose conduct was or is deemed to be the same as the disabled employee's -**
- **(iii) and the conduct gave rise to the reason for the treatment by the employer: Mayor and Burgesses of the London Borough of Lewisham v Malcolm (2008) UKHL 43.**

In **Dartford Borough Council v Richardson (2009)** EAT (Case No.0031/09), (judgment was given on 04 November 2009), Underhill J., the President of the Employment Appeal Tribunal, clarified the differences in **Clark v Novacold (1999)** and that of **Lewisham v Malcolm (2008)**. In effect, he said that in **Malcolm (2008)** the House of Lords made an important change to the way the Disability Discrimination Act 1995 was previously understood and how the Act should be applied thereafter.

In **Lewisham v Malcolm (2008)**, heard on 25th June 2008, the House of Lords overruled the longstanding 1999 Court of Appeal decision in the case of **Clark v Novacold (1999)** (that was the first Court of Appeal case under the Disability Discrimination Act). The Court of Appeal had ruled that it would be unlawful discrimination to dismiss a person who has been off work for a long time because of a disability on the basis that that person was being treated less well than a non-disabled person (who, because he is not disabled, would not have taken take time off). The House of Lords ruled in **Malcolm (2008)** that this was wrong. The correct comparison is with a non-disabled person who had taken the same amount of time off as the disabled person: if the non-disabled person would have been dismissed, then dismissal of the disabled person could not be discrimination as they would have both been treated identically.

The effect of the House of Lords' decision was, therefore, that the correct comparator in a disability discrimination case, where a person with a disability is dismissed for long sickness absence, is a non-disabled person who is absent for the same period. Needless to say, this interpretation of the law made it substantially more difficult in many cases for a disabled employee to win a disability-related discrimination case under s.3A(1), DDA 1995 than before.

The House of Lords' decision in 2008 came after the hearing by an employment tribunal in the case of **Dartford Borough Council v Richardson (2009)** and after the initial decision had been reached 24 hours later, but before the tribunal's delayed written judgment and reasons. The tribunal took the decision to apply the law as it was understood to be in April 2008 and thus disregard the House of Lords interpretation of the 1995 Act.

The EAT called this 'an elementary error.' The House of Lords was not making 'new' law – instead, it was saying that the Court of Appeal's interpretation in 1999 was wrong and that the correct interpretation, **at all times**, was that which the House of Lords promulgated in 2008 (meaning that possibly many cases had been wrongly decided during the previous nine years).

The facts in **Malcolm (2008)** were that Mr Malcolm was a tenant of Lewisham Council and he was diagnosed with schizophrenia. He exercised his right to buy his council flat but, just before completion, he sub-let the flat and moved out. Consequently, the council gave him notice to quit in accordance with the Housing Act 1985. Mr Malcolm claimed the eviction amounted to disability-related discrimination. The House of Lords affirmed the county court decision for the council and held that the eviction was not related to Mr Malcolm's schizophrenia and, in any case, he was not treated less favourably than any other person who sub-let his or her flat.

As mentioned, until the House of Lords' ruling in **Malcolm (2008)**, the established meaning of disability-related discrimination was set out in the ruling by the Court of Appeal in **Clark v Novacold (1999)**. Under the **Novacold (1999)** ruling, the reason for the less favourable treatment only needed to be related to the disability. Thus, according to the judgment in **Novacold (1999)**, if a café has a 'no dogs' rule, the reason for refusing entry to a blind man with his guide dog relates to his disability. Similarly, a customer who is told to leave a restaurant because she has difficulty eating as a result of her disability is so treated for a reason related to her disability. And a worker dismissed for long-term absence caused by a back-injury is dismissed for a reason related to his disability. In these examples, the comparator for assessing less favourable treatment is a person without the disability and without the 'reason,' i.e. without a dog; or without an eating difficulty; or without the long-term absence.

In **Malcolm (2008)**, the House of Lords disapproved of **Novacold (1999)** and held that the correct comparator in determining whether a disabled person was subject to less favourable treatment was a non-disabled person in the **same circumstances** as the claimant except for the disability. Hence, the treatment of Mr Malcolm should be compared to how the council would have treated a tenant without a disability who had sub-let. Accordingly, in the examples given in the paragraph above, the blind customer with a guide dog should be compared with a sighted customer with a dog; a customer with eating difficulties should be compared with a customer without a disability but who was a messy eater; and a worker who was long-term absent from work should be compared to a worker without a disability who was similarly long-term absent from work.

(By treating disabled and non-disabled the same, the effect - unless objectively justified - is that an employer or service provider would be discriminating against the disabled if the disabled were affected adversely by the equality of treatment, i.e. if no allowance was made to take account of disabled people's disabilities. What would be happening when a café refuses entry to a blind person with a dog is that the café would effectively be applying a 'provision, criterion or practice' which might constitute indirect discrimination but which nonetheless could be justified, say, on the grounds of health and safety. On the point of what constitutes indirect discrimination, direct disability discrimination would occur if the café proprietor displayed a sign at the entrance to the café that stated 'No blind or disabled people admitted.' Whereas indirect disability discrimination would occur if the café proprietor displayed a sign at the entrance that stated 'No guide dogs/walking frames/wheelchairs/etc admitted for health and safety reasons' and, as a result, the rule would make it difficult or impossible for disabled customers to satisfy that 'provision, criterion or practice' in order to gain entry to the café. When a provider of a service such as a café applies such a provision, criterion or practice, which potentially amount to indirect discrimination, and which places the disabled person concerned at a substantial disadvantage in comparison with persons who are not disabled, it is the duty of the café owner to take such steps as it is reasonable, in all the circumstances of the case, for him or her to take in order to prevent the provision, criterion or practice having that effect: ss.19 - 21, DDA 1995. So a disabled customer faced with the imposition of a provision, criterion or practice could often side-step the problem of trying to prove unlawful disability-related discrimination by asking the owner or occupier of the premises to make a reasonable adjustment (e.g. provide a non-slip coating to the floor or an entrance ramp or guide rails) and, if it can be made but it is refused, by making a claim for unlawful disability discrimination). In addition to the duty to make reasonable adjustment(s), the cafe owner would also need to objectively justify the imposition of the provision, criterion or practice.

3.6 Reversal by Parliament of the Law Lords' judgment in Malcolm (2008):

When the government published its Equality Bill on 27th April 2009 (when it was enacted, the Bill in the form of a single Equality Act brought together and re-stated nine major pieces of anti-discrimination legislation), it conceded that '... the House of Lords' judgment in the **Lewisham v Malcolm** case has disturbed the balance between the rights of the disabled person and the interests of those with duties under the legislation by making it harder for a disabled person to be able to demonstrate a prima facie case of disability-related discrimination.' On this matter, the government said that the Office of Disability Issues had consulted on how to address the problem that the **Malcolm (2008)** judgment created and accordingly proposed replacing disability-related discrimination with the model of indirect discrimination. In its consultation paper, the Office of Disability Issues defined indirect discrimination as:

> **'The concept of indirect discrimination takes the approach set out in Article 2(2)(b)(i) of the [European] Framework Employment Directive. [...] Indirect discrimination occurs where someone applies to both people in the protected group**

and to others an apparently neutral provision, criterion or practice –

- **which puts, or would put, persons sharing the protected characteristics at a particular disadvantage compared with other persons; and**
- **which put, or would put, an individual with the protected characteristics at that disadvantage,**
- **unless that provision, criterion or practice can be objectively justified as being a proportionate means of achieving a legitimate aim.**

When the comparison is made between the individual and the comparator group, there must be no material difference between the circumstances relating to each, apart from the protected characteristics, e.g. race, sex, etc.'

In response, the government stated that 'adopting the concept of indirect discrimination in the Equality Bill would achieve an appropriate level of protection for disabled people. In addition, it would improve consistency, within the Equality Bill, between the provisions for disability and those related to the other protected characteristics, such as age, race and sex.' However, the view of Cloisters, a barristers' chambers which specialises in discrimination and equality law, was that although indirect discrimination is an option, it would cause the following difficulties in the context of disability being:

- 'its possible inability to address individual, one-off acts.
- The potential for confusion, particularly in relation to the pool for comparison which must be identified for a claim of indirect discrimination to succeed. [...] a requirement to show a disparate impact, [...] may cause difficulties for disabled people who experience the effects of an impairment in different ways. Indirect discrimination is also a very complicated, time-consuming and expensive basis on which to bring a claim.'

Following **Malcolm (2008)** and responding to the consultation for the Equality Bill, many organisations, such as the CBI and the Housing Law Practitioners' Association, expressed a preference for the reinstatement of a modified form of disability-related discrimination based on the **Novacold** formulation with an objective defence of justification. When the Equality Bill was published at the end of April 2009, it contained Clause 14 (that became s.15 of the Equality Act 2010) and the Explanatory Notes which accompanied the Bill stated: 'This clause is a new provision. The Disability Discrimination Act 1995 provided protection from disability related discrimination but following the judgment of the House of Lords in the case of London Borough of Lewisham v Malcolm (2008) UKHL 43, those provisions no longer provided the degree of protection from disability related discrimination that is intended for disabled people. This clause is aimed at re-establishing an appropriate balance between enabling a disabled person to make out a case of experiencing a detriment which arises because of his or her disability, and providing an opportunity for an employer or other person to defend the treatment.' Accordingly, under the Equality Act 2010, s.15 provides a cause of action for those subjected to: 'Discrimination arising from disability.'

Discrimination – direct and indirect:

It may be helpful at this stage to explain in more detail two closely related forms of discrimination which are described as 'direct' and 'indirect.' Regardless of the reason for discrimination (e.g. being the person's sex, race, disability, age, etc), the same basic principles governing either 'direct discrimination' or 'indirect discrimination' apply if the ***reason*** why a person was subjected to unlawful discrimination was because of one or more of the nine protected characteristics that

(i) he or she has or
(ii) is perceived to have or
(iii) another person with whom he or she associates has.

For example, **direct discrimination** would occur if an employer refused to employ a Romanian gypsy because of the job applicant's ethnicity (ethnic or national origins being a protected characteristic, namely, one of race). **Indirect discrimination** would occur if the employer had a provision, criterion or practice which is that applications for jobs with the company can only be made by those whose names, on the basis of friendship or family connections, are put forward by the employer's present or past employees, 98% of whom are white British-born, thereby making it difficult or impossible for a Romanian gypsy newly arrived in the UK (or any other similar ethnic workers) to apply for a job with that particular employer. **Perceptive discrimination** (being direct discrimination) would occur if an employer dismissed one of its employees because he or she was perceived to be a Romanian gypsy. **Associative discrimination** (being direct discrimination) would occur if an employer dismissed one of its employees because of his or her association with a Romanian gypsy.

Before the Equality Act 2010 came into effect on the 01 October 2010, the law in this area was stated by Acts such as the Sex Discrimination Act 1975, the Race Relations Act 1976 and the Disability Discrimination Act 1995 as well as in statutory Regulations such as the Employment Equality (Age) Regulations 2006, SI.1031, the Employment Equality (Religion or Belief) Regulations 2003, SI.1660 and the Employment Equality (Sexual Orientation) Regulations 2003, SI.1661.

> **What constitutes direct discrimination is stated by s.13 of the Equality Act 2010: 'A person (A) discriminates against another (B) if, because of a protected characteristic, A treats B less favourably than A treats or would treat others.'**

Direct discrimination occurs where a person with one or more of the nine protected characteristics is treated less favourably than a similarly placed person, who does not have that protected characteristic or characteristics, on the grounds of the protected characteristic or characteristics. So, for example, **direct *disability* discrimination occurs where a person is treated less favourably than a similarly placed non-disabled person on grounds of disability.** Likewise, **direct *sex* discrimination occurs where a person is treated less favourably than a similarly place person of the opposite sex on grounds of sex.** This means that a reason for the less favourable treatment – not necessarily the only reason but one which is significant in the sense of more than trivial – must be one or more of the following protected characteristics: being the claimant's age, disability, gender reassignment, marriage or civil partnership, pregnancy or maternity, race, religion or belief, sex or sexual orientation.

'Because the allegation is that one person has been treated 'less favourably' than another, that treatment must be compared to the way another (called 'a comparator') was or would have been treated. In other words, a comparator is necessary. But in many cases of direct discrimination, it is not necessary for an employment tribunal to identify or construct a particular comparator (whether actual or hypothetical) and to ask whether the claimant would have been treated less favourably than that comparator. The employment tribunal can short circuit that step by focusing on the reason for the treatment. If it is a proscribed reason, such as disability, then in practice it will be less favourable treatment than would have been melted out to someone without the proscribed characteristic:' per Elias LJ, para.5 in **JP Morgan Europe Ltd v Chweidan (2011)** EWCA Civ 648, Court of Appeal.

Proving discrimination is a two-stage process:

In **Chweidan (2011)**, at para.6, Elias LJ goes on to say: ***'In practice, a tribunal is unlikely to find unambiguous evidence of direct discrimination. It is often a matter of inference from the primary facts found. The burden of proof operates so that if the employee can establish a prima facie case, i.e. if the employee raises evidence which, absent explanation, would be enough to justify a tribunal concluding that a reason for the treatment was the unlawful protected reason, then the burden shifts to the employer to show that in fact the reason for the treatment is innocent, in the sense of being a non-discriminatory reason: see Peter Gibson in Igen v Wong (2005) ICR 931, para.37.'***

Indirect discrimination occurs where an employer applies what used to be called a requirement or a 'must' that employees have to comply with. Whereas the majority of employees may well be able to comply with the employer's requirement, that is now referred to by a wider definition being 'a provision, criterion or practice,' some employees may find that they cannot do so because it is to their detriment in relation to one or more of their particular protected characteristics such as, for example, the protected characteristic of sex, being the ability (or inability) to continue to work full-time or continue to work a 12-hour day shift system when returning to work after taking maternity leave because of their childcare responsibilities; and the employer cannot justify the imposition of the particular provision, criterion or practice.

What constitutes indirect discrimination is stated by s.19 of the Equality Act 2010:

'(1) A person (A) discriminates against another (B) if A applies to B a provision, criterion or practice which is discriminatory in relation to a relevant protected characteristic of B's.

(2) For the purposes of subsection (1), a provision, criterion or practice is discriminatory in relation to a relevant protected characteristic of B's if –

(a) A applies, or would apply, it to persons with whom

B does not share the characteristic,

(b) **it puts, or would put, persons with whom B shares the characteristic at a particular disadvantage when compared with persons with whom B does not share it,**

(c) **it puts, or would put, B at that disadvantage, and**

(d) **A cannot show it to be a proportionate means of achieving a legitimate aim.'**

To succeed with an indirect discrimination claim under s.19, Equality Act 2010, a claimant must show that he or she is not the only person with the protected characteristic in question who is disadvantaged by the employer's provision, criterion or practice. The use of the plural 'persons' in s.19 demonstrates that the claimant must show that (i) there are others who have that particular protected characteristic and (ii) they would be similarly disadvantaged, i.e. that there were a sufficient number of people who shared the claimant's protected characteristic to constitute a 'group' amounting to 'a group disadvantage' (a case authority in which the claimant could not show that she was one member of a group that was disadvantaged by the provision, criterion or practice applied by her employer which was that a religious emblem being a Christian cross must not be worn visibly was: **Eweida v British Airways (2010)** EWCA Civ 80): **Chatwal v Wandsworth Borough Council (2011)** EAT (Case No.0487/10).

The reason why members/believers/followers of other religions such as Muslims or Sikhs are able lawfully to insist on wearing religious clothing and symbols at work which denote their belief in a particular religion is because they are able and willing to group together and assert that it is a requirement of their religion that they do so. In contrast, the claimant in **Eweida (2010)** was the only Christian in BA's workforce who insisted that the visible wearing of the Christian cross was a requirement of her religion.

So some practical examples of unlawful indirect discrimination would be where an employer insisted that all potential employees must be at least six feet tall. This would likely discriminate against (i) a women and (ii) women as a group, more of whom in relation to men are generally less than six feet tall. If the employer could not justify this provision, criterion or practice then it would be unlawfully discriminatory. Or an employer might insist that all employees working in a particular department should be able to move and carry articles which weigh up to 25 kilos. This would be a provision, criterion or practice which (i) an employee with a particular disability, for example, who has or has had a slipped disc and

(ii) others being a group who have or have had slipped discs and related back injuries, would be unlikely to be able to comply with and, for that reason, would be to his or her and their detriment and, again, would be unlawfully discriminatory if the employer could not justify the provision, criterion or practice or failed to take steps which were reasonable (such as providing lifting equipment) to remove the disadvantage for the disabled employee so that he or she could continue to do his or her job. As for age discrimination, an employer might have a provision, criterion or practice which is that all employees doing a certain job must retire at age 55. This would be unlawful discrimination on the ground of age unless the employer could objectively justify the provision, criterion or practice and do so, maybe, on the grounds of health and safety or by showing that a certain standard of physical or/and mental (cognitive) fitness was required to do the job satisfactorily, safely and competently and that only people below the age of 55 would generally have that ability.

3.7 Novacold (1999) was followed before the case of Malcolm (2008):

Returning once more to the decision of the Court of Appeal in Novacold (1999):

the Employment Appeal Tribunal applied analysis of the Court of Appeal given in **Novacold (1999)** to **Cosgrove v Caesar & Howie (2001)** IRLR 653. C, a legal secretary, was absent from work owing to depression. The EAT found that the material reason for C's dismissal was her long-term absence (15 months) and, further, held that this reason related to C's disability. Finally, the EAT considered whether C & H would have dismissed another employee to whom the reason for C's dismissal did not apply. Looking to the then correct comparator – a non-disabled employee who had not been absent from work - the EAT found that there would have been no reason to dismiss an employee who was attending work unless some other grounds for dismissal existed. The EAT therefore found that C had been subjected to less favourable treatment for a reason relating to her disability.

3.8 Commentary on Malcolm (2008):

Commenting on the Law Lords' majority decision in **Malcolm (2008)**, Michael Rubenstein wrote in the editorial of the 09 September 2008 edition of the Industrial Relations Law Reports (IRLR):

> ***'On the Malcolm reasoning, if a non-disabled person would***

> ***have been treated the same, there is no disability-related reason, and if a non-disabled person would have been treated more favourably, there will be direct discrimination "on the ground of" disability, rather for a reason which relates to disability. According to Malcolm, the correct comparator in such a case is with a non-disabled person with the same amount of absence. If they would also be dismissed, there is no disability-related discrimination'.***

Rubenstein added: ***'...the result of Malcolm is to emasculate disability-related discrimination as a ground of complaint.'*** He concluded by expressing the view that: ***'The result is that, unless and until Parliament overrides Malcolm, the focus in DDA cases will now shift almost entirely to reasonable adjustments, where the concept that disability is to be treated differently from other strands by discrimination law is expressly recognised. In particular, we can expect cases that will argue that the adjustment duty encompasses changes to policies and procedures which would otherwise lead to a disabled employee's dismissal.'***

3.9 Post-Malcolm (2008):

After the case of **Malcolm (2008)**, many commentators correctly forecasted that there was likely to be a significant reduction in the protection provided by s.3A(1) after the House of Lords' laid down a narrower test for disability-related discrimination in **Malcolm (2008)** wherein their Lordships declared that the comparators as defined in **Novacold (1999)** were **incorrect** and that an employee who has a statutory disability and makes a disability claim alleging that his or her employer treated him or her less favourably for a reason which relates to his or her disability should compare his or her treatment with comparators:

(i) who **did not** have a statutory disability;
(ii) and who is in the same circumstances as the disabled employee.

That is to say, a **disabled employee** was to be compared with **non-disabled employees** (the comparators) who were deemed to have done what the disabled employee did. For example, in **Novacold (1999)** where the claimant was dismissed for sickness absence arising from his disability, the treatment of such an employee should be compared with that of a non-disabled person who had also been absent. There is a suggestion in **Malcolm (2008)** that the employer can treat both disabled and non-disabled the same **unless** the reason for the treatment of the disabled employee by the employer is **closely related** (maybe wholly related) to the disabled employee's disability in which case, if the latter occurred, liability for disability discrimination would arise: **Lord Scott at paragraph 33**.

Despite the House of Lords' judgment in **Malcolm (2008)**, the statutory provisions of the Disability Discrimination Act 1995 still needed to be followed by adopting a step-by-step approach as stated by HH Judge Peter Clark in **Macklin (2008)** so that if, during the comparison stage, the employment tribunal found that the disabled employee had **not** been treated less favourably by the employer than it would have treated its non-disabled comparator employees, there still remained a further statutory requirement that was to consider whether the employer discriminated against the disabled employee contrary to s.4A(1) and s.3A(2) of the Disability Discrimination Act by applying a provision, criterion or practice (or there is a feature of the employer's premises) which the disabled employee could not comply with because it placed the disabled employee at a substantial disadvantage in comparison with the employer's non-disabled employees who could or can so comply. If this was the case, the employer had a duty to consider what **reasonable adjustments** (per 18B) it could make to prevent the provision, criterion or practice (or feature) having the effect of placing the disabled employee at a substantial disadvantage compared to its non-disabled employees.

However, it has to be stressed that the judgment of the House of Lords in **London Borough of Lewisham v Malcolm (2008)** - that was a **tenancy case** in which the tenant alleged that he had been **treated less favourably** by Lewisham Council **for a reason** which related to his disability - meant that unless a claim was made that the employer failed to take steps to make reasonable adjustments, Courts needed only to determine the first stage, being the comparator stage, by examining whether the disabled claimant was treated less favourably than non-disabled comparators for a reason which relates to the disabled claimant's disability in circumstances where both parties (the disabled claimant and the non-disabled comparator) were deemed to be in the same position or had done the same thing.

If there is a finding that the disabled claimant was not treated less favourably than the non-disabled comparators because both the disabled claimant and the non-disabled comparators were or would have been treated the same, then there is no need for Courts to proceed any further and consider the question of whether the disabled claimant was placed at a substantial disadvantage by a provision, criterion or practice applied by the landlord or property owner which would have placed the landlord or property owner under the duty to take steps to make reasonable adjustments to remove the provision, criterion or practice (or feature of the premises) from having that effect.

Immediately following the case of **Malcolm (2008)**, the legal commentators said that it remained to be seen whether employment tribunals, the Employment Appeal Tribunal and the Court of Appeal would determine employees' disability discrimination claims in the same way as the House of Lords determined a tenant's disability discrimination claim in **London Borough of Lewisham v Malcolm (2008).** Subsequence cases showed that this would be the result as predicted, at paragraph 158 of **Malcolm (2008)**, by Lord Neuberger who said:

> ***'As Lord Brown points out in para 111, the principle reasons for rejecting the wider construction of section 24(3) is its potentially extraordinary penal consequences for property owners and the apparent pointlessness of the comparison exercise, and the same arguments apply to the wider construction of section 5(1)(a)*** [now s.3A(1)(a)(b)] ***in relation to employers.'***

At the Employment Appeal Tribunal on 26 November 2008 in **Countrywide Estate Agents and others (2008)** (Case No.0393/08), HHJ Birtles referred to **Malcolm (2008)** by saying:

- ***'... despite the fact that it was a housing discrimination case, it is clear that it applies to employment matters as well... The remarks of the members of the House of Lords in the Malcolm case are equally applicable to employment law cases.***
- ***... the effect of Malcolm, as is well known, is to limit the range of comparators in disability discrimination cases. Suffice it to say that we are not able to find that the (tribunal's) judgment either sets out the law accurately in relation to the appropriate comparator or indeed internally...'***

In **Countrywide Estate Agents and others (2008),** the EAT was not prepared to decide who the proper comparators should be. Instead it decided to leave that question to be answered by the employment tribunal to whom it remitted the case.

Similarly, at the Employment Appeal Tribunal on 05 February 2009 in **Child Support Agency v Truman (2009)** (Case No.0293/08), HHJ Peter Clark remarked that this was the first time that it had been required to consider the law ***'... as it has now been revealed...'*** by the House of Lords in **Malcolm (2008)**.

The case of **Child Support Agency (2009)** had been heard by an employment tribunal at first instance in December 2007 that was well before the House of Lords decided **Malcolm (2008)** in June 2008. In **Child Support Agency (2009)** the employment tribunal upheld the claimant's (Mrs Truman's) claim of disability discrimination. The respondent Child Support Agency appealed to the EAT, the appeal having particular significance in view of the Law Lords' decision in **Malcolm (2008)**.

At the appeal hearing, the key question for the EAT was whether the decision in **Malcolm (2008)** applied only to housing matters or to employment issues as well. If **Malcolm (2008)** did apply to the latter, the question that arose to be considered was what was the status of the previous case authority of **Clark v Novacold (1999)** ICR 951? HHJ Peter Clark made the position crystal clear at paragraph 22 of the Employment Tribunal Appeal judgment by saying:

> ***'In our judgment the narrower comparator favoured by the majority in*** **Malcolm** ***applies equally in the employment context. The wider comparator used in*** **Novacold** ***should no longer apply (unless and until the legislation is further amended by Parliament).'***

HHJ Peter Clark said that there were a number of reasons why the EAT considered that this must be the case, in particular the policy considerations of arriving at a situation where a narrower comparator was used in housing cases than in employment cases, adding:

> ***'… that is a matter for Parliament. If it is thought necessary to further amend the legislation so as to provide for different comparators in different contexts so be it. For our part we are quite satisfied that, following*** **Malcolm*****, the wider comparator formulated by Mummery LJ in*** **Novacold** ***is incorrect. The narrower comparator is to be applied in employment cases such as the present, "however inconvenient," as Baroness Hale observed…'***

Thus, in **Child Support Agency (2009)**, the employment tribunal at first instance had approached the question of comparator incorrectly. This meant that at least some of the conclusions of the employment tribunal must be set aside. Accordingly, the respondent's appeal was allowed and the matter remitted to the tribunal for it to decide the correct comparator.

Further confirmation that employment tribunals had to follow the House of Lords' decision in **Malcolm (2008)** was stated by the Honourable Mrs Justice Slade in the EAT in the case of **Stockton-on-Tees Borough Council v Aylott (2009)** EAT, 11 March 2009 (Case No.0401/08) wherein the EAT held that an employment tribunal had erred in failing to apply **Malcolm (2008)**. As to the correct comparator for use in disability discrimination cases, Mrs Justice Slade cited the words of **Toulson LJ** in **N (R on the application of) v London Borough of Barking and Dagenham Independent Appeal Panel (2009)** EWCA Civ 108, Court of Appeal (24.02.09) wherein it was held that **Malcolm (2008)** overruled **Novacold (1999)** (see para 44) in that the **Malcolm (2008)** comparator is:

> ***'... someone who had behaved in the same way as the person concerned, but did not suffer from that person's disability.'***

So, to use one of the examples given previously being that of a blind person who relied on a guide dog to get around, it would be lawful for a cafe owner who had a no dogs' rule to refuse entry to a blind person who had a guide dog just as the cafe owner would refuse entry to an able-bodied dog owner who tried to take a dog into the cafe.

Postscript: it could be said, perhaps, that if the **Malcolm** case had been about discrimination on the ground of sex rather than disability and the Law Lords had decided that an employee who was absent from work for a reason relating to her pregnancy or maternity leave but whose treatment, nonetheless, was to be compared to the way an employer treated or would treat an employee who was neither pregnant nor absent on maternity but was nevertheless absent from work, there would probably have been an outcry from those who represent and advocate women's rights. On the other hand, it is unlikely that a court or tribunal would allow a pregnant woman or an employee absent from work on maternity leave to use the protective rights granted to her under the anti-discrimination legislation as a legal weapon to defeat the legal rights of another, being a landlord, as the litigant in **Malcolm** sought to do.

3.10 Justification test under the Disability Discrimination Act 1995 (1):

Under the Disability Discrimination Act 1995, disability-related discrimination amounting to less favourable treatment was only unlawful if it was not justified. Treatment would only be justified if the reason for it was both material to the circumstances of the particular case and substantial: s.3A(3) of the DDA 1995 as amended by the Regulations.

The question of justification applied at two stages. The first was the **comparator stage** when considering whether the disabled employee was treated less favourably by the employer for a reason which relates to the disabled person's disability and the reason does not or would not apply to the non-disabled employees and the employer cannot show that the treatment in question is justified.

Justification applied also at the **reasonable adjustments' stage**. An employer was under a duty to take steps to make reasonable adjustments if the employer had applied a requirement that placed the disabled employee at a substantial disadvantage compared to its non-disabled employees or there was any physical feature of the employer's premises that had that effect. If, for example, the employer applied a requirement (that now had a wider meaning being 'a provision, criterion or practice') that all employees absent for six months or more will be dismissed, and that requirement placed a disabled employee at a substantial disadvantage because, unlike the employer's non-disabled employees, the disabled employee – for a reason which relates to the disabled employee's disability – could not comply with the requirement, the employer had a statutory duty under s.4A(1)(a)(b) **'... to take such steps as it is reasonable, in all the circumstances of the case, for him** (the employer) **to have to take in order to prevent the provision, criterion or practice, or feature, having that effect.'** An employer would discharge that statutory duty by taking any reasonable steps which it could take to prevent 'a provision, criterion or practice' it had applied (or any feature of the premises it occupies) from having the effect of placing the disabled employee at a substantial disadvantage compared to its non-disabled employees. If there were no reasonable steps which the employer could take, the employer might have been able to show that - (i) its treatment of the disabled employee was justified because the reason for the treatment was both material to the circumstances of the particular case and substantial: s.3A(3); and (ii) the employer complied with its statutory duty under s.4A to consider any reasonable adjustments but none could be made: s.3A(6).

3.11 Justification test under the Disability Discrimination Act 1995 (2):

Section 5(3) DDA 1995 (that became s.3A(3)) stated that less favourable treatment of a disabled person is justified **"... if, but only if, the reason for it is both material to the circumstances of the particular case and substantial.'** The burden of proof was on the employer to show that the reason for the less favourable treatment satisfied the statutory criteria: **Baynton v Saurus General Engineers Ltd (2000)** ICR 375, EAT.

For 'justification' see: **Jones v Post Office (2001)** IRLR 384 per s.5(3) DDA 1995. The Court of Appeal held that the role of the tribunal is confined to considering whether the **reason given by the employer** for the less favourable treatment can properly be described as both **'material to the circumstances of the case and substantial.'** The meaning of **'material'** is 'significant and relevant:' **Rainey v Greater Glasgow Health Board (1987)** ICR 129, HL - (an Equal Pay Act 1970 case).

'It would be justifiable to terminate the employment of an employee whose disability makes it impossible for him any longer to perform the main functions of his job, if an adjustment such as a move to a vacant post elsewhere in the business is not practicable or otherwise not reasonable for the employer to have to make:' paragraph 6.21 of the Code of Practice. But the Act also states that that less favourable treatment is only justified where specific criteria have been satisfied.

3.12 Different legal tests for 'reasonableness' and 'justification:'

The Court of Appeal said that **different legal tests** apply under the Disability Discrimination Act 1995 for (i) determining **'reasonableness'** (for the purposes of the duty to make reasonable adjustments) and (ii) **'justification'** (in relation to less favourable treatment). The important point is that the test for 'reasonableness' is **objective** while the test for 'justification' is **subjective**. This means that an employer's failure to make reasonable adjustments will render the employer liable to a disadvantaged employee who is suffering from a disability. The objective point of view is that of a disinterested person looking at the situation and asking himself or herself which were the reasonable adjustments that the employer could have made - this is the tribunal's viewpoint too. But less favourable treatment of a disabled employee can be justified subjectively - all that is required is that the reason for the treatment must fall within the 'band of reasonable responses' which a reasonable employer might have adopted. So, in effect, it is a limited degree of subjectivity. The subjective point of view is that of the employer but thinking and acting within the 'range of reasonable responses of a reasonable employer.' Case authority: **Smith v Churchills Stairlifts plc (2005)** EWCA Civ 1220, CA.

3.13 Reasonable adjustments under the Disability Discrimination Act 1995 - justification in relation to materiality and substantiality:

In **Nottinghamshire County Council v Meikle (2004)** Court of Appeal, EWCA Civ 859, Keene LJ held that the effect of s.5(5) (that became s.3A(6)) was to require the tribunal to consider what the position would have been if the employer had complied with its s.6 (and then 4A) duty. [Now **s.20(3)** and **s.4** and **s.39(5)** under the **Equality Act 2010**].

In **Collins v Royal National Theatre Board (2004)** EWCA Civ 144, the Court of Appeal held that (using the old section headings) s.5(4) DDA 1995 (the materiality and substantiality reason) does not permit an employer to justify a failure to comply with the s.6 duty to make reasonable adjustments by reference to factors which are properly relevant to establishing the s.6 duty and the breach of it.

That is to say the test under s.5(4) was not the same as the test of justification under s.5(3) as interpreted in **Post Office v Jones (2001)** IRLR 384, ICR 805.

In **Collins (2004)**, the Court of Appeal said that s.5(4) DDA 1995 only becomes relevant once an employer has been shown to have failed to comply with his s.6 duty to take reasonable steps to prevent an employee's disability resulting in substantial disadvantage. The effect of **Collins (2004)** was that employers were very unlikely to succeed with the s.5(4) defence for existing cases which were decided under the pre-1st October 2004 law. The s.5(4) justification defence available to employers in respect of a failure to make reasonable adjustments, provided the reason for the failure was both material to the circumstances of the particular case and substantial, was removed from the DDA 1995 on 1st October 2004 by the Disability Discrimination Act 1995 (Amendment) Regulations 2003, SI 2003/1673. However, the amended DDA allowed an employer to justify **any less favourable treatment** if the employer can show that the reason for the treatment was both material to the circumstances of the particular case and substantial: s.3A(3).

A tribunal, in determining whether justification had been made out in such a case, had to follow the approach laid down by the Court of Appeal in **Jones v Post Office (2001)** IRLR 384, CA: **Williams v J. Walter Thompson Group Ltd (2005)** IRLR 376, CA - i.e. the tribunal must not make an appraisal of the available evidence and decide for itself whether the employer was correct to impose the measure that led to the less favourable treatment. Instead, the tribunal must objectively consider the employer's subjective decision by using a test similar to the 'band of reasonable responses' test and, in doing so, must consider the materiality and substantiality of the employer's reason: s.3A(3), DDA 1995. See too: **Smith v Churchills Stairlifts plc (2005)** EWCA Civ 1220, CA.

The decision by the Court of Appeal in **Jones v Post Office (2001)** was widely criticised for setting a very low threshold for justification in DDA less favourable treatment claims. **Jones (2001)** limited employment tribunals to considering whether the reason given by an employer for less favourable treatment of a disabled person was material and substantial. But the real problem with **Jones (2001),** was that the Court of Appeal was asked to consider the issue of less favourable treatment alone, and was not asked to consider the reasonable adjustments provisions. The later cases of **Archibald (2004)** (HL) and **Meikle (2004)** (CA) redress that imbalance. **In both cases, the importance of first considering the issue of reasonable adjustments, before less favourable treatment, was emphasised.** (That is to say, read section 3A as: 3A(1)(a)(b) then (2) then (3) and finally but importantly (6)). This is the proper approach because it then enables the effect of any failures to be taken into account at the justification stage, as is required by the DDA 1995. **Therefore, in the majority of cases justification of less favourable treatment for a reason related to disability will depend upon reasonable adjustments**. It will only be in cases where a reasonable adjustment would have made no difference that the **Jones (2001)** test will apply.

3.14 'Discrimination arising from disability' per s.15, Equality Act 2010:

When the Equality Act 2010 was enacted on 01 October 2010, the section that applied to 'disability-related discrimination' being 3A(1)(a)(b), Disability Discrimination Act 1995 was not retained. Instead, in its place, a new statutory tort was enacted being 'discrimination arising from disability' that is stated in section 15, Equality Act 2010. A case authority on the meaning of 'discrimination arising from disability' is **Basildon & Thurrock NHS Foundation Trust v Weerasinghe (2015)** EAT 28/29 July 2015 (Case No.0397/14):

In **Basildon & Thurrock NHS Foundation Trust v Weerasinghe (2015)**, the President of the Employment Appeal Tribunal, Mr. Justice Langstaff, said of section 15, Equality Act 2010:

'24. The ingredients of a claim of "discrimination arising from disability" (as it is headed and as often referred to) are defined by statute. It is therefore to the statute, and not to any colloquial or shorthand representation of it that a Tribunal should have regard.

25. Section 15 (set out above in the judgment) involves no question of less favourable treatment. It is therefore distinct from direct discrimination, which does. Nor does section 15 concern discrimination "related to" disability. It would be a mistake to treat it as if it did, for that is a description of statutory provisions superseded by section 15 of the **Equality Act 2010**.

26. The current statute requires two steps. There are two links in the chain, both of which are causal, though the causative relationship is differently expressed in respect of each of them. The Tribunal has first to focus upon the words "because of something", and therefore has to identify "something" - and second upon the fact that that "something" must be "something arising in consequence of B's disability", which constitutes a second causative (consequential) link. These are two separate stages. In addition, the statute requires the Tribunal to conclude that it is A's treatment of B that is because of something arising, and that it is unfavourable to B. I shall return to that part of the test for completeness, though it does not directly arise before me.

27. In my view, it does not matter precisely in which order the Tribunal takes the relevant steps. It might ask first what the consequence, result or outcome of the disability is, in order to answer the question posed by "in consequence of", and thus find out what the "something" is, and then proceed to ask if it is "because of" that that A treated B unfavourably. It might equally ask why it was that A treated B unfavourably, and having identified that, ask whether that was something that arose in consequence of B's disability.

28. The words "arising in consequence of" may give some scope for a wider causal connection than the words "because of", though it is likely that the difference, if any, will in most cases be small; the statute seeks to know what the consequence, the result, the outcome is of the disability and what the disability has led to.

29. Two examples may be given from case law of the operation of these provisions. In the case of **Malcolm v London**

Borough of Lewisham (2008) IRLR 700 disability led to the Claimant wrongfully subletting his property; it was because of the effects of his mental condition (something arising in consequence of his disability) that he had sublet the property, and it was because of that that he was subject to eviction proceedings. Had the law been then as it is now, the Claimant would have succeeded in his claim that his eviction constituted unlawful discrimination against him. As it stood then, he failed.

30. The primary consideration in the case of **Trustees of Swansea University Pension & Assurance Scheme and Anor v Williams (2014)** EAT (Case No 0415/14) was as to the meaning of the word "unfavourably" in the context of the facts of that case, but at paragraph 29 there was a broader discussion of the effects of the wording of section 15(1)(a). In that an example was given of:

> **"29. A person who is asked, on pain of discipline, to perform at a rate which he cannot achieve because of his disability would be treated unfavourably if he were then to be subjected to that discipline, or threatened with it: this would not be directly because of his disability, but because of that which arose from it - his inability to perform work at the same speed or with the same efficiency."**

31. Once the question has been asked as to what the "something" is that is relevant that has arisen in consequence of disability and a Tribunal has decided that that something has been a consequence of the disability, this being a causal test, it will turn to ask whether the treatment complained of as unfavourable is because of that. It therefore needs to know what treatment has happened because of the something and whether it is unfavourable. As I have indicated, the argument may just as well be put the other way round and should be productive of precisely the same result. What unfavourable treatment is complained of? What was it because of? "Because of" is a causal test. A robust approach should be taken as is common throughout the law in respect of such a test.

32. Miss Ellenbogen QC submits that the wording "because of" is familiar territory in the **EqA 2010**. Though section 15 is a

new section designed to meet the inequity of the conclusion of the **Malcolm** appeal in the House of Lords, the definition of direct discrimination had been on the statute books for some 35 years before the **EqA 2010**. The words "because of" were not used in earlier formulations; the words "on the grounds of" were. There is now considerable case law to the general effect that the change in wording does not connote a change of substance. She argues that accordingly cases that stand as authorities in respect of the meaning of "on the grounds of" remain appropriate to consider in respect of the words "because of" and if this is so (as she contends) in relation to section 13, for instance, which is the provision relating to direct discrimination, so the same words in the same statute should be given the same force in section 15. Since the focus is on the treatment by A, A being the Respondent in this and most cases, the renowned discussion in particular of the meaning of "on the ground of" by Lord Nicholls in **Nagarajan v London Regional Transport** [2000] 1 AC 501 HL remains apposite.

33. There is some support for this when considering section 15 as a whole. Section 15(2) disapplies subsection (1) in any case in which A shows that A did not know and could not reasonably have been expected to know of the disability. That is strongly suggestive that the focus of the section is upon the thought processes, conscious or unconscious, of A. It therefore seems to me there is considerable force in this submission, though for present purposes I do not have to resolve it, and it may be that when there is closer focus upon it following more developed argument a different view might be taken.

34. Once a Tribunal has identified what is the treatment complained of and what is the something that has arisen in consequence of B's disability, the causal question invoked by "because of" as an explanation for A's treatment - and it may be thought processes, subconscious or unconscious - will be whether what happened was truly a consequence of the "something", and in turn that the "something" was a consequence of the disability. The approach therefore taken by the Tribunal here was, as the citations I have given above show, unacceptable. It impermissibly ran together the causal questions. It did so by looking for some "link", in terms that suggested it thought the link could be relatively

nebulous, between what had happened and was complained of on the one hand, and the disability on the other. The problem with such an approach is that it may insufficiently distinguish the context within which events occur from those matters which are causative. Thus the fact that in this case the Claimant had to seek permission to go to Sri Lanka could not, applying the two-stage test appropriately, sensibly be said to be a requirement imposed because of something arising in consequence of the disability. The disability made the Claimant sick, the consequence was that he was on sick leave, but the consequence of that was not obviously that he needed permission to go to Sri Lanka.

35. In the Claimant's response Miss Seymour pointed out that the Tribunal had correctly set out the issue at the start of its Decision. It said at paragraph 2.14: "did the Respondent treat the Claimant unfavourably because of something arising in consequence of his disability?" That set out the statutory words. Usually when a Tribunal sets out statutory words one may assume that it has correctly taken them into account and applied them. It is not always the case. Here, there are more than sufficient demonstrations that the Tribunal looked for a much looser general approach.

36. She drew attention to the **Code of Practice on Employment (2011)** made by the **Equality and Human Rights Commission**, which, though it is not binding, must be taken into account by Tribunals. Under the heading "What does 'something arising in consequence of disability' mean?" at paragraph 5.8 is said:

> **"The unfavourable treatment must be because of something that arises in consequence of the disability. That means that there must be a connection between whatever led to the unfavourable treatment and the disability."**

37. The second sentence of that is open to the criticism that it is not wholly faithful to the wording of the first. I do not think it was intended to be. It describes in very general terms what will be the effect of applying the statutory words, but it is the statutory words that must be applied, and in this area of all there is a danger in being too casual about seeking a connection between the conduct complained of

and the disability. The example, however, given immediately following makes this absolutely clear. It is:

"A woman is disciplined for losing her temper at work. However, this behaviour was out of character and is a result of severe pain caused by cancer, of which her employer is aware. The disciplinary action is unfavourable treatment. This treatment is because of something which arises in consequence of the worker's disability, namely her loss of temper. There is a connection between the 'something' (that is, the loss of temper) that led to the treatment and her disability. It will be discrimination arising from disability if the employer cannot objectively justify the decision to discipline the worker."

38. That is entirely correct and entirely faithful to the statute, but it does, as is obvious, require the application of the two-stage test:' **Basildon & Thurrock NHS Foundation Trust v Weerasinghe (2015)** EAT 28/29 July 2015 (Case No.0397/14).

Part 4

4.1 Duty to make adjustments under the Disability Discrimination Act 1995:

4A Employers: duty to make adjustments –

‘s.4A(1) Where –

a) any arrangements made by or on behalf of an employer, or
b) any physical feature of premises occupied by the employer, place the disabled person concerned at a substantial disadvantage in comparison with persons who are not disabled, it is the duty of the employer to take such steps as it is reasonable, in all the circumstances of the case, for him to have to take in order to prevent the provision, criterion or practice, or feature having that effect.

Equality Act 2010 –

‘s.20

(1) Where this Act imposes a duty to make reasonable adjustments on a person, this section, sections 21 and 22 and the applicable Schedule apply; and for those purposes, a person on whom the duty is imposed is referred to as A.
(2) The duty comprises the following three requirements.
(3) The first requirement is a requirement, where a provision, criterion or practice of A’s puts a disabled person at a substantial disadvantage in relation to a relevant matter in comparison with persons who are not disabled, to take such steps as it is reasonable to have to take to avoid the disadvantage.
(4) The second requirement is a requirement, where a physical feature puts a disabled person at a substantial disadvantage

in relation to a relevant matter in comparison with persons who are not disabled, to take such steps as it is reasonable to have to take to avoid the disadvantage.

(5) The third requirement is a requirement, where a disabled person would, but for the provision of an auxiliary aid, be put at a substantial disadvantage in relation to a relevant matter in comparison with persons who are not disabled, to take such steps as it is reasonable to have to take to provide the auxiliary aid.

(6) Where the first or third requirement relates to the provision of information, the steps which it is reasonable for A to have to take include steps for ensuring that in the circumstances concerned the information is provided in an accessible format.

(7) A person (A) who is subject to a duty to make reasonable adjustments is not (subject to express provision to the contrary) entitled to require a disabled person, in relation to whom A is required to comply with the duty, to pay to any extent A's costs of complying with the duty.'

It can be seen that the duty to make reasonable adjustments, set out in s.20 of the Equality Act 2010, comprises three aspects, the first two of which essentially replicate s.4A of the Disability Discrimination Act 1995 (where 'arrangements' are now called 'provision, criterion or practice.'). The third requirement, that before the coming into effect of the Equality Act 2010 used to apply only in respect of premises, goods and services, now extends to employment. Specifically, this is where, but for the provision of an auxiliary aid, a disabled person would be at a substantial disadvantage, the duty is to take such steps as it is reasonable to have to take to provide that auxiliary aid: s.20(5).

When the Equality Bill reached its Report stage in the House of Lords, section 20(6) was added. Section 20(6) provides that where the provision, criterion or practice or auxiliary aid relates to the provision of information, the steps which it is reasonable to have to take include steps for ensuring that the information is provided in an accessible format. In addition, s.20(7) states explicitly that a person who is under a duty to make reasonable adjustments is not (subject to an express provision to the contrary) entitled to pass on the costs of compliance to the disabled person.

With regard to employment (the Equality Act 2010 covers discrimination in other areas such as goods and services, education, transport, premises, etcetera), the basic requirement stated in s.20 is supplemented by Schedule 8 of the Act: Schedule 8, Work: Reasonable Adjustments, Part 1. In Part 3, it is stated that the duty to make reasonable adjustments will not apply where the employer could not reasonably be expected to know that an interested disabled person has a disability and is likely to be placed at one of the three disadvantages identified in s.20 or, in the case of job applicants, that an interested disabled person is or may be an applicant for the job in question.

18B Reasonable adjustments: supplementary

Note that there is no equivalent of s.18B(2), DDA 1995 (originally s.6, DDA 1995) in the Equality Act 2010. The duty to make reasonable adjustments is now contained in s.20 of the Equality Act 2010. This section essentially replicates s.4A(1) of the Disability Discrimination Act 1995 but makes a number of relatively minor changes. The Employment Code of Practice issued by the Equality and Human Rights Commission states that what is a reasonable step for an employer to take will depend on the circumstances of each individual case: para.6.29. As to any particular factors which should be taken into account when determining what amounts to a reasonable adjustment, the Equality Act 2010 does not specify any specific ones. Nonetheless, the examples previously given in s.18B(2), DDA 1995, are still likely to be relevant in practice and these are repeated in the Code issued by the EHRC. On this point, the Code suggests some further examples of what might constitute reasonable steps albeit these were not listed in s.18B(2), DDA 1995.

(1) In determining whether it is reasonable for a person to have to take a particular step in order to comply with a duty to make reasonable adjustments, regard shall be had, in particular, to –

a) the extent to which taking the step would prevent the effect in relation to which the duty is imposed;
b) the extent to which it is practicable for him to take the step;
c) the financial and other costs which would be incurred by him in taking the step and the extent to which taking it would disrupt any of his activities;
d) the extent of his financial and other resources;
e) the availability to him of financial or other assistance with respect to taking the step;

f) the nature of his activities and the size of his undertaking…

Note: the above is a ***'… balancing exercise required by s.18B(1) of the DDA:'*** per HH Judge Burke, QC in **London Borough of Camden v Price-Job (2007)**, EAT 18 December 2007 (Case No.0054/07).

(2) The following are examples of steps which a person may need to take in relation to a disabled person in order to comply with a duty to make reasonable adjustments -

a) making adjustments to premises;
b) allocating some of the disabled person's duties to another person;
c) transferring him to fill an existing vacancy;
d) altering his working hours;
e) assigning him to a different place of work;
f) allowing him to be absent during working or training hours for rehabilitation, assessment or treatment;
g) giving, or arranging for, training or mentoring (whether for the disabled person or any other person);
h) acquiring or modifying equipment;
i) modifying instructions or reference manuals;
j) modifying procedures for testing or assessment;
k) providing a reader or interpreter;
l) providing supervision or other support.'

See: **Morse v Wiltshire County Council (1998)** ICR 1023, wherein the EAT laid down a series of **sequential steps** which employment tribunals should follow when dealing with a reasonable adjustment claim. These are:

(1) whether the provisions of s.4A impose on the employer a duty to make reasonable adjustments in the circumstances of the particular case;
(2) if so, the tribunal must next decide whether the employer has taken such steps as it is reasonable, in all the circumstances of the case, for him to have to take in order to prevent the relevant arrangements or feature from placing the disabled applicant at a substantial disadvantage;

(3) the tribunal should then enquire whether the employer could reasonably have taken any of the above steps listed above (a) - (l).

The EAT thought that, in taking these steps, the tribunal must apply an objective test: i.e. what steps were reasonable; what was objectively justified; and what was material and substantial.

4.2 Duty to make adjustments under the Equality Act 2010:

s.20 Duty to make adjustments –

as mentioned above, the duty to make reasonable adjustments is now contained in s.20 of the Equality Act that essentially replicates s.4A(1) of the Disability Discrimination Act 1995. The Equality Act 2010 makes a number of relatively minor changes. Note that s.18B(2) of the Disability Discrimination Act 1995 is not reproduced in the Equality Act 2010.

s.20(3) '… where a provision, criterion or practice of A's puts a disabled person at a substantial disadvantage in relation to a relevant matter in comparison with persons who are not disabled, to take such steps as it is reasonable to have to take to avoid the disadvantage.'

The Equality Act 2010 does not specifically state any particular factors which should be taken into account when determining what amounts to a reasonable adjustment. Nonetheless, the examples previously given in s.18B(2) of the Disability Discrimination Act 1995 are still likely to be relevant in practice and, in this respect, are repeated in the Code of Practice issued by the Equality and Human Rights Commission. The Code gives further examples of reasonable steps which were not given in s.18B(2), Disability Discrimination Act 1995. As for the Equality Act 2010, the 'reasonable adjustments' provisions that used to be found in s.4A(1) are now to be found in subsections 20(3), 4 and 39(5) of the Equality Act 2010.

The 'Duty to make adjustments' as stated in s.20 of the Equality Act 2010:

s.20 Duty to make adjustments -

(1) Where this Act imposes a duty to make reasonable adjustments on a person, this section, sections 21 and 22 and the applicable Schedule apply; and for those purposes, a person on whom the duty is imposed is referred to as A.

(2) The duty comprises the following three requirements.

(3) The first requirement is a requirement, where a provision, criterion or practice of A's puts a disabled person at a substantial disadvantage in relation to a relevant matter in comparison with persons who are not disabled, to take such steps as it is reasonable to have to take to avoid the disadvantage.

s.21 Failure to comply with duty -

(1) A failure to comply with the first, second or third requirement is a failure to comply with a duty to make reasonable adjustments.

(2) A discriminates against a disabled person if A fails to comply with that duty in relation to that person.

(The reference in s.20(1) to 'applicable Schedule' is a reference to Schedule 8 (Work – Reasonable Adjustments). Part 2 of the Schedule states that the law in this area applies to employers of contract workers in that such employers must comply with the first, second and third requirements on each occasion when a contract worker is supplied to a principal to do contract work. This Schedule also refers employers to s.39 (employees and applicants or employees) that, inter alia, states that employers must not discriminate (because of a person's protected characteristic – e.g. disability - in the arrangements, terms or by not offering employment; must not victimise or harass; must observe the duty to make reasonable adjustments.)

4.3 Reasonable adjustments under the Disability Discrimination Act 1995 – when the duty arose and whether complied with:

How should employment tribunals determine whether:

(i) a duty to make reasonable adjustments arose and, if so,

(ii) whether an employer complied with the duty to make reasonable adjustments?

In **Romec Ltd v Rudham (2007),** EAT, 13 July 2007 (Case No.0069/07), the EAT cited the analysis given by a differently constituted EAT in **Smith Detection–Watford Ltd v Berriman (2005)** EAT (Case Nos. 0712/04; 0144/05) where, according to that decision, when determining the above questions, tribunals are required to identify the following:

- the relevant provision, criterion or practice applied by the employer;
- the relevant physical feature of the premises occupied by him;
- the identity of the non-disabled comparator (where appropriate);
- and the nature and extent of the substantial disadvantage suffered by the claimant.

On the immediate point above about how employment tribunals should determine a claim under the Disability Discrimination Act 1995, His Honour Judge Peter Clark, gave **guidance** when presiding as the legal member in the appeal of a case that was decided under the Disability Discrimination Act 1995 before the amendments were made to the Act by the 2003 Regulations, the case being **Secretary of State for Work and Pensions v Macklin (2008)** EAT (Case number 0370/07), judgment delivered on 28 February 2008, by saying:

'From the early days of the DDA the higher courts have indicated the need for Employment Tribunals to take a step-by-step approach to these statutory provisions. One such example is Morse v Wiltshire County Council (1998) ICR 1023 (EAT Bell J). More recently that requirement has again been emphasised in this EAT; see, pre-amendment, the judgment of HHJ Serota QC in Smith Detection-Watford v Berriman (2005) ALL ER (D) 56, followed and applied equally by a division presided over by HHJ McMullen, QC in a post-amendment case, London Borough of Barnet v Ferguson (2006) ALL ER (D) 192 and affirmed by Judge Serota in Environment Agency v Rowan (2008) IRLR 20, paras 26-27.

We repeat that guidance once more for the avoidance of doubt. Before finding that an employer has discriminated against a disabled Claimant in failing to comply with the duty to make reasonable adjustments an Employment Tribunal must identify:

a) ***the arrangements (now provision, criterion or practice under s.4A, DDA as amended) applied by or on behalf of the employer;***
b) ***the physical feature of premises occupied by the employer (if applicable; not in this case);***
c) ***the identity of non-disabled comparators (if appropriate);***
d) ***the nature and extent of the substantial disadvantage suffered by the Claimant.***

Only then will it be possible to determine the question as to what adjustments it would be reasonable for the employer to make, bearing in mind the extent to which such adjustments would prevent the arrangements made by the employer placing the disabled Claimant at a substantial disadvantage when compared with the non-disabled comparator.'

In **Macklin (2008)**, the employment tribunal, in error, when making a determination of the claim, simply proceeded to ask themselves - 'What steps the Respondent could have taken to improve matters for the Claimant?' - instead of asking themselves - 'How the Claimant was placed at a disadvantage in comparison with non-disabled employees engaged on the same project work?' The employment tribunal then went on in error to consider: 'What steps could be taken?' - instead of – 'What steps would probably prevent the disadvantage found?'

The EAT concluded that because the employment tribunal failed to follow the statutory steps required by s.6, the employment tribunal had, inter alia, fell into error.

Incidentally, the Claimant, who suffered from diabetes, was off sick throughout the relevant periods suffering from depression. So what was the relevant **arrangement** applied by the employer? The EAT suggested it must be the requirement for the Claimant to attend for work.

His Honour Judge Peter Clark also drew attention to the requirement under R30(6)(d) for employment tribunals, when giving written reasons, to include ***'... a concise statement of the applicable law.'*** He mentioned that the Employment Tribunal Rules of Procedure 2004, for the first time, set out mandatory requirements for the contents of an Employment Tribunal's written reasons: R30(6). He added: ***'... that concise statement will inevitably include a reference to the relevant statutory provisions which must be considered and applied to the facts as found by the Employment Tribunal (R30(6)(c)) so as to explain how the relevant findings of fact and applicable law have been applied in order to determine the issues in the case (R30(6)(e)).'***

In 2010, another employment tribunal erred by failing to follow the guidance stated in **Environment Agency v Rowan (2008) EAT ICR 218.** The outcome was that on appeal the EAT held that the employment tribunal was not in a position to determine which adjustments were reasonable for the employer to take in order to prevent the disabled person concerned being placed at a substantial disadvantage. The error on the part of the employment tribunal was that it had uncritically accepted the recommendations of two occupational health reports without analysing them in the light of the statutory obligation to make reasonable adjustments. In this regard, the EAT said that the employment tribunal should have set out how the particular recommendations in the occupational health reports would have prevented the substantial disadvantage to the claimant. Because the employment tribunal had accepted the occupational health reports at face value and had not carried out a thorough investigation of what amounts to reasonable adjustments in the particularly circumstances, the EAT set aside the findings of the employment tribunal as to reasonable adjustments and remitted the matter to the same tribunal for a rehearing: **Secretary of State for Work and Pensions v Wakefield (2010)** EAT 26 July 2010 (Case No.0435/09).

Following on what HHJ Peter Clark said in **Macklin (2008),** for a further case authority, in which the EAT referred to **Mid-Staffordshire General Hospitals NHS Trust v Cambridge (2003)** EAT, IRLR 566, the EAT said – ***'... a proper assessment of what is required to eliminate the disabled person's disadvantage is... a necessary part of the duty,'*** see: **Southampton City College v Randall (2006)** IRLR 18, EAT. An employer's duty under **s.4A(1), DDA 1995** is to make reasonable adjustments – but there is no duty upon the employer to ***consult*** with the disabled employee before making reasonable adjustments about steps which might be needed to eliminate any disadvantage in the workplace. In support of its view, holding that **Mid-Staffordshire General Hospitals NHS Trust (2003)** had been wrongly decided, the EAT thought it significant that the list of examples of reasonable adjustments given in s.18B(2), DDA 1995, makes no mention of a duty to consult a worker about potential adjustments: **Tarbuck v Sainsbury Supermarkets Ltd (2006)** IRLR 664, EAT. See too: **Scottish and Southern Energy plc v Mackay (2007)**, EAT 30 August 2007 (Case No. 0075/06).

The then new Regulations extended the duty to make reasonable adjustments beyond the pre-1st October 2004 statutory definition of 'arrangements' so that the duty covered the broader definition of 'provision, criterion or practice.' After 1st October 2004, the law no longer allowed the justification of failure to make reasonable adjustments, although for all practical purposes that had been the position since the case of **Collins v Royal National Theatre Board Ltd (2004)** IRLR 395.

The leading cases of **Archibald v Fife Council (2004)** IRLR 651 House of Lords and **Nottinghamshire County Council v Meikle (2004)** IRLR 703 Court of Appeal (see the case authorities in the following pages) have set out clear guidelines for employment tribunals to follow in reasonable adjustments claims; and these are as relevant to the legal position now as they were prior to 01 October 2004.

4.4 Failure to make a reasonable adjustment is an omission:

A failure by an employer to make a reasonable adjustment is an omission, ***not*** a continuing act. Accordingly, a claim against an employer runs from the date the employer made the decision not to make a reasonable adjustment, ***not*** from the date of the employee's resignation. Thus, such an employee has three months in which to make a claim to an employment tribunal: **Humphries v Chevler Packaging Ltd**, EAT, 24 July 2006 (Case No.0224/06). If the employee did not know when the employer made the decision not to make adjustments, an employment tribunal can extend time if it considers in all the circumstances that it is just and equitable to do so (s.111(2)(b), ERA 1996). (In **Matuszowicz v Kingston Upon Hull City Council (2009)** EWCA Civ 22, the Court of Appeal (para 14) said: ***'… in section 68(1) of the 1995 Act, "act" is defined as including a "deliberate omission."*** **Matuszowicz (2009)** gives a full exposition of the niceties of time limits in relation to omissions and how to identify the various dates on which omissions may or may not have occurred).

4.5 Failure to make reasonable adjustments – case authorities:

Failure to make reasonable adjustments - this was where an employer failed unjustifiably to comply with the section 6 duty that became **s.4A(1)** to make **reasonable adjustments** to accommodate a person's disability: was s.5(2) and became **s.3A(2) of the DDA 1995** as amended with supplementary provisions as to reasonable adjustments given at s.18B(2), DDA 1995.

Under the DDA 1995, an employer was under a duty to make reasonable adjustments where - '(a) any arrangements made by or on behalf of an employer, or (b) any physical feature of the premises occupied by the employer, places the disabled person concerned at a substantial disadvantage in comparison with persons who are not disabled, it is the duty of the employer to take such steps as it is reasonable, in all the circumstances of the case, for him to have to take in order to prevent the provision, criterion or practice, or feature, having that effect:' **s.4A(1), DDA 1995**.

The duty to make reasonable adjustments was a legal responsibility under the DDA 1995. It applied to people such as employers, service providers and education providers and was intended to make sure that disabled people did not face substantial difficulties in employment, education or when using services. Failure to make reasonable adjustments can be a form of adverse discrimination and is unlawful.

The DDA 1995 defined a reasonable adjustment as a reasonable step taken to prevent a disabled person suffering a substantial disadvantage compared with people who are not disabled. For example, in the case of employers, the duty applied to any disadvantage caused by a provision, criterion or practice applied by, or on behalf of, the employer, or any physical feature of premises occupied by the employer. A 'substantial disadvantage' is one that is not 'minor' or 'trivial.' The term 'provision, criterion or practice' covers an employer's policies on offering work, terms and conditions, managing and dismissing staff, and the way in which these are carried out.

Why does the law require an employer, in certain circumstances, to consider and, if reasonable, take the necessary steps to make an 'adjustment?' The answer to this question was given by the Employment Appeal Tribunal that said:

> ***'35. The purpose of the reasonable adjustment is to prevent whatever provision, criterion or practice from placing the disabled person at a substantial disadvantage: this follows from the wording of section 4A.***
>
> ***36. If the substantial disadvantage arises from arrangements for interview (see section 4(1)(a) of the 1995 Act) and relates to the ability of the disabled person (compared to persons who are not disabled) to perform in interview for a job, then the purpose of the reasonable adjustment is to remove that disadvantage – in other words, to eliminate the practical difficulty and embarrassment which the PCP has caused and create a level playing field for the disabled person in interview. If a reasonable adjustment should have been made for this purpose it is not fatal to the disabled person's case that he or she would still not have obtained the job:' Noor v Foreign & Commonwealth Office (2011) EAT (Case No.0470/10).***

The DDA 1995 did not define **'reasonable'** nor gave a complete list of what reasonable adjustments may be. Ultimately, it was up to the courts to decide. This was because an adjustment is related to a particular individual, his or her experience of their impairment and the situation he or she is in. However, it did set out **four tests of reasonableness** being:

- the effectiveness in preventing disadvantage. How much will a reasonable adjustment reduce the disadvantage? The more effective an adjustment is in reducing disadvantage, the more reasonable it is likely to be;
- the practicality of the step. It is more likely that an employer will be expected to take a step that is easy, than to take a step that is hard. If disadvantage can easily be removed by changing the way things are done, or the equipment that is used, then the adjustment is likely to be considered reasonable;
- the financial and other costs and the extent of any disruption caused. When trying to decide whether an adjustment would be reasonable, the cost of the adjustment and any disruption it might cause should also be considered;
- the extent of an organisation's financial and other resources. An organisation with big financial resources would be more likely to have to make a reasonable adjustment than one with fewer resources.

Note: financial help from government schemes, such as **Access to Work**, was available to help in providing reasonable adjustments for employees. These funds were required be to taken into account when deciding how 'financially reasonable' an adjustment was.

4.6 The reasonableness of taking steps to make adjustments:

The duty on an employer is only to take such steps as it is **reasonable** (i.e. rational) to take in all the circumstances of the case to prevent a provision, criterion or practice applied by or on behalf of an employer or any physical feature of premises occupied by the employer from placing the disabled employee at a substantial disadvantage: s.4A(1) DDA 1995. [Now **s.20(3)** and **s.4** and **s.39(5)** under the **Equality Act 2010**].

Determining the 'reasonableness' of making adjustments consists of weighing the various factors such as practicality, cost and benefit. These are listed in the Code of Practice: 6(4).

A survey in the USA in September 1994 showed that there are many effective adjustments which can be made and which cost nothing or very little yet were of considerable benefit to disabled employees: Job Accommodation Network Survey.

Sickness absences or the inability to perform the job because of illness/disability are the most common reasons given by employers for dismissing employees. Where an employee is too ill to work and where it is unlikely that the employee will be able to return to work in the foreseeable future, employment tribunals generally accept that an employer was justified and did act reasonably by dismissing the employee (see para.76, **Griffiths v The Secretary of State for Work & Pensions (2015)** EWCA Civ 1265 per Elias LJ). In common law terms, it could be said that the contract of employment was brought to an end by the doctrine of frustration. However, statute law in the form of the provisions of the DDA 1995 (and since 01 October 2010 by the disability discrimination provisions in the **Equality Act 2010**) now ousts the common law doctrine of frustration in this area of the law. That being so, the Code of Practice made clear that a dismissal for this reason (incapability), that included compulsory early retirement on grounds of ill-health, must be justified by the employer in that the employer did consider the question of whether any reasonable adjustment could have been made to enable the employee to remain in employment: paragraph 6.21.

4.7 Disability discrimination - some case authorities:

1 Failure to make reasonable adjustments –

This form of unlawful discrimination occurred where an employer failed unjustifiably to comply with the duty placed upon an employer by section 4A(1) of the DDA 1995 which was to take reasonable steps to carry out adjustments to prevent a disabled person from being placed at a substantial disadvantage by an employer's working arrangements: **s.3A(2) DDA 1995**. Such adjustments include transferring an employee to fill an existing vacancy; assigning an employee to a different place of work; and allowing an employee to be absent during working hours for rehabilitation, assessment or treatment: **s.18B(2) DDA 1995**.

In **Beart v HM Prison Service (2003)** IRLR 238, the Court of Appeal upheld the decision of an employment tribunal (ET) that an employee who was off work suffering from depression was subjected to disability discrimination when the employer failed to transfer her to a different workplace. The fact that the s.4A(1) duty to relocate arose during disciplinary proceedings in which the employee's dismissal was in issue did not justify the failure.

In **Archibald v Fife Council (2004)** UKHL 32, the House of Lords held that where an employee becomes so disabled that she can no longer meet the requirements of her job description, the employer is required to take steps to help her which the employer is not required to take for others. One such step would be to treat the disabled employee more favourably by removing the disadvantage that is attributable to the disability. This necessarily entails a measure of positive discrimination such as moving the employee from a physical job she is no longer able to do to a sedentary one at a slightly higher grade that she is qualified to fill but without requiring her to undergo a competitive interview.

Jones v Jewson Ltd (2011) Cardiff Employment Tribunal 06 July 2011 - A claimant was awarded nearly £400,000 in compensation for disability discrimination that was, until 2011, the highest award that had ever been given in Wales. The claimant, Jonathon Jones, was awarded £390,870.58 after successfully suing his employer for disability discrimination. Mr. Jones, aged 55, was the branch manager in Cardigan, Wales, for builders' merchant Jewson Ltd and was dismissed on the grounds of incapacity five months after he suffered a severe stroke in April 2009. Mr. Jones had been averaging over 60 hours working time per week. He had not been taking his full entitlement of holidays and had been consistently carrying over a considerable proportion of untaken holidays each year.

Mr. Jones had signed a 48-hour opt-out agreement and there was a clear expectation that branch managers would work far in excess of their contracted hours. He had been in the industry most of his working life and had been employed by Jewson Ltd for 22 years. Jewson Ltd is part of the global business of Saint Gobain that has a turnover of £20 billion and employs 140,000. In the UK, Jewson Ltd is a nationwide business with a staff of over 10,000 and its HR department is based at the UK head office of Saint Gobain.

After Jones' stroke, he was instructed by his doctor that in order to return to employment he must avoid stress at work. However, Jewson felt that there was no role in the company that was void of stress and therefore dismissed him. The claimant's solicitor, Stephen Jackson of Jackson Osborne, stated that the doctor's report did not say that Jones would 'never' make a full recovery from his stroke. He also commented on Jewson's statistics on sickness absence rates and found that 204 other employees had been allowed more than 6 months' absence and 64 employees had been allowed more than 12 months' absence. Given that Mr Jones made a full recovery within 11 months it was 'common sense' that he should have been given the time to recover. Jewson, however, argued at the tribunal that there was a difference between the 204 other employees and Jones, in that Jones was unable to return to his existing role whereas the other employees had a favourable prospect of returning to their jobs.

Employment tribunal: at a liability hearing in August 2010 the

employment tribunal, sitting in Cardiff and chaired by employment judge Wayne Beard, decided that the dismissal was unfair and amounted to disability discrimination by reason of failure to make reasonable adjustments.
Remedies hearing: this was held on 06 July 2011 at which the employment tribunal ordered Jewson Ltd to pay Mr. Jones £390,870.58 that included £15,000 for injury to feelings plus an uplift of approximately £18,000, being effectively a penalty for unreasonable failure to follow the ACAS Code of Practice on Disciplinary and Dismissal Procedures.

Commenting on the decision, Stephen Jackson, solicitor and principle of Jackson Osborne, said Jewson Ltd was complacent in accepting that its existing working practices of long hours were necessary. The company also assumed that Mr. Jones' condition was so severe that his health was at risk if he returned to work in any role. Although during the five months' of his absence Mr. Jones' recovery was slow and his prospects appeared poor, he in fact made a complete recovery within eleven months of the stroke. On this point, if Jewson Ltd had waited, Mr. Jones would not even have come within the definition of disability that is necessary to make a disability discrimination claim albeit there is the possibility that his condition may recur: s.6(4) & Schedule 1, para.9, Equality Act 2010. Concluding, Mr. Jackson said that employers should recognise that they may be acting unfairly and discriminating unlawfully where they fail to obtain specialist and up to date medical evidence and that requirement is nearly always going to be essential to keep them on track in any incapacity procedure.

Apart from the **Jones v Jewson Ltd (2011)** disability discrimination award made in Wales, there have been larger compensation awards for disability discrimination cases in the UK, including an award of £792,000 to a disabled football journalist for unfair dismissal and unlawful harassment.

2 disability-related discrimination –

This is where an employer, for a **reason** which relates to a disabled person's disability, treats that person less favourably than he treats or would treat others to whom that **reason** does not or would not apply, and the employer cannot show that the treatment is justified: **s.3A(1) DDA 1995**. For example, there were a number of ways in which an employer could treat someone less favourably. Unlike direct disability discrimination, less favourable treatment was able to be justified by an employer if it was able to show that the reason for the treatment was both material to the circumstances of the particular case and substantial:

s.3A(3). The old s.4(2)(b) of the Act made it unlawful for an employer to discriminate against a disabled employee by subjecting him or her to a detriment (a disadvantage), that includes not providing the employee with opportunities for receiving benefits: para 6.7 of the Code of Practice. In **Jenkins v Legoland Windsor Park Ltd**, EAT (Case No.1155/02), the EAT decided that an employer subjected an employee to a detriment when it presented him with a Lego model of himself depicting his **disability** whereas other employees were given models of themselves depicting a feature of their **work**. Another common example of less favourable treatment was where an employer dismissed an employee for a reason relating to or connected with the employee's disability (also a breach of s.3A(1)): **BT plc v Pelling (2004)** EATS 0093/03 (Scottish EAT).

Note that the s.3A, DDA 1995 'disability-related discrimination' provision no longer exists as a cause of action because the government decided not to re-enact it in the Equality Act 2010 when that Act repealed the Disability Discrimination Act 1995 on 01 October 2010. Instead, a new cause of action under s.15, Equality Act 2010, being 'Discrimination arising from disability,' gives the same or a better level of protection for a disabled worker where (i) his or her employer treats the worker unfavourably (ii) because of something arising in consequence of his or her disability and, (iii) if the employer knows that the worker is disabled, (iv) the employer cannot justify the unfavourable treatment.

Equality Act 2010 - duty to make adjustments (s.20); discrimination arising from disability (s.15):

Case authority: one employer that failed to take steps which are reasonable to take to make reasonable adjustments was, surprisingly perhaps, the Government Legal Service.

The facts: the claimant was a 33 years old law graduate with a 2.2 degree who had applied for a trainee solicitor's post under the trainee recruitment scheme with the respondent, the Government Legal Service, and she won her case both at the ET and at an EAT appeal hearing at which the respondent sought to reargue the facts of the case, which is a fundamental error, instead of presenting its appeal on points of law. The crux of the claimant's case was that she has a disability, namely, Asperger's Syndrome and said she was disadvantaged unlawfully by being required to sit the first-stage competitive assessment test, being a multiple choice 'Situational Judgment Test,' that was to be marked by a computer. So she made a request to the respondent to allow her to answer the questions in the SJT in the form of narrative short written answers and that the respondent should have made an adjustment to allowed her to answer the questions in that way. The requirement to pass the Situational Judgment Test at the required pass mark of 14 out of a possible 22 was the provision, criterion or practice (PCP). The claimant achieved a score of 12. For the PCP not to be unlawfully indirectly discriminatory, the respondent had to show that the PCP was objectively justified.

Employment Tribunal: the ET found that the respondent had indirectly discriminated against the claimant; had failed to comply with the duty to make reasonable adjustments; and had treated her unfavourably because of something arising in consequence of her disability. The ET ordered the respondent to pay compensation to the claimant and made a recommendation, under s. 124(2), Equality Act 2010, that the respondent issue a written apology to the claimant and review its procedures in relation to people with a disability applying for employment, with a view to greater flexibility in the psychometric testing regime. Specifically, the ET considered the question of whether the PCP put people such as the claimant, as a group, at a disadvantage compared to those who did not have Asperger's and concluded that it did. There was no appeal to the EAT against that finding. The ET went on to find that the PCP put the claimant, in particular, at such a disadvantage. That finding was challenged on appeal to the Employment Appeal Tribunal on this point. The ET then considered the issue of justification and concluded that while the PCP served a legitimate aim - in that the SJT was there to test a fundamental competency required of GLS trainees, namely the ability to make effective decisions - the means of achieving that aim were not proportionate to it and, accordingly, the complaint of indirect discrimination succeeded. The claim in respect of reasonable adjustments also succeeded on similar reasoning. Finally, the claim for discrimination because of something arising in consequence of a disability, the ET found, stood or fell with the indirect discrimination claim and, accordingly, that succeeded as well.

Employment Appeal Tribunal: the claimant had presented her claim at the employment tribunal as one of indirect discrimination (s. 19, Equality Act 2010) and of discrimination by failure to make the reasonable adjustment (s. 20) of permitting short written answers to questions instead of multiple choice questions. There was also a third claim, for discrimination under s. 15, Equality Act 2010 because of something arising in consequence of the claimant's disability. The EAT dismissed the respondent's (The Legal Government Service) appeal. The decisions of the employment tribunal which was that the respondent had indirectly discriminated against the claimant; had failed to comply with the duty to make reasonable adjustments; and had treated her unfavourably because of something arising in consequence of her disability; were unassailable and correct in law. The EAT concluded by saying the appeal raises no point of law and is dismissed: **The Government Legal Service v Brookes (2017)** EAT 28 March 2017 (Case No.0302/16).

The essential point found by the ET was that the purpose of the SJT test was to assess a candidate's analytical abilities but that could be done, where necessary, by other means, such as by narrative short written answers, other than solely using the SJT test. That was the reasonable adjustment that could have been made.

It could be said that by succeeding in her claim at the ET where she represented herself there and at the EAT, a claim that was held to be correct in law by the EAT at the appeal, showed that the claimant would have been a suitable person for the Government Legal Service to have accepted onto its trainee recruitment scheme and shows, explicitly, that a person with a disability can compete with and succeed against those who assert that they are the finest in the legal profession. She had been awarded a 2.2 law degree upon graduation, a class of degree that is below that which many commercial law practices require of applicants. But evidence shows that many law graduates who achieve first-class law degrees do not always succeed particularly well professionally. One particular barrister who had a 2.2 law degree was Sir John Donaldson who became Lord Donaldson of Lymington and who, during the course of his career, became the first president of the National Industrial Relations Court that was the forerunner to the EAT. He then went on to become Master of the Rolls, the third most senior judge in England and Wales, who presides over the Court of Appeal.

Part 5

5.1 Disability-related claims after Malcolm (2008):

What effect did the House of Lords' judgment in Malcolm (2008) have on disability-related claims?

In its judgment in **Malcolm (2008)**, the Appellate Committee of the House of Lords considered at length the question of who are the correct comparators for the purpose of s.3A(1) (and the other similar sections) of the Disability Discrimination Act 1995. The majority concluded that the comparator in **Clark v TDG Ltd t/a Novacold (1999)** ICR 591 had been **wrongly decided.**

Whereas the Court of Appeal in **Novacold (1999)** had held nine years earlier that the correct comparator was:-

> **... a non-disabled person who had not been absent from work and who would not have been dismissed ....**

...the House of Lords in **Malcolm (2008)** held on 25 June 2008 that the **correct comparator**, for the purposes of s.3A(1), was:

> **... a secure tenant of the council without a mental disability who has sublet his property...**

this wording, transposed for employment cases under s.3A(1), means that the correct comparator is:

> **... an employee or worker of the employer who is not disabled who has been absent from work for a similar amount of time as the disabled claimant and who would also have been dismissed.**

The difference in comparators between **Malcolm (2008)** and **Novacold**

(1999) was that in the latter an employee dismissed for sickness absence arising from his or her disability would, applying section 3A(1) of the Disability Discrimination Act 1995 as interpreted by the Court of Appeal in **Novacold (1999)**, be compared with (i) a non-disabled employee (ii) who had not been absent from work and who, accordingly, (iii) would not have suffered a detriment such as being dismissed.

It could be said that the judgment of the Court of Appeal in **Novacold (1999)** applied the disability discrimination legislation as intended by Parliament. On this point, Lady Hale, in her dissenting opinion in **Malcolm (2008)**, after reviewing the Parliamentary history of the disability legislation, said:

> ***'This confirms that the construction chosen by the Court of Appeal in Clark v Novacold Ltd was indeed the construction which Parliament intended... Furthermore, Parliament has since legislated on the basis that it (Clark v Novacold) is correct.'***

If compared with other discrimination provisions, the comparator as stated in **Novacold (1999)** seems unassailable. For example, if the word 'disability' in s.3A(1) is replaced with the words 'pregnancy' and 'maternity,' the section would read like this:

(1) … a person discriminates against a pregnant person if –

- a) for a reason which relates to the person's pregnancy or maternity, he treats her less favourably than he treats or would treat others to whom that reason does not or would not apply, and
- b) he cannot show that the treatment in question is justified.

The 'reason' in (a) above could be an absence from work which relates to the person's pregnancy or maternity. That 'reason' could not and would not apply either to a man or a non-pregnant woman, either of whom would be the comparator. Would the law allow an employer to say that the reason it dismissed such an employee was not because of a pregnancy/maternity-related illness but the absence from work itself, i.e. not an illness-related absence but an absence from work per se? On point (b), the employer's provision, criterion or practice (being something that an employee must comply with), would be the requirement not to be absent from work for too long or too often or a requirement to attend work regularly. Where an employer imposes a PCP, the employer would be required to objectively justify the PCP by showing that it was (i) objectively and reasonably justified by a legitimate aim (ii) and if the means of achieving that aim are both appropriate and necessary.

The law (but in a different format to the example given) requires employers to omit or ignore the fact of the employee's pregnancy-related absence or maternity leave absence when considering whether to take disciplinary action against the employee or dismiss her. If the then disability discrimination law under **Malcolm (2008)** had been framed or interpreted in the same way as sex discrimination law, employers would have be prohibited from taking into consideration for disciplinary or dismissal purposes a disabled employee's absence from work for a reason that relates to his or her disability. The 'others' in the above example are employees who are not pregnant and have not been absent from work for a pregnancy-related reason or on maternity leave.

But the House of Lords in **Malcolm (2008)** had to give a judgment according to the wording of a poorly drafted law that did not, when properly interpreted, give protection against detrimental treatment to those whom it sought to protect.

5.2 Disability-related discrimination - history of Novacold (1999):

The history of **Novacold (1999)** that led to the judgment in **Malcolm (2008)** was summarised by Lord Justice Hooper in **O'Hanlon v Commissioners for HM Revenue & Customs (2007)** EWCA Civ 283 (see para.83+) wherein his Lordship said of **Novacold (1999)**:

> ***'In that case, the employee was dismissed after he had become disabled following an accident at work. The employers were informed the likelihood was that he would be unable to resume work for about a year. The employers accepted that he was disabled within the meaning of the Disability Discrimination Act. The Employment Tribunal found that there was no disability-related discrimination because the employers would have treated any employee equally who had been sick for a similar length of time, whether he was disabled or not. In other words, the appropriate comparator was held to be someone absent for the same length of time, but for a reason other than disability.'***

[Following the House of Lords' judgment in **Malcolm (2008)**, this was the correct comparator for the purpose of s.3A(1), DDA 1995 until the Equality Act 2010 came into effect on 01 October 2010 when s.15 of this latter Act provided similar protection to disabled workers as s.3A(1) of the DDA 1995 had done prior to Malcolm (2008)].

Hooper LJ continued:

'The Employment Appeal Tribunal accepted that this was the correct approach when considering the appropriate comparator… The Court of Appeal upheld the employee's appeal and held that this was an improper construction of the section. The proper approach to determining the question of whether or not there was disability-related discrimination was identified in the following way by Lord Justice Mummery (at page 961 to 962, but substituting the current statutory provisions):

"The two questions posed by the statutory provisions are:

Was the applicant dismissed for a reason which relates to his disability?

If so, did the employers treat him less favourably than they would treat others to whom that reason would not apply?

Question (1) is one of fact. It is common ground that "dismissal" is caught by section [3A(1)]: see section 4(2)(d). The finding of the industrial tribunal on the reason for dismissal is stated above. It is clear that that was a reason which related to his disability. In order to answer question (2), it is necessary to compare the employers' treatment of the applicant with the treatment of others to whom "that reason" would not apply. What is meant by "that reason?"

Mummery LJ then analysed the possible interpretations of "that reason" in what is now section 3A(1)(a).

Did it simply mean the reason for the treatment and no more? In this case that would mean that the reason was the fact of being absent for the requisite period and thus the comparison would be with someone not absent for that period.

Or did it mean the reason for the treatment but embracing the causal link to the disability? In this case that would mean that the reason was absence connected to disability and the comparison would be with those absent for the same period but for a reason not connected with any disability.

The analysis is crucial. If the first interpretation is correct then there is less favourable treatment because a person not absent for the requisite period will still receive full pay.

If, on the other hand, the second approach is right then there is

no less favourable treatment since all absentees are treated alike (save where the absence stemmed from an accident which was work related)'.

Hooper LJ added that:

'The Employment Tribunal and the EAT in that case had both preferred the latter interpretation. The Court of Appeal held that they were wrong to do so. Mummery LJ accepted that the term was ambiguous, but considered that it should be construed in the manner which would best give effect to the purpose of the legislation. He then continued as follows (p.963F to H):

"The result of this approach is that the reason would not apply to others even if their circumstances are different from those of the disabled person. The persons who are performing the main functions of their jobs are "others" to whom the reason for dismissal of the disabled person (that is inability to perform those functions) would not apply.

In the context of the special sense in which "discrimination" is defined in section [3A] of the Act of 1995 it is more probable that Parliament meant "that reason" to refer only to the facts constituting the reason for the treatment, and not to include within that reason the added requirement of a causal link with disability: that is more properly regarded as the cause of the reason for treatment than as in itself a reason for the treatment. This interpretation avoids the difficulties which would be encountered in many cases in seeking to identify what the appeal tribunal referred to as "the characteristics of the hypothetical comparator."'

In **Novacold (1999)**, both the ET and the EAT decided that the relevant section was aimed at a specific circumstance that was, in the case of the claimant in **Novacold (1999)**, limited to an absence cause by and related to the claimant's disability and not any other kind of absence. The comparator, not having a disability, could not be absent from work for a disability-related reason but could or would be absent for a non-disability reason. This is why the ET and EAT decided that the correct comparator was a person who was not disabled but who had been absent from work for a similar period as the claimant. So the 'reason' for dismissal was specific and limited being a dismissal of someone who was absent from work for the very precise reason which related to his or her disability. That 'reason which relates to the disabled person's disability' could not and did not apply to the hypothetical comparator who, however, was or would be deemed to be similarly absent from work. Questions which could have been asked about s.3A(1) were:

(i) Did the 'reason' (that, in **Novacold (1999)**, was an absence from work) relate or was connected to the disabled person's disability? The answer is 'yes.'

(ii) Did that 'reason' apply or would have applied to others (the comparators), i.e. were they or could they have been similarly absent from work for a reason related or connected to their disabilities? The answer is 'no' because they were not disabled and so could not have been absent for a reason related or connected to disability.

(iii) That being so, was the disabled person treated less favourably in relation to the others?

(iv) The result was that a decision had to be made by the employment tribunal and the higher courts about the way the employer treated two parties, one being the disabled person and the other being the non-disabled ones. The disabled person was dismissed while the non-disabled ones were not. The reason why the employer dismissed the disabled person was because he was absent from work for a reason that related or was connected to his disability. The others were not disabled and were not and could not be absent from work for that reason. So, in essence, the employer had a group of employees (the 'others') who were not disabled and who were not and could not be absent from work because of a reason related or connected to disability. Another employee who was disabled was, however, absent from work for a reason related or connected to his disability. By dismissing **that employee** for **that reason** that did not and could not apply to its other non-disabled employees, the employer would have been treating that employee less favourably. For a dismissal or any other detriment to have been lawful under s.3A(1), an employer would have needed to have ignored any reason that related or was connected to the disabled worker's disability. By doing that the employer would avoid treating the disabled worker less favourably than its other non-disabled workers. This is the analysis that should have been done in **Novacold (1999)**. Put simply, the dismissed employee was disabled; the comparators were not; the disabled employee was absent for a reason related to his disability; the others were not and could not be absent from work for that reason; he, the disabled employee, was treated less favourably by the employer for that combined reason than the employer treated or would have treated its other non-disabled employees. Essentially, s.3A(1) prohibited employers from treating disabled workers less favourably than non-disabled workers who, not being disabled, would not and could not do what disabled workers did which was be unable to do something, such as doing their work, because of a reason related or connected to their disabilities.

The point here is that there were two groups in **Novacold (1999)** between which a comparison had to be made: the person in one group had a certain characteristic (disability) that those in the other group did not have. If the person in the first group was treated less favourably because of the characteristic, then the employer would have discriminated unlawfully against that person. Those in the second group (the comparators) did not and could not have that certain characteristic and therefore could not have been treated less favourably for that reason by the employer. Put another way, the law prohibited employers from treating disabled workers less favourably (in comparison with non-disabled workers) if it was for 'a reason which relates to the disabled person's disability.'

The stopgap in s.3A(1) in any case, that would have prohibited employers from treating disabled workers less favourably than employers would have treated non-disabled ones, was s.3A(1)(b) that required employers to justify less favourable treatment. What is relevant about this subsection is that it gives rise to the question: Can the employer justify its less favourable treatment of the disabled worker even after considering its duty that was to take steps that it is reasonable to take to prevent a provision, criterion or practice the employer applied from placing the disabled worker concerned at a substantial disadvantage in comparison with its other workers who are not disabled? For example, an employer might have a provision, criterion or practice which is that its employees must achieve a 98% attendance record. An employee who has a statutory disability might not be able to comply with such a provision, criterion or practice. If that is the case, an

> employer may need to take steps which are reasonable to remove or lessen the disadvantage to which the disabled employee is subjected by the imposition of such a provision, criterion or practice. So, in a case where a disabled worker had absences from work for a reason that related or was connected to his or her disability, did the employer consider its s.4A(1) duty by taking steps which were reasonable to take to help the worker to continue to do his or her job and to do it despite his or her occasional or frequent disability-related absences? This s.4A(1) consideration seemed to be absent from **Novacold (1999)** as it was in **Jones v Jewson (2011).**

In summary: section 3A(1) of the Disability Discrimination Act 1995 states –

> **'... a person discriminates against a disabled person if – (a) for a reason which relates to the disabled person's disability, he treats him less favourably than he treats or would treat others to whom that reason does not or would not apply...'**

As a matter of logic, such a reason can never apply to an employer's non-disabled workers. Such a reason can only ever apply to the employer's disabled ones. This can be confirmed by substituting the word 'reason' with the full reason being 'an absence from work which relates to the disabled person's disability' which shows that a non-disabled worker can never be absent from work for that reason so that reason could never apply to such a person. And if a disabled worker is treated less favourably by the employer for such a reason, that would constitute unlawful disability discrimination – if,

> **'... and (b) he** (the employer) **cannot show that the treatment in question is justified.'**

Section 3A, DDA 1995, along with the Act itself, is now repealed so the arguments as to the correct interpretation of that section is now purely of academic interest.

The raison d'être of disability discrimination is that disabled workers are not treated the same as able-bodied workers just as workers who are pregnant or on maternity leave are not treated the same as those not pregnant or on maternity leave but, in both cases, if necessary are treated more advantageously to remove the disadvantage caused by their respective conditions, be it disability or pregnancy/maternity.

5.3 Questions which employment tribunals needed to ask post-Malcolm (2008):

After the House of Lords' judgment in **Malcolm (2008)**, it seemed that when determining a claim for disability discrimination, employment tribunals needed to consider the following questions:

- Did the claimant have a statutory disability at the time the alleged dismissal or detriment occurred?
- Was the claimant dismissed or subjected to any other detriment?
- Did the reason for the dismissal or detriment relate to the claimant's disability?
- Did the employer have knowledge of the claimant's disability?
- If so, who are the statutory comparators?
- When comparing the way the employer treated the claimant with the way the employer treated or would treat its non-disabled employees, did the employer treat the claimant less favourably?
- If it is found at the comparator stage that the employer did not treat the claimant less favourably than it treated or would treat its non-disabled employees who are deemed to have done what the claimant did, did the employer nonetheless treat the claimant less favourably by applying a provision, criterion or practice that had the effect of placing the claimant at a substantial disadvantage compared to the employer's non-disabled employees and, if so, did the employer consider and take any reasonable steps to make adjustments that would have prevented the provision, criterion or practice (or physical feature of its premises) from having that effect?
- If it is found that the employer did treat the claimant less favourably for a reason which relates to the disabled claimant's disability or the employer failed to take any steps which were reasonable for it to take to make adjustments to prevent the provision, criterion or practice that it applied from placing the claimant at a substantial disadvantage vis-à-vis its non-disabled employees, is the defence of justification available to the employer if the employer had complied with the duty to take steps to make reasonable adjustments?

In more detail, the suggested questions which needed to be determined were:

- identify who were the statutory **comparators** and **compare** the way the employer treated them, being non-disabled employees, with the way the employer treated the claimant who is or was the disabled employee.
- In doing this, a tribunal would need to identify the **reason** why the employer treated the claimant the way that the claimant alleged and whether the reason **related** to the claimant's disability. The employer must have knowledge of the claimant's disability.
- If the reason did so relate, the tribunal would then ask whether the claimant had been treated **less favourably** than the non-disabled comparators to whom that reason did not or would not apply.
- It may be that in applying s.3A(1)(a)(b), the tribunal has found that the employer treated both the comparators and the claimant the same so that the claimant was not treated less favourably.
- Nonetheless, following the long line of cases which tribunals and the higher courts have determined under the DDA 1995 per His Honour Judge Peter Clark in **Macklin (2008)**, a tribunal would need to ask whether a duty arose under s.3A(2) that required the employer to take steps as it is reasonable to make adjustments in relation to the disabled person. This duty could arise in one of two ways, the first being if the employer had applied a requirement, being 'a provision, criterion or practice,' that placed the disabled employee at a substantial disadvantage in comparison with non-disabled employees and, in all the circumstances of the case, it would have been reasonable for the employer to have taken those steps to make reasonable adjustments to prevent the provision, criterion or practice having that effect. The second way the duty could arise is if there was any physical feature of the premises occupied by the employer that similarly placed the disabled employee at a substantial disadvantage and, if so, whether the employer could have taken steps which were reasonable to take to prevent the feature having that effect
- If the employer was found to have treated the claimant less favourably at this stage, a tribunal would have needed to ask whether the employer could **justify** the treatment.

- Under s.3A(3) of the Act, an employer was able to justify the treatment but only if the reason for the treatment was both material to the circumstances of the particular case and substantial and, if applicable, the employer considered and/or took steps which were reasonable to make adjustments to prevent the employee being placed at a substantial disadvantage by a requirement applied by the employer or a feature of the employer's premises.
- Moving on to s.3A(6) of the Act, the tribunal would have needed to consider subsection (6) that relates back to subsection (1). So, if the tribunal made a finding that the claimant was treated less favourably than the comparators for a reason which relates to the claimant's disability and the reason did not apply to the comparators and, in the circumstances the employer was under a duty to make reasonable adjustments (regarding any physical feature of the employer's premises or a provision, criterion or practice applied by the employer that placed the claimant at a substantial disadvantage in comparison with the employer's non-disabled employees), the tribunal would have needed to ask if the employer failed in its duty in this respect and, if so, the employer was not permitted to justified the reason for its treatment of the claimant under subsection (3) unless the reason the employer failed to comply with the duty was because there were no reasonable steps which it could have taken, in which case the employer was permitted to justify its treatment of the claimant under subsection (3).

5.4 Reasonable adjustments duty under the Disability Discrimination Act 1995:

With regard to the last paragraph, under the Disability Discrimination Act 1995 as under the Equality Act 2010 that replaced it, an employer was and still is under a statutory duty to consider and then, if reasonable, take steps to prevent the requirement applied by the employer (or the physical feature of the employer's premises) from having the effect of placing the disabled employee at a substantial disadvantage compared to the employer's non-disabled employees. But, if the employer failed to do that, the employer could not thereafter say that what it did (perhaps it dismissed the employee) was justified in that its actions were based upon a reason that was material and substantial to the circumstances of the particular case (in that the employee was unlikely to be fit for work in the foreseeable future), unless there were no reasonable adjustments which could be made or, if reasonable adjustments had or could have been made, these would have made no difference or insufficient difference in preventing the requirement applied by the employer from placing the claimant at a substantial disadvantage. In simpler words, if any reasonable adjustments had or could have been made, these would have made no difference or insufficient difference in that they would not have helped or enabled the disabled employee to continue to do his her or work.

For confirmation as to how an employer, when dealing with an employee who may have a disability, is under a statutory duty firstly to consider what steps can be taken to make reasonable adjustments and, if none can be taken or made, then and only then can the employer rely on the defence of justification of less favourable treatment, see below the case authorities of **Archibald (2004)** and **Meikle (2004)**).

The way section 3A worked can be explained by two practical examples given by the Code of Practice. The first shows how an employer, who is under a duty to make reasonable adjustments, **cannot** justify discrimination if he fails to make the adjustment while the second (in analogous factual and legal circumstances) shows a situation in which an employer **can** justify discrimination.

The first example is per paragraph 4.7 of the Code of Practice -

> 'An applicant for a typing job is not the best person on the face of it, but only because her typing speed is too slow due to arthritis in her hands. If a reasonable adjustment - perhaps an adapted keyboard - would overcome this, her typing speed would not in itself be a substantial reason for not employing her. Therefore the employer would be unlawfully discriminating if on account of her typing speed he did not employ her and provide the adjustment.'

The second example per paragraph 4.7 of the Code of Practice -

> 'An employer refuses a training course for an employee with an illness which is very likely to be terminal within a year because, even with a reasonable adjustment to help in the job after the course, the benefits of the course could not be adequately realised. This is very likely to be a substantial reason. It is clearly material to the circumstances. The refusal of training would therefore very likely be justified.'

If, in the first example, the employer refuses the applicant the job because of her disability, the refusal would, prima facie, be for a reason that was related to or was connected with her disability and, therefore, it would constitute a breach of s.3A of the Disability Discrimination Act 1995. On the other hand, the situation could be that the employer decides to employ the applicant even though he knows that she has a disability but believes that the disability will not greatly impede her in doing her work. However, he then discovers subsequently that her typing rate is well below the speed of his other comparable typists. It is at this point that the employer realises that he must either dismisses her for the reason of (in)capability or, alternatively, he must make a reasonable adjustment that would enable her to increase her typing speed. If he dismisses her, s.3A(3) prevents him from putting forward the justification defence that the dismissal

> 'was material to the circumstances of the case and substantial because s.4A(1) DDA 1995 places him under a duty to make a reasonable adjustment but he has unjustifiably failed to do so. In once sense such a dismissal would be 'material to the circumstances of the case and substantial.'

But the employer's response, that of dismissing his disabled employee, would not be 'within the range of reasonable responses of a reasonable employer' because the reasonable employer would ascertain the law and then take the necessary steps to carry out his s.4A(1) duty by making a reasonable adjustment. The first step that an employer must take is to consider and then make any reasonable adjustment; if there is no reasonable adjustment that can be made or an adjustment would make no difference, then it is at that stage that an employer can contend that the failure to make a reasonable adjustment was justified in that his course of action was material to the circumstances of the particular case and substantial.

By contrast, the second example shows that the employer's response - being a failure to make a reasonable adjustment - is: (i) justifiable, (ii) material to the circumstances of the case and substantial and (iii) reasonable and therefore is not a breach of s.3A.

Part 6

6.1 Leading case authority under the Disability Discrimination Act 1995:

Apart from **Malcolm (2008)**, the leading case under the Disability Discrimination Act 1995 is **Goodwin v The Patent Office (1999)** IRLR 4 that was heard by the President of the EAT, Morison P. who gave the decision of the tribunal and set out guidance as to the Tribunal's approach with regard to the determination of the issue of disability.

At paragraph 22 he said:

> **'The tribunal should bear in mind that with social legislation of this kind, a purposive approach to construction should be adopted. The language should be construed in a way which gives effect to the stated or presumed intention of Parliament, but with due regard to the ordinary and natural meaning of the words in question. With this legislation, tribunals are given explicit assistance in two forms, which should detract from the need to adopt a loose construction of the language.**

Guidance issued on 25 July 1996 under s.3 of the Act by the Secretary of State (Statutory Instrument No.1996/1996) with statutory effect from 31 July 1996; and a Code of Practice issued on 25 July 1996 but with statutory effect from 2 December 1996.

At paragraph 26, Morison P. set out the four different conditions which have to be satisfied before a tribunal can find that an applicant has a disability within the meaning of the Act:

> **'(1) The impairment condition -**
> **Does the applicant have an impairment which is either mental or physical?**
> **(2) The adverse effect condition -**
> **Does the impairment affect the applicant's ability to carry out normal day-to- day activities in one of the**

respects set out in para 4(1) of Schedule 1 to the Act, and does it have an adverse effect?

(3) The substantial condition -
Is the adverse condition (upon the applicant's ability) substantial?

(4) The long-term condition -
Is the adverse condition (upon the applicant's ability) long-term?'

He continued at paragraph 35:

'The focus of attention required by the Act is on the things that the applicant either cannot do or can only do with difficulty, rather than on the things that the person can do. The Act is looking to see whether the capacities listed in para 4(1) have been affected. These capacities are those which will be required, to a greater or lesser extent, to carry out normal day-to-day activities, whether at home or at work.'

At paragraph 40 he defines the term 'substantial' as meaning more than minor or trivial (per both the Guidance and the Code of Practice). At paragraph 42, Morison P. considered the effect of medical treatment - the so-called "deduced" effect - setting out the position thus:

'The tribunal will wish to examine how the applicant's abilities had actually been affected at the material time, whilst on medication, and then to address their minds to the difficult question as to the effects which they think there would have been but for the medication: the deduced effects. The question is then whether the actual and deduced effects on the applicant's abilities to carry out day-to-day activities is clearly more than trivial.'

Note: the Disability Rights Commission replaced the 1996 version of the Guidance with a revised 'Guidance on matters to be taken into account in determining questions relating to the definition of disability' that came into force on 01 May 2006. The then new Guidance reflected the changes introduced by the DDA 2005 on 05 December 2005. These changes included the removal of the requirement that a mental illness be 'clinically well-recognised' as well as a specific provision that progressive illnesses such as cancer, HIV infection and multiple sclerosis are disabilities under the Act from the point of diagnosis.

6.2 Disability discrimination – two more leading case authorities:

Case authorities (old section numbers used):

(1) Archibald v Fife Council (2004) IRLR 651; (2004) ICR 954 (HL);
(2) Nottinghamshire County Council v Meikle (2004) IRLR 703 (CA).

(1) The House of Lords, for the first time, considered the provisions of the Disability Discrimination Act 1995 in the case of **Archibald v Fife Council (2004).** Like the Court of Appeal case of **Meikle (2004)** that was decided shortly after **Archibald (2004),** this case provided new and authoritative guidance as to the understanding and interpretation of the DDA 1995 which assisted employment tribunals during the remaining period that the DDA 1995 was in force and which still assist tribunals with regard to the disability discrimination provisions of the Equality Act 2010. Both cases highlighted the importance of the reasonable adjustments provisions and, in so doing, set in proper context the case of **Jones v Post Office (2001)** IRLR 384.

Archibald v Fife Council (2004) IRLR 651 (HL).

The facts: Susan Archibald was a road sweeper employed by Fife Council. She became unable to walk after a routine surgical procedure and thus unable to do her job. The Council placed her on its redeployment list. Because of her disability, the only suitable type of work that she could do was sedentary or office-based. A problem arose in that the Council's redeployment procedure allowed redeployment without competitive interview only to posts of the same or lower pay grade. But Mrs Archibald's pay rate was slightly lower than that of the lowest pay grade for office-based jobs. This meant that, technically, a move to an office-based job would amount to a promotion. That being so, under s.7 of the Local Government and Housing Act 1989, appointments must be made on merit which meant that existing staff seeking a promotion had to apply via a competitive interview. She applied for a large number of jobs but, despite being suitable for office work, she was unsuccessful in being appointed to a position. Mrs Archibald thought that her manual work background, rather than her disability, was the reason she failed to gain an appointment. Nonetheless, her case was that when she became disabled and unable to do her previous job, her employer should have considered transferring her to office-based work that she could do particularly as she had the necessary skills to do such work. However, because of the redeployment policy, no such transfer was made. Because she was unable to carry out her previous job and because she was unsuccessful with her applications for office-based work, the Council dismissed her.

Employment tribunal: Mrs Archibald made a claim to an employment tribunal against the Council for disability discrimination for (1) failure to make reasonable adjustments and (2) less favourable treatment for a reason related to her disability. The ET dismissed her claim for the reason that it considered that the reasonable adjustment proposed constituted more favourable treatment and that such advantageous treatment was not allowed by virtue of what was then s.6(7) of the DDA 1995. However, s.6(7) states: 'Subject to the provisions of this section, nothing in this Part is to be taken to require an employer to treat a disabled person more favourably than he treats, or would treat others.' The opening words - 'Subject to the provisions of this section' - make it clear that the subsection is subject to the specific requirement of s.6 that is the duty to make reasonable adjustments. In other words: 'Subject to the provisions to make reasonable adjustments, nothing in this Part…' In addition to dismissing her claim that the Council had failed to make reasonable adjustments, the tribunal also held that her dismissal was justified.

Scottish Employment Appeal Tribunal: the tribunal dismissed her appeal for the reason that she had not been placed at a substantial disadvantage by the Council's redeployment policy because it applied to all the Council's staff.

Court of Session: the grounds of her appeal changed slightly and focused on whether the scope of the reasonable adjustments provisions extended to a situation where an employee could no longer carry out the essential functions of their job because of their disability.

Held: if an employee becomes disabled and is no longer able to carry out the essential functions of their job, that occurrence does not constitute 'an arrangement made by or on behalf of an employer' for the purposes of the reasonable adjustments provisions of the DDA 1995. The Court thought that the steps which an employer might have to take in order to comply with the reasonable adjustments duty would not extend to transferring an employee to a completely different job, regardless of the fact that one of a non-exhaustive list of examples of steps that an employer might need to take in order to comply with the duty under the DDA 1995 is 'transferring him to fill an existing vacancy.'

House of Lords: the Law Lords unanimously allowed Mrs Archibald's appeal and, in doing so, stated some important principles. These are:

> the Law Lords said that the DDA 1995 does not operate the same way as other anti-discrimination legislation and that it is not intended to do so. Baroness Hale, in setting out the background to the issues in question, compared disability discrimination to sex and race discrimination and said:
>
> ***'In the latter two, men and women or black and white, as the case may be, are opposite sides of the same coin. Each is to be treated in the same way. Treating men more favourably than women discriminates against women. Treating women more favourably than men discriminates against men. Pregnancy apart, the differences between the genders are generally regarded as irrelevant. The 1995 Act, however, does not regard the differences between disabled people and others as irrelevant. It does not expect each to be treated in the same way. It expects reasonable adjustments to be made to cater for the special needs of disabled people. It necessarily entails an element of more favourable treatment. The question for us is when that obligation arises and how far it goes.'***

The first question that the House of Lords considered was: **'When is the duty to make reasonable adjustments triggered?'** The DDA 1995 states that the duty to make adjustments is triggered where any arrangements made by or on behalf of the employer, or any physical feature of premises occupied by the employer, place the disabled person concerned at a **substantial disadvantage** in comparison with persons who are not disabled.

During the course of the appeal, the argument advanced for the Council was that Mrs Archibald was asking for adjustments which would amount to positive discrimination. In contrast, the argument put forward for Mrs Archibald by the Disability Rights Commission that represented her was that the purpose of the DDA 1995 is to achieve equality of outcome - and that this requires differential treatment. At the appeal hearing in the Court of Session, the Court decided that the duty to make reasonable adjustments did not arise where an employee can no longer carry out the essential functions of their job. The House of Lords rejected this proposition. **The Law Lords emphasised the breadth of the term 'arrangements' and said that the relevant arrangement was the express or implied contractual term that anyone who becomes incapable of fulfilling their job description is liable to be dismissed.** Having defined the arrangement in this way, the House of Lords concluded that Mrs Archibald was substantially disadvantaged compared to other employees who are not disabled when she became liable to be dismissed because she could not carry out her existing job. Answering the question as to who was the correct non-disabled comparator, the Law Lords said that the most helpful approach would appear to be to focus upon identifying the arrangement correctly rather than focus on the correct comparator.

The second question that the House of Lords considered was: **'What is the scope of the duty to make reasonable adjustments?'** In particular, did the duty to make reasonable adjustments include transferring a disabled employee to fill an existing vacancy that was at a slightly higher grade without requiring the employee to undergo a competitive interview?

The Law Lords noted that that transfer is merely an example of a step that it might be reasonable to take. Thus, the scope of potential steps is broader than the examples contained in s.6(3) (that then became s.18B(2)(c)) of the DDA 1995.) The Lords held that 'transferring him to an existing vacancy' was not limited to the same kind of work or to a job of the same grade - a transfer could be upwards as well as sideways or downwards. They concluded that such a transfer might be a reasonable adjustment.

Having so concluded, the question then became whether it might have been reasonable, in all the circumstances, to transfer Mrs Archibald without competitive interview to an office-based job that she was capable of carrying out. This question was remitted to an employment tribunal.

Next, the House of Lords considered the arguments as to what might be the 'control mechanism' for determining the scope of the duty. The Lords accepted the arguments advanced on behalf of Mrs Archibald that the 'control mechanism' consists of the duty to do only what is **reasonable** in the circumstances of a particular case. In other words, an employer must or need only take steps which are reasonable (or are rational to take) in the particular circumstances of a case. So that the duty to consider and take reasonable steps arises as soon as the employer's arrangements substantially disadvantage a disabled employee. If steps can be taken and should be taken then, to comply with the law, an employer should take steps to make adjustments which are reasonable.

The third question that the House of Lords considered was: **'Does the making of reasonable adjustments in this way amount to more favourable treatment?'**

In the opinion of their Lordships, they said that the tribunal's interpretation of s.6(7) of the DDA 1995 was wrong. **They held that the opening words - 'Subject to the provisions of this section...' mean that to the extent the duty to make reasonable adjustments require it, the employer is not only permitted but obliged to treat a disabled person more favourably than others.** This is a very important finding and it is central to the way that the duty to make reasonable adjustments operates. The nature of the duty is such that it requires a difference in treatment between a disabled person and a person who is not disabled. This is required when disability is an issue because equality of treatment may not lead to equality of outcome - hence the need for reasonable adjustments.

The last question that the House of Lords considered was: **'Justification.'**

Their Lordships looked at two aspects of justification as it arose in: (1) the duty to make reasonable adjustments, and (2) less favourable treatment. (Note: as from 1st October 2004, the DDA 1995 no longer made any provision for justification of failure to make reasonable adjustments. This was because of amendments brought about by the Disability Discrimination Act 1995 (Amendment) Regulations 2003. At the time this case was being heard, it was technically possible to argue justification in the reasonable adjustments context. But the case of **Collins v Royal National Theatre Board Ltd (2004)** IRLR 395 had established that justification in reasonable adjustments cases would be of very narrow scope indeed, a finding that the House of Lords endorsed).

In considering justification, the House of Lords concluded that the question of whether Mrs Archibald had been discriminated against by being dismissed could not be determined until after the question of reasonable adjustments was resolved. The House of Lords stressed the importance of first considering the issue of reasonable adjustments, before the issue of less favourable treatment. This is the proper approach because, by so doing, it then enables the effect of any failures to be taken into account at the justification stage as is required by the DDA 1995. Thus, if a reasonable adjustment would have made a difference, less favourable treatment will not be justifiable.

In the majority of cases, justification of less favourable treatment for a reason related to disability will depend upon reasonable adjustments. It will only be in cases where a reasonable adjustment would have made no difference that the test in **Jones v Post Office (2001)** IRLR 384 will apply. In **Jones (2001),** employment tribunals are limited to considering whether the reason given by an employer for less favourable treatment of a disabled person is material and substantial. But the problem with **Jones (2001)** was that the Court of Appeal, when hearing that case, was asked to consider the issue of less favourable treatment alone, but was not asked to consider the reasonable adjustments provisions. The cases of **Archibald (2004)** and **Meikle (2004)** correct that imbalance.

Nottinghamshire County Council v Meikle (2004) IRLR 703 (CA).

The facts: the Claimant, Mrs Gaynor Meikle, was a teacher. Her eyesight deteriorated in 1993. She made a request to the school at which she worked which was whether it would make reasonable adjustments so as to enable her to carry out her job. None of these adjustments would have been costly or difficult. However, there was a persistent failure by the school to make these adjustments and, after working in inappropriate conditions for a long period of time, Mrs Meikle went off sick in June 1993 with stress and eye strain. During the period that she was off sick, her sick pay was reduced to half as a consequence of her employer's sick pay policy. She eventually resigned, having concluded that the remaining reasonable adjustments she had requested were not going to be made. She presented a claim to an employment tribunal for disability discrimination and constructive dismissal.

Employment tribunal: it made a finding in favour of Mrs Meikle in respect of a number of failures to make reasonable adjustments and held that she was correct to believe that the remaining adjustments were not going to be made. But the employment tribunal dismissed a part of Mrs Meikle's claim which was that her employer's policy of reducing her pay during her sickness absence amounted to a failure to make a reasonable adjustment and also amounted to less favourable treatment for a reason related to her disability. In addition, the tribunal made a finding which was that she had not been constructively dismissed. That latter claim depended on whether the Council, by its conduct, committed a breach of contract which allowed Mrs Meikle to terminate the contract of employment, with or without notice (per s.95(1)(c), ERA 1995), that existed between her and the Council.

Employment Appeal Tribunal: Mrs Meikle appealed against the findings in respect of constructive dismissal and the employer's policy of reducing sick pay of employees who were absent from work on sick leave because of the effects of their disabilities. **Held:** the EAT allowed the appeal. In so doing, the EAT held that the term 'dismissal' in the DDA 1995 included constructive dismissal. The EAT also substituted a decision that she had been constructively unfairly dismissed and that, by reducing her pay when she was on long-term sickness absence, her employer had (i) treated her less favourably and (ii) had failed to make reasonable adjustments.

Court of Appeal: her employer appealed against the findings of the EAT. **Held:** the Court of Appeal dismissed the local authority's appeal on all grounds. The reasons for the Court of Appeal's decision were:-

(1) that repudiatory conduct did not need to be the only reason for the employee's resignation in a constructive unfair dismissal claim;

(2) that considering whether the conduct concerned was an 'effective cause' of the resignation was also an incorrect approach as this could lead to questions about the employee's motives. That the proper approach, once repudiation of the contract had been established, was to ask whether the employee had accepted the repudiation by treating the contract of employment as at an end. (Note: in discrimination cases, it is not appropriate to consider the question of what happened in terms of causation, i.e. 'but for.' Rather, in trying to establish what happened, the question should be based upon an answer to the phrase 'by reason that.' In other words, ask: 'Why did the alleged discriminator act as he did? What, consciously or unconsciously, was his reason? Unlike causation, this is a subjective test. Causation is a legal conclusion. The reason why a person acted as he did is a question of fact:' per Lord Nicholls at para 29 in **Chief Constable of West Yorkshire Police v Khan (2001)** ICR 1065, 1072. See also - **Pantry v The Home Office (2004)** EAT Case No.0083/04 18.10.04, para 7);

(3) that the test for whether or not there has been a breach of the implied term of trust and confidence is an objective test, a principle established by the case of **Malik and another v BCCI (1997)** IRLR 462;

(4) that 'dismissal' in s.4(2)(d) of the DDA1995 includes constructive dismissal thus resolving conflicting EAT authorities being: **Catherall v Michelin Tyres plc (2003)** IRLR 61; **Commissioner of Police for the Metropolis v Harley (2001)** IRLR 263; **Derby Fabrication Ltd v Burton (2001)** IRLR 69;

(5) that where there is a discriminatory constructive dismissal claim, the time for lodging a complaint to the employment tribunal runs from the date the employment terminated rather than from the date(s) when the act(s) of discrimination took place. In deciding this, the CA declined to follow the approach suggested by Auld LJ in **Cast v Croydon College (1998)** IRLR 318. (This should have a significant impact on the way that tribunals approach the question of limitation in all discrimination cases where constructive dismissal is alleged. But note the decision of the EAT in **Coutts and Co plc and another v Cure and another (2004)** EAT 17 September 2004 (Case No.0395/04), wherein the EAT held that that the three-month limitation period begins with the date on which the act, consisting of a detriment, occurred, thereby following the Court of Appeal's guidance on time limits in sex discrimination cases from **Cast v Croydon College (1998)** IRLR 318. However, an employee must act promptly in any event by terminating the contract of employment when he or she has reasonable grounds for so doing because of the employer's repudiatory conduct; and an employee must also act promptly, i.e. no later than three months less one day, when making a claim for unlawful discrimination to an employment tribunal);

(6) that s.6(11) of the DDA 1995 did not apply to sick pay paid by an employer. In deciding this, the CA upheld the reasoning of the EAT in the case of **London Clubs Management v Hood (2001)** IRLR 719 as regards the scope of s.6(11) in that s.6(11) applies only to occupational pension schemes and benefits provided under third-party insurance services and does not, therefore, extend to benefits such as contractual sick pay. The local authority argued that sick pay is exempt from the reasonable adjustments provisions of the DDA 1995 because s.6(11) of the DDA 1995 states that the reasonable adjustments provisions do not apply to 'any benefit under an

occupational pension scheme or any other benefit payable in money or money's worth under a scheme or arrangement for the benefit of employees in respect of... accident, sickness or invalidity.' **But the CA held that s.6(11), DDA 1995 was intended to exempt an employer from the duty to make reasonable adjustments in relation to benefits under occupational pension schemes and similar schemes, such as insurance schemes, which are not administered by the employer.** Keene LJ pointed out that other sections of the DDA 1995 - i.e. ss.17 and 18 - formed the counterpart of s.6(11) in as much as they made provision for non-discrimination by trustees of occupational pension schemes and imposed liability on insurers who discriminate on the ground of disability when providing benefits to employees under insurance arrangements with their employer. It made sense for the 'reasonable adjustments' s.6 duty to be disapplied because protection of the employee is secured by ss.17 and 18 and because the employer will often not be in a position to make adjustments to a pension or insurance scheme. Such duties as there need to be fall more appropriately on those administering the schemes. But no such reason existed for excluding direct payment of sick pay by an employer to an employee, in respect of which the employer does have control. For these reasons, the CA concluded that there had been a failure to make a reasonable adjustment in respect of the sick pay policy;

(7) that the justification defence under s.5(5) DDA 1995, the effect of which is to make the question of justification of less favourable treatment subject to consideration of the effect of any failure to make reasonable adjustments, is only to be considered after all the reasonable adjustments had been made. The CA found that the evidence pointed towards Mrs Meikle's lengthy absence being the consequence of the prolonged failure by her employer to take appropriate steps to cope with her disability. If those steps had been taken, she would not have been off sick. Therefore, there was unlawful discrimination under s.5(1) (that became s.3A(1)) of the DDA 1995 being less favourable treatment for a reason related to disability in respect of the decision to reduce Mrs Meikle's pay to half-pay.

The effect of the judgments in **Archibald (2004)** and **Meikle (2004)** emphasised the importance of the reasonable adjustments provisions of the DDA 1995. The issue of reasonable adjustments was central to most if not all DDA 1995 claims and is also central to such claims under the disability discrimination provisions of the Equality Act 2010. These provisions were what made the DDA 1995 different from other legislation designed to combat discrimination and, in this regard, the DDA 1995 – and now, since its repeal, the Equality Act 2010 - would be ineffective without them.

Archibald (2004) and **Meikle (2004)** redress the imbalance that arose from the Court of Appeal case of **Jones v Post Office (2001)** IRLR 384 that was widely criticised for setting a very low threshold for justification in DDA 1995 less favourable treatment cases. **Jones (2001)** restricted employment tribunals to considering whether the reason given by an employer for less favourable treatment of a disabled employee is material and substantial. But the problem with **Jones (2001)** was that the Court of Appeal was asked to consider the issue of less favourable treatment alone; and was not asked to consider the reasonable adjustments provisions. In both **Archibald (2004)** and **Meikle (2004)**, the importance of first considering the issue of reasonable adjustments, before less favourable treatment, was emphasised. This is the proper approach because it then enables the effect of any failures to be taken into account at the justification stage, as is required by the Act. If a reasonable adjustment would have made a difference, less favourable treatment will not be justified. Therefore, in the majority of cases, justification of less favourable treatment for a reason related to disability will depend upon reasonable adjustments. It will only be in cases where a reasonable adjustment would have made no difference that the test in **Jones (2001)** will apply.

On the matter of sick pay, sickness pay schemes are now susceptible to the s.6 duty (that became s.4A(1) and, under the Equality Act 2010, is now s.20) to make reasonable adjustments in respect of employees who are off work for a disability-related reason. Typically, such schemes provide for the payment of full pay for a limited period only, after which benefits are usually substantially reduced or discontinued altogether. Disabled employees will often be substantially disadvantaged by such reduction rules since they are more likely to experience greater levels of sickness-related absence than non-disabled employees. In the light of the Court of Appeal's judgment, employers may well find that they are unable to justify reducing benefits to disabled employees. This is so particularly in a case such as **Meikle (2004)** wherein the employer failed to make other reasonable adjustments which could have resulted in a far lower level of sickness absence incurred by the employee. But note: this is a narrow rule that applies to employees who have a statutory disability and are absent from work because of the effects of their disability, rather than a wide rule that applies to employees generally who are absent from work because of sickness.

6.3 Principles derived from disability discrimination case authorities:

Various other principles can be derived from the **case authorities** -

- the Guidance issued pursuance to s.3 DDA 1995 is only meant to be illustrative and not exhaustive: **Vicary v British Telecommunications plc (1999)** IRLR 680 and **Leonard v Southern Derbyshire Chamber of Commerce (2001)** IRLR 19.
- following the amendments to the Disability Discrimination Act 1995, mental impairments are established in the same way as physical impairments in that the claimant only has to show that he or she has a physical or mental impairment and will not have to show the **cause** of that impairment or that he or she suffers with a particular illness: DDA 2005;
- a tribunal must provide sufficiently detailed reasons to show its thinking and its findings in that parties must understand why they have lost or won; a tribunal must give reasons as to why it reached the conclusions that it did: **Meek v City of Birmingham District Council (1987)** IRLR 250; see also the later cases of **Tran v Greenwich Vietnam Community (2002)** IRLR 735; **English v Emery Reimbold and Strick (2002)** EWCA Civ 605;
- an employer should take such steps as are sensible according to the circumstances to consult an employee and to discuss with him or her and to inform themselves of the true medical condition before acting upon a decision to dismiss: **East Lindsey District Council v Daubney (1977)** IRLR 181 and 184;
- where there is a lack of proper current medical evidence, a respondent will not act fairly and may discriminate unlawfully and be guilty of failing to make reasonable adjustments, if it fails to obtain the necessary opinion. 'Reasonableness'

includes tests similar to those in the unfair dismissal regime: **Jones v Post Office (2001)** IRLR 304;

- an employment tribunal may err if it decides that a dismissal on the basis of permanent incapacity for medical reasons disqualifies an applicant from some but not all relevant employment: **Bank v IBM (UK) Ltd (2003)** EAT (Case No. 389/03) 9 September 2003;
- in deciding whether employers meet pre-dismissal obligations, in the context of a well-developed ill-health procedure, to make reasonable adjustments under section 6 (then s.4A; now s.20, Equality Act 2010), a tribunal must consider the extent to which, if at all, adjustments proposed by the applicant could have overcome medical symptoms which otherwise prevent a return to work: **Fu v London Borough of Camden (2001)** IRLR 186;
- on the subject more generally about reasonable adjustments, the duty to make reasonable adjustments applies to dismissals. The Disability Discrimination Act was amended in 2003 to give effect to the EU Equal Treatment Framework Directive (No.2000/78). Following that amendment, tribunals and courts are obliged, wherever possible, to interpret the reasonable adjustment provisions in s.4A, DDA 1995 in a way that complies with the Directive. Note that Article 3(1)(c) of the Directive expressly states that it applies to dismissals; therefore, the statement by Mummery LJ in **Clark v Novacold (1999)** in which he held that dismissal was not a breach of the duty to make reasonable adjustments is no longer correct law. This means that the act of dismissal can amount to unlawful disability discrimination where the dismissal is because of a failure to make a reasonable adjustment: **Aylott v Stockton-on-Tees Borough Council (2010)** EWCA Civ 910.
- in deciding whether a reason for less favourable treatment does not or would not apply to others, it is simply a case of identifying others to whom the reason for the treatment does not, or would not, apply. The test of less favourable treatment is based on the reason for the treatment of the disabled person and not on the fact of the disability: **Clark v Novacold (1999)** IRLR 318. But see the leading authority under the now repealed DDA 1995 in this area of the law being **Mayor and Burgesses of the London Borough of Lewisham v Malcolm (2008)** UKHL 43;
- an employer can only discriminate against a disabled

employee if the employer treats the employee differently for a reason – present in the employer's mind – that is related to the employee's disability: **City of Edinburgh Council v Dickson (2009)** EAT 02.12.09 (Case No.0038/09);

- the Employment Appeal Tribunal held that an employment tribunal had erred in finding that it had no jurisdiction to hear a claim of disability discrimination against an employee by another employee. An employee can, as a matter of law, make a disability discrimination claim against another employee with whom he or she works and that includes a claim for victimisation (the latter being that the discriminating employee took retaliatory action against the disabled employee because he or she took some kind of action such as making a complaint or a claim about disability discrimination.) Such a claim by one employee against another employee came within Part 11 of the Disability Discrimination Act 1995 whereby s.17A(1)(b) specifically gave an employment jurisdiction to hear such a claim against a person who fell within s.57(1)(2) and s.58(1)(2), DDA 1995. These latter sections are now found in the Equality Act 2010 being: s.57(1), DDA 1995 is now s.112(1), Equality Act 2010; s.57(2), DDA 1995 is now s.110(1), Equality Act 2010; s.58(1), DDA 1995 is now s.110(2) and 109, Equality Act 2010: **Barlow v Stone (2012)** EAT 01 June 2012 (Case No. 0049/12);
- where an employer or prospective employer takes retaliatory action against one of its employee or an applicant for employment because the employee or applicant brought proceedings under the Equality Act 2010, or gave evidence under the Act, or did any other thing in connection with the Act, or made an allegation under the Act, this is called 'victimisation.' Bringing or giving evidence in support of a discrimination claim is a 'protected act' under s.27, Equality Act 2010. If a prospective employer held a previous case against a job applicant, or reject the job application because the applicant made an ET claim against his or her previous employer, this would be unlawful victimisation. The remedy is an award for injury to feelings (i.e. for the upset and mental distress caused) and, if dismissed unfairly, an award of compensation: s.27(1) and (2), Equality Act 2010;
- in a case where it is contended by a respondent that it operated its standard procedure, the tribunal should consider whether the applicant was refused the particular benefit for a reason

which related to his disability rather than whether he was receiving what was ordinarily due to him for that reason: **London Clubs Management Ltd v Hood (2001)** IRLR 719;

- in considering whether an employer discriminated unlawfully, the test of whether it knew of the disability is objective and includes an examination not only of the actual knowledge of the respondent but of factors which might indicate the manifestation of such a condition without the employer expressly being told of it: **H. A. Heinz v Kenrick (2000)** IRLR 144; **Mayor and Burgesses of the London Borough of Lewisham v Malcolm (2008)** UKHL 43 (**Kenrick (2000)** overruled by HL in **Malcolm (2008)**: knowledge now required);
- where an employer lacks knowledge of the employee's disability, the employer cannot be liable for any form of discrimination relating to disability if it was not, and could not reasonably have been, aware at the material time that the employee suffered from a disability - per Underhill P: **Wilcox v Birmingham CAB Services Ltd (2011)** EAT 23 June 2011 (Case No.0293/10).
- it is not the duty of the tribunal to obtain evidence or to make sure that adequate medical evidence is obtained by the parties; the onus is on the applicant to prove the impairment on the conventional balance of probabilities; it is for the applicant to show what would have happened if he had not been prescribed medication or received other medical treatment which he received: **McNicol v Balfour Beattie Rail Maintenance Ltd (2002)** ICR 1498, EWCA Civ 1074;
- in a disability discrimination case, the onus of proving disability lies on a claimant to demonstrate that he was disabled at the time of the alleged detrimental treatment; it is not for the respondent to prove that he was not. Furthermore, in deciding the question, the tribunal must not take account of developments after that date: **SG Baker Ltd v Haggart (2011)** EAT 09 November 2011 (Case No.0007/11);
- the point of time at which to assess disability is at the time of the alleged discrimination: **Cruickshank v VAW Motorcars Ltd (2002)** IRLR 24 (per HH Judge Altman at para 26 & 27); **Richmond Adult Community College v McDougall (2008)** EWCA Civ 4, CA; **Mahon v Accuread Ltd (2008)** EAT, 01.07.08 (Case No.0081/08); **Mayor and Burgesses of the London Borough of Lewisham v Malcolm (2008)** UKHL 43

- per Lord Bingham at 6;

- the section 6 duty to make reasonable adjustments and consider whether any could be made is on the employer, not the employee. The test is an objective one: **British Gas Services Ltd v McCaull (2001)** IRLR 60; **Morse v Wiltshire County Council (1998)** IRLR 352 (para 41-47);
- a section 6 duty refers to what is generally described as the duty to make reasonable adjustments. In fact it is a duty under section 6 to take certain steps: **Freer Bouskell v Brewster (2003)** EAT (Case No.0377/03) (per McMullen J at para 9);
- an adjustment will constitute a reasonable adjustment where there is a 'real prospect' that the adjustment could or would remove the disabled employee's disadvantage. But that does not mean that a prospect less than a real prospect would not be sufficient to make the adjustment a reasonable one. It may, in all the circumstances, still be enough: **Leeds Teaching Hospital NHS Trust v Foster (2011)** EAT 14 June 2011 (Case No.0552/10).
- the duty to make reasonable adjustments for a disabled employee can extend to continuing to pay a higher salary when an employee is moved to a lesser role held the EAT in **G4S Cash Solutions (UK) Ltd v Powell (2016)**. Because of his disability, the claimant had been moved from an engineering role maintaining cash machines to a less skilled 'key runner' role. After initially having his pay protected, the respondent proposed reducing the claimant's pay by around 10%, dismissing the claimant when he refused the pay cut. The employment tribunal found the dismissal to be discriminatory and unfair, and that the reasonable adjustments required extended to maintaining the claimant's former pay in his new role. The EAT found no reason in principle why the duty to make reasonable adjustments would not extend to protecting an employee's pay (along with other measures) to counter a disabled employee's disadvantage. The objectives of the legislation plainly envisage an element of cost to the employer, and 'pay protection' was but one form of cost to an employer. The question will always be whether it is reasonable for an employer to have to take that step to avert a disabled employee's disadvantage. However, the EAT did not expect that requiring employers to make up pay would be an 'everyday event' for tribunals, and in changed circumstances such an adjustment may cease to a reasonable one an

employer has to make: **G4S Cash Solutions (UK) Ltd v Powell (2016)** EAT 26 August 2016 (Case No.0243/15).

- a failure by an employer to make a reasonable adjustment under the disability discrimination legislation is an omission, not a continuing act and, that being so, the time limit for bringing a disability discrimination claim starts to run from when the employer takes the decision not to make the adjustment: **Humphries v Chevler Packaging Ltd (2006)** EAT 24 July 2006 (Case No.0224/06);
- in contrast, a disabled employee succeeded at an employment tribunal in his claim for disability discrimination, being a failure by the employer to make reasonable adjustments. The EAT overturned the decision for the reason that the failure to make reasonable adjustments was **not** a continuing omission and was therefore out of time. The Court of Appeal, however, held that the employer's failure **was** a continuing omission and was not out of time. Sedley LJ highlighted a point of general importance from the judgment: ***'... unfortunately not a readily obvious one...'*** of paragraph 3, schedule 3, DDA 1995 the effect of which is to eliminate continuing omissions from the computation of time by deeming them to be acts committed at a notional moment. This prevent ***'... a situation of neglect from dragging on indefinitely...'*** but can of course ***'... create very real difficulties for claimants.'*** To avoid this problem, Sedley LJ suggested that it would thus be prudent for an employee, once a potentially discriminatory omission has been brought to the employer's attention, ***'... to issue proceedings sooner rather than later unless an express agreement is obtained that no point will be taken on time for as long as it takes to address the alleged omission.'*** He also suggested that tribunals might be ***'sympathetic'*** to an application for an extension of time in relevant cases: **Matuszowicz v Kingston upon Hull City Council (2009)** EWCA Civ 22 (judgment 10 February 2009). See s.68(1), DDA 1995;
- section 68(1), DDA 1995, prohibited discrimination by employers against those in their employment or those applying to them for employment. The definition of 'employment' in s.68 was broad, covering individuals working under a contract of employment, apprentices, and anyone working under a contract to do work personally. But the section did not cover volunteers who have no protection from discrimination by

employers; and this applies to all other strands of discrimination law: **X v Mid Sussex Citizens Advice Bureau and another (2011)** ICR 460, Court of Appeal. (This case was granted leave to appeal to the Supreme Court on 27 June 2011.) The same definition of employment as stated under s.68, DDA 1995 is now found at s.83(2), Equality Act 2010.

Note: Under para.3(1), Sch.3, Disability Discrimination Act 1995, the normal time limit for a disability discrimination claim was three months from when the act complained about took place: para.3(1), Sch.3, Disability Discrimination Act 1995.

Time limits in the **Equality Act 2010** are stated in s.123 which are that: 'Proceedings on a complaint within section 120 (that states that employment tribunals have jurisdiction to determine claims relating to a contravention of Part 5, being work) may not be brought after the end of the period of 3 months starting with the date of the act to which the complaint relates or such period as the employment tribunal thinks just and equitable.'

The previous law was that if a **statutory grievance** was made by the employee or by his or her representative to the employer about the discrimination and a procedure was still ongoing at the expiry of the three-month claim period, then Reg.15(2) of the Employment Act 2002 (Dispute Resolution) Regulations 2004 applied to extend the time limit by an extra three months. Note that the statutory dispute resolution procedures were repealed as of 06 April 2009 which is the date when the ACAS Code of Practice on Disciplinary and Grievance Procedures came into force by virtue of the Employment Act 2008.

- there is a duty to pay attention to relevant guidance issued by the Secretary of State and also to consider the Code of Practice. The relevant provision of the Code of Practice is paragraph 3(2) which provides as follows:

"It will probably be helpful to talk to each disabled person about what the real effects of the disability might be, or what might help. There is less chance of a dispute where the person is involved from the start. Such discussions should not, of course, be conducted in a way which would itself give the disabled person any reason to believe that he was being discriminated against" - in **Freer Bouskell v Brewster (2003)** EAT (Case No.0377/03) (per McMullen J at para 10);

- an employer who is under the duty to make reasonable adjustments cannot put forward the defence of justification under s.5(2)(b) DDA 1995, being that the reason for dismissing an employee for a reason related to or connected with her disability was material to the circumstances of the case and was substantial, if the employer failed to consider or make reasonable adjustments in the form of offering the applicant part-time working: **Francis v London Borough of Hammersmith & Fulham (2004)** EAT (Case 0942/03);
- an employer is under a duty to make adjustments where any provision, criterion or practice (PCP) that it applies, or any physical feature of premises that it occupies, places a disabled person at a substantial disadvantage in comparison with those who are not disabled. Once this duty is triggered, the employer must take steps such as it is reasonable for it to take to prevent the PCP or physical feature having the disadvantageous effect. In two separate cases, the EAT gave guidance to assist employment tribunals applying these provisions which is that in establishing a breach of duty to make reasonable adjustments, tribunals must identify - (i) the offending PCP or physical feature, (ii) the non-disabled comparators (where appropriate), (iii) the nature and extent of the substantial disadvantage suffered by the disabled employee, and (iv) the 'step' the employer has allegedly failed to take to remedy that disadvantage, and (v) whether it was reasonable to take that step by reference to the matters set out in s.18B, DDA 1995: **Environment Agency v Rowan (2008)** IRLR 20; **HM Prison Service v Johnson (2007)** IRLR 951. The case of **Environment Agency v Rowan (2008)** was cited and approved in **Secretary of State for Work and Pensions v Wakefield (2010)** EAT judgment 13 September 2010 (Case No.0435/09) wherein HH Judge Ansell presiding allowed the respondent employer's appeal and remitted the case back to the same employment tribunal for the reason that the employment tribunal when making a finding that the employer had failed to make reasonable adjustments under the Disability Discrimination Act 1995, failed to follow the guidance set out in **Environment Agency v Rowan (2008)** ICR 218;
- In a disability discrimination reasonable adjustments claim, an employment tribunal must identify exactly what it is about a provision, criterion or practice that was applied by the employer and which caused the disabled person to suffer a

substantial disadvantage: **Chief Constable of West Midlands Police v Gardner (2011)** EAT 18 October 2011 (Case No.0174/11).

- on the point of what constitutes a 'provision, criterion or practice' (PCP), their Lordships in the House of Lords' case of **Archibald v Fife Council (2004)** ICR 954, confirmed that the terms, conditions and arrangements relating to the essential functions of the disabled person's employment are a PCP. This means that where an employee becomes incapable of performing the duties of the job he or she previously carried out, an employer will be under a duty to make reasonable adjustments such as transferring the employee to another job;
- internal disciplinary and other procedures come within the definition of a 'provision, criterion or practice:' **Bid v KPMG LLP (2009)** ET Case No.1300313/09; **Cumbria Probation Board v Collingwood (2008)** EAT (Case No.0079/08);
- where a claimant claims that the employer failed to comply with its duty to make reasonable adjustments, the claimant must shift the burden of proof onto the employer by (i) establishing that the duty has arisen and (ii) by showing that there are facts from which it can be reasonably inferred, in the absence of an explanation from the employer, that the duty has been breached so that, (iii) when the case is heard before an employment tribunal, there must be some apparently reasonable adjustment that could be made: **Project Management Institute v Latif (2007)** IRLR 579;
- where a claimant makes a claim for disability discrimination, being a failure by the employer to make reasonable adjustments and direct discrimination, it is appropriate for the employment tribunal to order the claimant to discloses details of the actual medical condition so that the respondent and the tribunal can properly and fairly assess whether or not the claimant has a statutory disability, per Lord Justice Pill: **Leeks v St Georges Healthcare NHS Trust (2011)** EWCA Civ 1551, Court of Appeal 17 November 2011;
- there is no requirement in law that a provision, criterion or practice need be specifically applied to the disabled person. In disability discrimination 'reasonable adjustments' cases, the primary question is whether a provision, criterion or practice (PCP) was applied by the employer that placed the disabled person at a substantial disadvantage - if so, the duty to make reasonable adjustments is triggered. There is no requirement

that the PCP needs to be actually applied to the disabled person. A substantial disadvantage may still be caused even if the disabled person has been specifically exempted from it. The headline summary by the Employment Appeal Tribunal in this case was: 'The Tribunal misapplied section 4A of the Disability Discrimination Act 1995 by holding that the provision, criterion or practice in question was not applied *to the Claimant*, and therefore that no duty was owed to him under section 4A. The Tribunal should have followed the statutory wording and asked whether a provision, criterion or practice applied by the Respondent placed the Claimant at a substantial disadvantage in comparison with persons who are not disabled. A provision, criterion or practice applied by the Respondent may affect a disabled person without being directly applied to him:' **Roberts v North West Ambulance Service (2012)** EAT 24 January 2012 (Case No.0085/11);

- an employer who decides to dismiss an employee on the grounds of ill-health before obtaining a full medical report does so unfairly: **East Lindsey District Council v G.E. Daubney (1977)** IRLR 181 (per Phillips J at para 18);
- must the parties accept the evidence of a joint expert or can each party call their own expert? The factors a judge should consider when faced with such a request by one or both parties that is or are not satisfied with the joint expert can be found in the judgment of **Daniels v Walker (2000)** 1 WLR 1382, CA, the guidance of which was adopted and applied by Neuberger J. in **Cosgrove v Pattison (2001)** C.P. Rep 68, who gave nine factors which should be considered before a decision is given: **Saunder v Birmingham City Council (2008)** EAT 21 May 2008 (Case No. 0591/07);
- the two terms 'sickness' and 'disability' cannot be treated as meaning the same thing. When choosing the word 'disability,' the legislature (when passing the Framework Directive in 2000 that was given effect in the UK by the DDA 1995) had deliberately chosen a word that differed from 'sickness.' The two terms, therefore, could not be treated as meaning the same. Therefore, an employee who was dismissed by her Spanish employer after being unable to work through sickness for six months was unable to make a claim of disability discrimination: **Chacón Navas v Eurest Colectividades SA (2006)** IRLR 706, Case C-13/05, ECJ. This case also established a uniform definition of disability throughout the

European Union;

- less favourable treatment, being the dismissal of a disabled employee, can only be justified if it can be shown that it was unconnected with the medical condition, or, unavoidable: **Jones v Post Office (2001)** IRLR 384;
- if a tribunal is not satisfied with an employer's reasons for its detrimental treatment of a disabled employee, it should draw the inference that that treatment was for a reason related to the employee's disability, and is not justified: **Rowden v Dutton Gregory (2002)** EAT, ICR 971;
- the duty under the DDA 1995 to consider adjustments and medical opinion is solely upon the employer: **Cosgrove v Caesar & Howie, (2001)** EAT, IRLR 653;
- there is no duty upon an employer to consult with the employee prior to making any reasonable adjustments. Accordingly, **Mid-Staffordshire General Hospitals NHS Trust v Cambridge (2003)** EAT, IRLR 566 was wrongly decided. However, an employer would be wise to consult with a disabled employee so as to be better informed of all factors which may be relevant to determining what adjustments should reasonably be made. Failure to do this increases the risk that, out of ignorance, the employer will not make appropriate adjustments: Elias P. in **Tarbuck v Sainsbury Supermarkets Ltd (2006)** EAT 08 June 2006 (Case No.0136/06);
- a tribunal does not have to decide (a) if an adjustment would have worked or (b) if medical opinion would have supported an adjustment, but simply that to comply with the DDA 1995 there is a duty on the employer to investigate (a) and (b): **Wilding v BT (2002)** Court of Appeal EWCA Civ 349;
- the need under the DDA 1995 for disability cases to involve medical advice is detailed in the Employer's Code of Practice; and the requirement on a tribunal to consider questions about medical advice has been made clear by the Employment Appeal Tribunal: **London Borough of Hillingdon v Morgan (1999)**;
- a failure by the employer to obtain suitably qualified and expert medical opinion about an employee covered by the DDA 1995 and not considering medical advice which is available, are grounds to decide that unfair discrimination took place, contrary to the DDA 1995: **Surrey Police v Marshall (2002)** EAT, IRLR 843;

- the fact that a claimant had been awarded a disability living allowance by a Social Security Appeals Tribunal (SSAT) on the basis that she was suffering with post-traumatic stress disorder was not conclusive of the issue of whether she was disabled for the purposes of the DDA 1995. In the view of the Court, there is no rule or principle of law that an employment tribunal is bound to follow decisions of the SSAT and, further, it was for the tribunal to make up its own mind on the evidence before it: **Hill v Clacton Family Trust Ltd (2006)** ICR 12, Court of Appeal. But see: **Mahon v Accuread Ltd (2008)** EAT 01 July 2008 (Case No.0081/08);
- an employer should obtain specialist information about an employee's condition before considering dismissal. A tribunal held that an employee had been subjected to less favourable treatment, that was not justified as being for a material and substantial reason, when the employer, prior to dismissing the employee, failed to obtain a specialist's report: **Holmes v Whittingham and Porter Ltd (1997)** ET Case No.1802799/97;
- where there was a conflict of views between two doctors, it would be unreasonable for the employer to reject the suggestion that a third consultant be asked to advise: **British Gas plc v Breeze** (unreported, 13 September 1988) (at 6E-7C);
- the onus is on the employer to justify its discriminatory actions: **HM Prison Service v Beart (2002)** EAT 21 May 2002;
- whether a person is a disabled person as so defined in the Act is a matter of law based on all the facts including the medical evidence. It is for the tribunal and not for any medical expert to make a finding taking account of all relevant material. The nature of any illness suffered by an applicant is one factor but the effects of that illness and whether they are long-term, substantial and adverse as regards ability to carry out day-to-day activities are for the tribunal to determine: **Bush v Zurich Financial Services (2004)** EAT (Case No.0832/03);
- where a claimant suffers a personal injury that was caused by unlawful discrimination by the employer, an employment tribunal can award a sum to the claimant to compensate him or her for that injury and there is no requirement that the employment tribunal must hear expert medical evidence before making such an award: **Hampshire County Council v**

Wyatt (2016) EAT 13 October 2016 (Case No.0013/16);

- it is not necessary for an employer to know that an employee has a disability in order to be potentially liable for discrimination within the meaning of s.5(1)(a) of the DDA 1995: **H.J. Heinz Co Ltd v Kenrick (2000)** EAT, ICR 491; **but the House of Lords have held that knowledge of disability is necessary to found liability** - per Baroness Hale at 86: **Mayor and Burgesses of the London Borough of Lewisham v Malcolm (2008)** UKHL 43; see too, s.15(2), Equality Act 2010 – liability for unlawful disability discrimination does not arises against an employer if the employer did not know, and could not reasonably have been expected to know, that the person had the disability;
- an appeal from a decision of an employment tribunal to the Employment Appeal Tribunal that the decision of the employment tribunal was perverse would only succeed where an overwhelming case is made out that the employment tribunal reached a decision which no reasonable tribunal, on a proper appreciation of the evidence and the law, would reach: **Yeboah v Crofton (2002)** IRLR 634 (93) (per Mummery LJ).
- In **Nottinghamshire County Council v Meikle (2004)** Court of Appeal, EWCA Civ 859, the Court confirmed that 'dismissal' includes constructive dismissal in s.4(2)(d) of the DDA 1995 thereby resolving conflicting EAT authorities on this point: **Catherall v Michelin Tyres plc (2003)** IRLR 61; **Commissioner of Police for the Metropolis v Harley (2001)** IRLR 263 and **Derby Fabrication Ltd v Burton (2001)** IRLR 69. The Court of Appeal also confirmed that the test for whether or not there has been a breach of the implied term of trust and confidence is an objective test, a principle established in the case of **Malik and another v BCCI (1997)** IRLR 462. In addition, the Court of Appeal decided that where there is a discriminatory constructive dismissal, the time for lodging a complaint to an employment tribunal runs from the date the employment terminated rather than from the date(s) when the act(s) of discrimination took place. This decision overruled that of Auld LJ in **Cast v Croydon College (1998)** IRLR 318. The effect of the decision by the Court of Appeal is that tribunals now have clear and authoritative guidance when considering the question of limitation in all discrimination cases where constructive dismissal is alleged;
- in the same case, the Court of Appeal held that the duty to

make reasonable adjustments under s.6 (that became s.4A and, under the Equality Act 2010 is s.20) extends to contractual sickness benefits so that it would be unlawful (and unreasonable) for an employer to reduce or terminate the payment of a contractual sickness benefit to an employee who has a statutory disability after a stated period of sickness absence by relying on the terms and conditions of such a policy. The s.6 duty is not excluded by s.6(11) that applies only to occupational pension schemes and benefits provided under third-party insurance services, the non-discriminatory provision of which are provided for by ss.17 and 18 DDA 1995;

- giving a greater level of sick pay (or full pay) to a disabled employee would **not** be a reasonable adjustment, except in 'a rare case indeed,' so that the discrimination was lawfully based on material and substantial reasons being: (i) significant cost to the employer; (ii) a requirement that tribunals should not usurp the management functions of employers; (iii) to treat the disabled as objects of charity might act to discourage them from returning to work; and (iv) it was not one of the examples of reasonable adjustments given in s.18B(2) of the DDA. Accordingly, although such a disabled employee was treated less favourably than an employer would treat other non-disabled employees, the treatment in question in this case was objectively justified: **O'Hanlon v Commissioners of HM Revenue and Customs (2006)** EAT, 04.08.06, Case No. 0109/06. See too the decision of the Court of Appeal in this case: **(2007)** EWCA Civ 283; IRLR 404;
- a person dismissed on account of absence from work due to sickness was not discriminated against on the ground of 'disability' and therefore was not protected by the disability provisions of the EC Equal Treatment Directive. Nor could 'sickness' be regarded as a protected ground of discrimination in addition to those provided in the Framework Directive: **Chacón Navas v Eurest Colectividades SA (2006)**, IRLR 706 European Court of Justice;
- the EAT stated what factors a tribunal should consider when assessing whether an impairment is long-term and/or is likely to recur: **McDougall v Richmond Adult Community College (2007)** EAT 13 July 2007 (Case No.0589/06);
- the EAT has held that dyslexia is a statutory disability under the Disability Discrimination Act 1995: **Paterson v**

Commissioner of Police of the Metropolis (2007) EAT 23 July 2007 (Case No. 0635/06); (2007) ICR 1522. An employment tribunal ordered the accountancy firm KPMG to pay £45,000 in compensation for an act of disability discrimination against an accountancy trainee whom it dismissed before awaiting the results of a dyslexia test that confirmed that she suffered from that disability: Accountancy Age, 06 October 2009;

- the cost of the reasonable adjustments must be considered: **Shaw & Co Solicitors v Atkins (2009)** EAT (Case No.0224/08), judgment 11 February 2009;
- non-remunerated work does not fall within the definition of 'work' or 'occupation' in the Equal Treatment Framework Directive 2000/78/EC. Accordingly a volunteer (unless they have a contract to work personally for those to whom they provide their services) does not fall within the wide definition of 'employment' in the Disability Discrimination Act 1995 *(or since 01 October 2010 in s.83, Equality Act 2010)* and cannot bring a discrimination claim: **X v Mid Sussex Citizens Advice Bureau and another (2011)** EWCA Civ 28, Court of Appeal 27 January 2011;
- an employer who conceded pre-hearing that the employee is a disabled person was under a duty to make reasonable adjustments to the working environment and an employment tribunal hearing the claim for disability discrimination because of the employer's failure to make reasonable adjustments does not have to consider thereafter what were now irrelevant considerations such as whether any of the specific provisions of the Disability Discrimination Act 1995 have been met (such as substantial effect, day-to-day activities, how long the effect of the disability was likely to last): **Bowers v William Hill Organisation Ltd (2009)** EAT (Case No.0046/09), judgment 10 July 2009;
- the European Court of Justice has ruled that **'associative' disability discrimination** is unlawful, i.e. treating an employee or prospective employee less favourably because he or she is associated with or provides care to a disabled person: **Coleman v Attridge Law (2008) ECJ Case C-303/06.** An employer who discriminates against an employee in this way would be in breach of the EC Equal Treatment Framework Directive 2000/78/EC and, in the UK, of the Disability Discrimination Act 1995 that implements the provisions of the

Directive into UK law. The wider effect of the decision by the ECJ is that acts of unlawful associative discrimination by employers now encompass acts such as treating less favourably or harassing employees because they are associated with a person of a certain sexual orientation, an older or old person or, indeed, have a relationship with a person much younger than himself or herself, a person who holds certain religious or other beliefs as well as a person who is disabled and needs the provision of care. In the case of **Coleman v Attridge Law (2008)**, the relevant provision of the DDA 1995 was s.3A(5) being: **'A person directly discriminates against a disabled person if, on the ground of the disabled person's disability, he treats the disabled person less favourably than he treats or would treat a person not having that particular disability whose relevant circumstances, including his abilities, are the same as, or not materially different from, those of the disabled person.'** However, to ensure UK law is compliant with EC law as required by the Directive and the judgment of the ECJ, the South London employment tribunal that heard Ms Coleman's disability discrimination claim decided that it could and should interpolate additional words into s.3A(5) so that the section did complied with EU law. The tribunal accepted Ms Coleman's barrister's submission that to give effect to the Directive in UK law the wording of s.3A(5) could and should be read as: **'A person directly discriminates against a disabled person *or a person associated with a disabled person* if, on the ground of the disabled person's disability, he treats the disabled person *or a person associated with the disabled person* less favourably than he treats or would treat a person not having that particular disability *or association (as the case may be)* whose relevant circumstances, including his abilities, are the same as, or not materially different from, those of the disabled person *or the person associated with the disabled person.*'**

The **Coleman (2008)** case returned to the Employment Appeal Tribunal on 30 October 2009 where the President, Underhill, J., sitting alone, handed down his judgment being: ***'The Disability Discrimination Act 1995 can be interpreted so as to apply to 'associative' discrimination as required by the decision of the European Court of Justice (2008) ICR 1128.'***

The judgment of the President confirmed that the Disability Discrimination Act 1995 should be interpreted by inserting words making it unlawful for an employer to discriminate against an employee who is primary carer of a disabled person by reason of that person's disability. When hearing the appeal on the 30 October 2009, the President of the EAT agreed with the employment judge, Mary Stacey, who chaired the case at the South London employment tribunal, holding that, on a proper interpretation of the Disability Discrimination Act 1995, employment tribunals do have jurisdiction to determine claims of this kind. The result was that the claimant, Ms. Coleman, could proceed with her claim to an employment tribunal for a hearing on its merits.

The reason for the above appeal to the EAT in **Coleman (2008)** was that the ruling given by the European Court of Justice when it heard **Coleman v Attridge Law (2008)** required Member States to outlaw 'associative discrimination.' But this judgment was directly binding only on public authority employers, not on employers in the private sector. By interpreting the domestic law provisions of the Disability Discrimination Act 1995 as he has done, the President of the Employment Appeal Tribunal ensured that the same rules are now binding on private sector employers as well.

In order to ensure that the domestic law of the UK gives effect to the judgment of the ECJ and thereby complies with European law in the form of the Equal Treatment Framework Directive (2000/78/EC), the President of the EAT at paragraph 15 of his judgment stated the wording to be interpolated into the Disability Discrimination Act 1995 is that to s.3A should be added a sub-section (5A) in the following terms:

s.3A (5A) A person also directly discriminates against a person if he treats him less favourably than he treats or would treat another person by reason of the disability of another person.

s.3B (3) A person also subjects a person (A) to harassment where, for a reason which relates to the disability of another person (B), he engages in unwanted conduct which has the purpose or effect of –

a) violating A's dignity, or

b) creating an intimidating, hostile, degrading, humiliating or offensive environment for him.

Subsection (2) applies to this sub-section, save that the relevant perception is that of A.

Plus appropriate consequential adaptations of s.4 subsections (1), (2) and (3).

EBR Attridge Law LLP (1) (formerly Attridge Law) (2) v Coleman (2009) EAT, 30.10.09, (Case No.0071/09).

As a matter of interest, the case of **Attridge Law v Coleman (2009)** was remitted to an employment tribunal for a hearing on its merits following the decision by the Employment Appeal Tribunal but before the merits hearing took place the case was settled for £12,000: Bates, Wells and Braithwaite 29th April 2010.

Bates, Wells and Braithwaite issued the following Press Release:

Coleman v Attridge Law: Settlement

29 April 2010

The long-running case of Sharon Coleman v Attridge Law has recently settled, after 5 years of litigation, including two trips to the Employment Appeal Tribunal and one to the European Court of Justice. The case established that people associated with disabled people (such as carers) have protection from direct discrimination and harassment under the Disability Discrimination Act 1995. Sharon Coleman received £12,000 under the terms of the settlement.

Case example: associative disability discrimination -

An employer dismissed an employee whom it had employed for exactly one year for the reason that the employee's primary customer had been dissatisfied with the employee's work. The dismissal was for the reason of (lack of) capability per s.98(2)(a), Employment Rights Act 1996. The employee challenged the employer's reason for dismissing him and succeeded at the employment tribunal with his claim for associative disability discrimination. The facts were that he and his wife have a disabled daughter. His wife was the main carer for their disabled daughter who has cystic fibrosis but his wife was unable to continue that role because she was starting her own business. Therefore, for that latter reason, he was in the process of becoming the carer for his daughter. The reasons the employment tribunal found in the claimant's favour on the balance of probabilities were: that, as an employee, he had good appraisals; before dismissing him, the employer had not put in place a performance improvement process; there was no indication from the employer's managers that they or his primary customer were dissatisfied with the claimant's work performance; and he was dismissed on the very day that he completed one year's service with the employer which, coincidentally, was the very day he became a 'qualifying employee' entitled to take up to four weeks a year parental leave until his child's 18th birthday. As the carer of a disabled child he would also have been entitled, in an emergency, to take dependant care leave per ss.57A and 57B, ERA 1996 which would last as long as it took him to deal with the emergency: **Truman v Bibby Distribution Ltd (2014)** ET case 2404176/2014.

See book sections 3.3 for associative and perceptive disability discrimination.

6.4 Occupational requirements:

What, you might ask, are 'occupational requirements?' The meaning of 'occupational requirements' is that an employer can stipulate that it is a requirement for the occupation on offer that only a job applicant with a particular 'protected characteristic' is eligible to apply for and to be appointed to a particular job where the protected characteristic is an essential requirement of the job – e.g. a male for the position of priest in the Roman Catholic Church; a Negro female to play a role in a stage production that requires for authenticity a person who is both female and a Negro; a deaf person to provide support and teach sign language to people who have become deaf; a female carer to provide intimate personal care for an elderly lady; a male carer to do the same for a young severely disabled man.

It is important to be aware that the Equality Act 2010 allows employers to lawfully discriminate against job applicants and workers where certain jobs are concerned ***if*** these employers can show that a requirement, being one of the statutory 'protected characteristics' that the employer deems to be essential for the occupation, is an **occupational requirement** for the job in question and that the occupational requirement is objectively justified in that it is a proportionate means of achieving a legitimate aim. The Act provides a number of statutory exceptions to the general principle of non-discrimination. Compared to the previous anti-discrimination legislation that existed prior to the coming into force of the Equality Act 2010, these exceptions from the requirement not to discriminate have been simplified and harmonised by applying a general **'occupational requirement'** test consistently across all the strands of discrimination, including disability discrimination. One well-know exception to the anti-discrimination legislation that was permitted under the Employment Rights Act 1996, the Employment Equality (Age) Regulations 2006 and the Equality Act 2010 until the exception was repealed and revoked on 06 April 2011 was the age discrimination exception, being the default retirement age exception, in that employers were allowed to lawfully dismiss for the reason of retirement employees who had reached or were over the age of 65 and employers could do this by using the statutory compulsory retirement dismissal procedure. Employers could also dismiss other workers who were not of employee status if they could show that such dismissals for the reason of retirement were objectively justified – and this is the current rule that applies to all workers of whatever age, including employees, now. Effectively, a contractual retirement age imposed by an employer is a provision, criterion or practice which may constitute indirect discrimination unless the PCP can be objectively justified.

Another exception that is not quite so well-known is that which is permitted in respect of organised religions. Many of the major long-standing religions have traditionally discriminated against people because of their gender or sexual orientation. Notably, Roman Catholics and Muslims have a requirement that only people of one gender, males, are eligible for appointment to the post of priest or imam. As for the Church of England, it will appoint both genders to its junior clergy but has an **occupational requirement** that it will appoint to its senior clergy, such as to the post of bishop, (i) males of any sexual orientation but, (ii) once appointed, only heterosexual males are allowed to practice their sexuality so that (iii) males whose sexual orientation is homosexual are eligible for appointment but (iv) only on the condition that they do not actively practice their sexuality. This occupational requirement would, except for the statutory exceptions, ordinarily be unlawful discrimination on two grounds: that of sex and that of sexual orientation. See below for a further explanation of whether or not the requirement by the Church of England is lawful under the Equality Act 2010.

Buried away at the back of the Equality Act 2010 in Schedule 9, Part 1, Paragraph 1 – **Occupational Requirement Defence** – are the provisions which permit employers to discriminate lawfully if they can show that the job in question qualifies for an exception under the **Occupational Requirements** exceptions. Although under s.13(3) (direct discrimination) it is not unlawful discrimination for an employer to treat a disabled worker more favourably than a worker who is not disabled, nonetheless the **occupational requirements** apply to the protected characteristic of disability. So in respect of a person with a disability: (1) an employer does not contravene a provision mentioned in this part of the Equality Act 2010 by applying in relation to work a requirement to have or not to have a particular protected characteristic (e.g. disability) if the employer shows that having regard to the nature or context of the work, (a) it is an occupational requirement and (b) the application of the requirement is a proportionate means of achieving a legitimate aim and (c) the person to whom the employer applies the requirement does not meet it (or the employer has reasonable grounds for not being satisfied that the person meets it): para.1(1), Schedule 9, Equality Act 2010.

In respect of the protected characteristic of disability, employers are allowed to treat job applicants differently because of a protected characteristic in the arrangements made for the purposes of determining who should be offered employment, or by refusing to offer or deliberately not offering employment. When training people for a post or when promoting, transferring or dismissing employees, an employer may also rely on the exceptions. But an employer is not permitted, however, to discriminate against an employee in the terms of employment afforded or offered to him or her, or by subjecting him or her to any other detriment: para.1(2) of Schedule 9.

Disability as an occupational requirement – an example where this would be lawful so that an employer can require someone, before offering him or her work, to have a particular disability that counts as an occupational requirement is given in the Explanatory Notes of the Equality Bill that accompanied the Bill before it became an Act and which state: '… an organisation for deaf people might legitimately employ a deaf person who uses British Sign Language to work as a counsellor to other deaf people whose first or preferred language is BSL.' The word 'deaf' in this example can be replaced with nouns naming other disabilities (or any statutory protected characteristic other than disability) and this shows that employers can legitimately insist that, as an occupational requirement, they will employ only people with a particular disability for certain work albeit work that involved working with people who share that disability or it is essential that the worker has a particular disability for an objective reason such as being an actor in a performance. Similarly, an occupational requirement can be cited as a defence to **direct and indirect discrimination** by employers where they offer work based on the worker being of a particular race or ethnic or national origin, religion or belief, sexual orientation or age and these protected characteristics are an (i) occupational requirement and (ii) objectively justified. Hence, a general 'occupational requirement' is a defence for all grounds of discrimination if an employer can show that it is 'a proportionate means of achieving a legitimate aim.' Note that the general occupational requirement defence in the Equality Act 2010 applies only to direct and indirect discrimination; it does not apply to claims of harassment and victimisation.

To return to the exceptions allowed under the religion or beliefs exceptions which usefully show how the exceptions work and which are permitted and those which are not, para.2 (1) states in respect of 'religious requirements relating to sex, marriage, etc., sexual orientation' that an employer does not contravene a provision mentioned in sub-paragraph (2) (work arrangements for employee and applicants) by applying in relation to employment a requirement to which sub-paragraph (4) (requirements as to sex, transsexual, marriage or civil partner, sexual orientation) applies if the employer shows that (a) the employment is for the purposes of an organised religion (b) the application of the requirement engages the compliance or non-conflict principle, and (c) the person to whom the employer applies the requirement does not meet it (or the employer has reasonable grounds for not being satisfied that the person meets it).

The problem for the Church of England under this exception is that the Equality Act 2010 allows the Church to appoint people to its clergy and to make it a requirement that these people be of a certain gender or/and of a certain sexual orientation but does not permit an employer, like the Church of England, to go further and require that a person of a certain sexual orientation must not actively practice his or her sexual orientation as a requirement for appointment to a post. To do the latter would be a breach of a person's human rights under Articles 8 and 14 of the European Convention on Human Rights and Fundamental Freedoms as transpose in the Human Rights Act 1998.

Schedule 9 of the Equality Act 2010 continues by stating: 'Other requirements relating to religion or belief' – para.3. 'A person (A) with an ethos based on religion or belief does not contravene a provision mentioned in paragraph 1(2) [access or appointment to work] by applying in relation to work a requirement to be of a particular religion or belief if A shows that, having regard to that ethos and to the nature or context of the work – (a) it is an occupational requirement; (b) the application of the requirement is a proportionate means of achieving a legitimate aim; and (c) the person to whom A applies the requirement does not meet it (or A has reasonable grounds for not being satisfied that the person meets it).

Part 7

7.1 Time limits within which to make claims:

Time limits within which to present a claim of disability discrimination under the Disability Discrimination Act 1995 -

The general rule was that a complaint had to be presented to a tribunal within the period of **three months** beginning with the date of the act complained of: paragraph 3(1), Schedule 3 DDA 1995. For example, if an employee was dismissed for the reason of disability on, say, March 13, the last day on which a complaint had to be presented to a tribunal was June 12. Employment tribunals had the power to grant extensions if, in all the circumstances, an extension of time would have been just and equitable. s.3(2), Schedule 3 DDA 1995 (See **Matuszowicz v Kingston Upon Hull City Council (2009)** EWCA Civ 22, Court of Appeal). However, an act of disability discrimination may be treated as done at the end of a period if it is an act 'extending over' that period (Schedule 3, para.3(3)(b), DDA 1995): **Barclays Bank plc v Kapur & others (1991)** ICR 208.

An employment tribunal does not have jurisdiction to hear a complaint of unlawful discrimination unless the complaint is presented within three months of the discriminatory act complained of: s.123(1), Equality Act 2010. Sometimes, however, there will be a course of discriminatory conduct or a 'continuing act' rather than an isolated incident. As a result, s.123(3)(a) stipulates that, where an act or acts of discrimination extend over a period, they are treated as having occurred at the end of that period. Therefore, time does not start to run until the end of the course of discriminatory conduct: **Khetab v AGA Medical Ltd and others (2010)** EAT (Case No.0313/10).

Note: as stated above, a complaint of disability discrimination had to be presented to an employment tribunal within three months of the act complained of: para 3(1), Schedule 3, Disability Discrimination Act 1995. If a complaint was presented outside the three-month period, an employment tribunal had no jurisdiction to hear the claim unless it considered that, in all the circumstances, it was just and equitable to do so: para 3(2); case authority – **Department of Constitutional Affairs v Jones (2007)** EWCA Civ 894, Court of Appeal; (the applicant in this case was, inter alia, reluctant to admit to himself and others that his depression was severe enough to amount to a statutory disability.)

Equality Act 2010: time limits in the **Equality Act 2010** are given in s.123 which are that: 'Proceedings on a complaint within section 120 (that states that employment tribunals have jurisdiction to determine claims relating to a contravention of Part 5, being work) may not be brought after the end of the period of three months starting with the date of the act to which the complaint relates or such period as the employment tribunal thinks just and equitable.'

Under the Equality Act 2010, proceedings (i.e. being the claim or claims which are subject to the time limits) by those serving in the armed forces per s.121(1) may not be brought after the end of (a) the period of six months starting with the date of the act to which the proceedings relate, or (b) such other period as the employment tribunal thinks just and equitable: s.123(2).

Note: presenting a statutory grievance under the now revoked and repealed dispute resolution procedures (e.g. being about an employer's failure/refusal to deal reasonably about a disability matter) had the effect of extending the time limit by an extra three months if, at the expiry of the three-month time limit, a procedure was still ongoing: Reg.15(1) and (3), Employment Act 2002 (Dispute Resolution) Regulations 2004. That is to say, the normal time limit of three months in which a claim had to be presented to the tribunal office for it to be heard by an employment tribunal was extended by three months thereby giving a claimant six months (less one day) in which to present a claim. **Note that the three-stage statutory dispute resolution procedures were repealed on 06 April 2009 by the Employment Act 2008 and replaced on the same day by the ACAS Code of Practice on Disciplinary and Grievance Procedures that was issued under s.199, Trade Union and Labour Relations (Consolidation) Act 1992. It replaces the Code issued in 2004.**

ACAS early conciliation scheme – compulsory from 06 May 2014.

Early conciliation – summary:

As part of the reform by the Coalition Government (that was in office from May 2010 to May 2015) of the employment tribunal system with the aim of reducing the number of tribunal claims, a compulsory early conciliation (EC) service was introduced on 06 April 2014.

From that date tribunal claimants will have to submit details of their claim to ACAS at first, at which point they will be offered the option of EC. If it is refused by either party, or is unsuccessful, the claimant will be able to make their tribunal claim. The period for EC will end after one month.

While the requirement for prospective claimants to contact ACAS before they can lodge proceedings at the employment tribunal will be mandatory, the decision whether to accept the offer of EC will be entirely voluntary.

ACAS will have a duty to conciliate pre-claim, rather than a power. It will retain its duty to provide post-claim conciliation.

Background to the Scheme –

In 2013 the Department for Business, Innovation and Skills (BIS) asked ACAS to provide Early Conciliation due to the success of a similar voluntary ACAS service called Pre Claim Conciliation (PCC). In July 2013 ACAS published a new evaluation of PCC alongside studies on Early Conciliation Support Officers (ECSOs) who undertake the new ACAS early conciliation service from its introduction in April 2014. Highlights of the study show that:

- nearly nine out of ten employers who used PCC said that they would use it again;
- two thirds of employees would advise a friend or relative to use PCC if they were involved in a similar dispute;
- eight out of ten users said that ACAS was important in helping to resolve their dispute;
- service users reported that PCC was cheaper, easier or more convenient, less traumatic or stressful and resolved their issue more quickly than submitting an employment tribunal claim.

ACAS Chief Executive Anne Sharp said: "These studies demonstrate how much the public value the benefits of our Pre Claim Conciliation service and the skills and experience of our conciliation staff".

Requirements of the Scheme –

Section 7 of the Enterprise and Regulatory Reform Act 2013 (ERRA 2013) inserts new sections 18A and 18B into the Employment Tribunals Act 1996 (ETA 1996). Section 18A of the ETA 1996 sets out a mandatory four-stage Early Concilation (EC) procedure under which prospective Tribunal claimants in most types of proceedings will be required to contact ACAS before issuing relevant proceedings (those listed in section 18(1) of the ETA 1996).

The draft Employment Tribunals (Early Conciliation: Exemptions and Rules of Procedure) Regulations were published, detailing the procedure for EC:-

> **Stage 1:** the prospective claimant must send "prescribed information" on the prescribed ACAS form.
> **Stage 2:** after an EC Support Officer has made initial contact with the prospective claimant and confirmed that they wish to proceed, the claimant's information is sent to a conciliation officer.
> **Stage 3:** the conciliation officer must try to promote a settlement within the "prescribed period" (up to one calendar month, although this can be extended for a further period of up to 2 weeks with the agreement of both parties).
> **Stage 4:** if a settlement is not reached, either because the conciliation officer considers that settlement is not possible, or because the prescribed period expires, the conciliation officer must issue an Early Conciliation Certificate ("ECC") to that effect. Without this ECC, prospective claimants will be unable to pursue most Tribunal claims.

Even where the parties reach a settlement, ACAS will draw up an agreement recording the settlement and will still issue an ECC. This is because if only some of the matters in dispute are settled, the prospective claimant would still need an ECC to be able to bring a Tribunal claim for the remaining issues in dispute.

Time limits for ET claims –

To take account of the EC period, Schedule 2 to the ERRA 2013 inserts new sections into primary legislation providing for the extension of the time limit for presenting certain identified claims. Although the wording of the amendment differs for each piece of legislation, the effect on time limits will be the same:

Where EC is required, a specified period will "stop the clock" in calculating time limits for bringing ET proceedings. This period begins with the day after the prospective claimant contacts ACAS and ends on the day when they receive an ECC from ACAS (or are deemed to have received it by virtue of the Early Conciliation Regulations).

The time limit for bringing proceedings will be extended so that where the normal time limit for bringing the claim would expire in the period which begins with the day when the prospective claimant contacts ACAS and ends a month after receipt of the EC certificate from ACAS (or deemed receipt it by virtue of Regulations), the time limit expires one month after the receipt (or deemed receipt) of the ECC from ACAS. Tribunals will retain their existing discretion in terms of extending time for late claims.

7.2 Claims - disability discrimination or unfair dismissal?

Should the claim be for disability discrimination or unfair dismissal or both?

An employer can dismiss an employee for the reason of (in)capability that is a potentially fair reason for dismissal under the Employment Rights Act 1996: s.98(2)(a). Whether the dismissal will be fair depends on whether the employer had a **fair reason** (per s.98(1)(2) ERA 1996) and followed a **fair procedure** when taking the decision to dismiss and, in all the circumstances including the size and administrative resources of the employer, acted **reasonably** in treating the reason as a sufficient reason for dismissing the employee (per s.98(4), ERA 1996) and the question will be determined in accordance with equity and the substantial merits of the case. See: the Unfair Dismissal Law book in this series: ISBN 978-1-291-85782-5.

The potentially fair reason 'capability' (per s.98(2)(a) ERA 1996) covers both incapability on ill-health grounds as well as unsatisfactory work performance. Commonly, employers may also dismiss employees who are or have been ill or have a disability 'for some other substantial reason' (per s.98(1)(b) ERA 1996) instead of or as well as 'capability.'

Well-advised employers will be aware that the dismissal of a disabled employee for one or more of the potentially fair reasons under the ERA 1996 could also potentially involve them in an unjustifiable act of discrimination under the DDA 1995 (or, from 01 October 2010, under the disability discrimination provisions of the Equality Act 2010.) Some illnesses, for example, may constitute disabilities which are defined as such by the Act. Similarly, a disability may manifest itself in poor work performance, absences or misconduct. Therefore, the dismissal of an employee with a disability for one or more of the potentially fair reasons in s.98 ERA 1996 could give rise to two separate causes of action being: (1) unfair dismissal and (2) unlawful disability discrimination. In practice, the well-advised employee will usually present a claim to an employment tribunal for reinstatement/re-employment or seek recompense for his or her financial losses to an employment tribunal by making claims under both heads. As a matter of good employment procedure, an employer who decides to dismiss an employee who has a disability (or an illness that might satisfy the statutory definition of a disability) for one or more of the potentially fair reasons listed in s.98 ERA 1996 must consider whether the employee in question comes within the provisions of the DDA 1995 (or since 01 October 2010 the Equality Act 2010.) If the employer thinks that the employee potentially may do so, the employer must ensure that the requirements of the DDA 1995 (and now the Equality Act 2010) are complied with. By doing this, the employer will save considerable time and expense in defending either a disability discrimination claim or an unfair dismissal claim or both. It is important for employers to remember that a discrimination claim can cover pre-dismissal issues (such as failure to promote, offer training or provide work-related benefits and so on) as well as the dismissal itself. Both are potential detriments. Note that uncapped awards can be made by employment tribunals for stigma and victimisation both of which may result in future employment loss (a 'Chagger' claim): **Chagger v Abbey National plc (2010)** ICR 397; **Small v Shrewsbury and Telford Hospitals NHS Trust (2017)** EWCA Civ 882, CA.

7.3 Eligibility to make a claim for disability discrimination:

To make a claim under the DDA 1995 (before it was repealed and replaced on 01 October 2010 by the Equality Act 2010), an employee **did not** need to have been continuously employed by the employer for at least one year as required in a claim for unfair dismissal. Note that the qualification period (being the period of continuous employment required with the employer before being eligible to bring a claim of unfair dismissal in the employment tribunal) was one year for employees who began their contract of employment with their employer before 06 April 2012. The qualification period was increased by the Conservative-Liberal Democrat Coalition Government (May 2010-May 2015) to two years for employees who began their contract of employment with their employer on or after 06 April 2012: **The Unfair Dismissal and Statement of**

Reasons for Dismissal (Variation of Qualifying Period) 2012; SI.2012/989. Likewise, an employee who was over the contractual retirement age or the State retirement age before (or, indeed, after) 06 April 2011 could also present a disability claim. The provision that (i) prevented an employee who had reached his or her employer's contractual retirement age or (ii) the State retirement age from making an unfair dismissal claim or (iii) being entitled to a statutory redundancy payment, being s.109, Employment Rights Act 1996, was repealed when the Employment Equality (Age) Regulations 2006 came into force on 01 October 2006. (Note that from 06 April 2011, as regards age discrimination, a dismissal for the reason of retirement is prohibited unless an employer can objectively justify such discrimination: Employment Equality (Repeal of Retirement Age Provisions) Regulations 2011. Discrimination on the grounds of age was also prohibited with regard to recruitment, employment and vocational training as from 01 October 2006: Employment Equality (Age) Regulations 2006 (most of these provisions are now subsumed into the Equality Act 2010.)

The statutory tests which an employment tribunal had to apply to determine whether a dismissal was either (1) unfair under the ERA 1996 or (2) unlawful discrimination under the previous DDA 1995 (and now the Equality Act 2010) were and still are different. As stated, in a case of **unfair dismissal**, a tribunal had to consider the **reason** for the dismissal and the **reasonableness** of the employer's actions and whether the employer's response to the matter relating to the employee was 'within the range of reasonable responses of a reasonable employer.' In a case of a dismissal that resulted in an allegation that it constituted **disability discrimination**, a tribunal had to consider the employer's **reason** for treating the disabled employee **less favourably** than a non-disabled employee to whom that reason did not apply. An employer could justify such a dismissal if the reason for the treatment was both **material to the circumstances of the case and substantial** and the disadvantage suffered by the disabled employee could not be removed by **a reasonable adjustment**. In **Jones v Post Office (2001)** IRLR 384, Court of Appeal, Pill LJ thought that there was not much difference between considering the reasonableness of the employer's action under s.98 ERA 1996 and considering the materiality and substantiality of the employer's actions under s.5(3) (that then became s.3A(3)) of the DDA 1995. In other words, the test for both types of claim was one of reasonableness. This meant that tribunals had to apply the statutory test and consider the reasonableness of an employer's response and not substitute their own view of what the employer should have done; i.e. do what the Administrative Court does when conducting a judicial review which is to examine the employer's decision-making procedure to see if the employer followed correctly the statutory or/and contractual procedures. For this reason, if a tribunal found that an employer unlawfully dismissed an employee in breach of the provisions of the DDA 1995 for an unjustifiable disability discrimination reason it is likely that such a dismissal would have been unfair under the ERA 1996 because no minimum period of employment was required when making a disability discrimination claim (and likewise no minimum period of employment is required under the Equality Act 2010 to make a disability discrimination claim).

Tests under the Equality Act 2010 -

For '**Direct discrimination,**' the test under s.13 of the Equality Act 2010 is whether or not, because of the disability, the employer treated the complainant less favourably than he treats or would treat others (hence a comparator is required.) This section does not permit an employer to justify direct disability discrimination.

For **'Discrimination arising from disability,'** the test under s.15 of the Equality Act 2010 consists of the first limb that is whether or not the discriminator treated the disabled person '... unfavourably because of something arising in consequence of the claimant's disability,' meaning that no comparator is required; and the second limb of the test is whether or not the discriminator can show that the treatment was objectively justified, being '... a proportionate means of achieving a legitimate aim.' In **Basildon and Thurrock NHS Foundation Trust (2015)** EAT (Case No.0397/14) the judge said that s.15 gave rise to two causation tests which are (1) the need to identify what was the 'because of' and (2) what was the 'something?'

For **'Indirect discrimination,'** the test under s.19 of the Equality Act 2010 is whether or not the employer applies to the disabled person a provision, criterion or practice which is discriminatory in relation to the disability that the complainant has; the employer applies or would apply it to others with whom the complainant does not share the disability; it puts or would put persons with whom the claimant shares 'the disability' at a particular disadvantage when compared with others with whom the claimant does not share it; it puts or would put the claimant at that disadvantage; and the employer cannot show it to be a proportionate means of achieving a legitimate aim (hence the employer is given the opportunity to objectively justify the particular provision, criterion or practice.)

Note that with reference to s.19, Equality Act 2010, section 6(3)(b) makes clear that in relation to disability, '... a reference to persons who share a protected characteristic is a reference to persons who have the same disability.' This means that for indirect discrimination purposes, the 'particular disadvantage' must affect those who share the claimant's particular disability. The problem with this requirement is that even people who have the 'same disability' cannot easily be treated as one particular class because the way in which the 'same disability' manifests itself will probably differ from person to person, thereby making it difficult for a disabled person to show a group disadvantage. Instead of attempting to rely upon s.19, a disabled person who is being or has been, because of his or her disability, subjected to a detriment by his or her employer would probably find it easier to bring a claim for recompense for any loss suffered by making a claim under s.15 being 'Discrimination arising from a disability' or under s.20 'Duty to make adjustments.' Both of these latter heads of claim are less complex than indirect discrimination, are easier to prove, as well as being specific to the disability strand of discrimination.

As for the **'Duty to make reasonable adjustments,'** the test under s.20 of the Equality Act 2010 is whether or not the employer - where a provision, criterion or practice or a physical feature or the lack of an auxiliary aid puts a disabled person at a substantial advantage - took or should have taken steps to make an adjustment or adjustments where the taking of a step or steps is or would have been reasonable to take to avoid the disadvantage for the disabled person.

7.4 Compensation for an unfair dismissal:

If the tribunal decides that a dismissal is unfair, the tribunal can award financial compensation to the claimant under s.123 of the Employment Rights Act 1996; i.e. -

> 's.123(1) Subject to the provisions of this section and sections 124, 126, 127 and 127A(1), (3) and (4), the amount of the compensatory award shall be such amount as the tribunal considers just and equitable in all the circumstances having regard to the loss sustained by the complainant in consequence of the dismissal in so far as that loss is attributable to action taken by the employer.
>
> ...
>
> (6) Where the tribunal finds that the dismissal was to any extent caused or contributed to by any action of the complainant, it shall reduce the amount of the compensatory award by such

proportion as it considers just and equitable having regard to that finding.'

The **compensatory award** has a statutory maximum limit of **£80,541 or the claimant's gross annual pay, whichever is the smaller**: for the year from **06 April 2017**. This amount now generally increases on the 06 April each year instead of 01 February as before. (Note: there is no statutory maximum if the reason for the dismissal was because the complainant (a) acted as a health and safety representative; (b) made a protected disclosure; (c) was selected for redundancy for either of those reasons. In addition, the maximum basic award is £14,670 for the year from 06 April 2017).

7.5 Compensation for a disability discrimination dismissal:

> 's.8(3) Where a tribunal orders compensation under subsection (2)(b), the amount of the compensation shall be calculated by applying the principles applicable to the calculation of damages in claims in tort or (in Scotland) in reparation for breach of statutory duty.' DDA 1995.

Under the **Equality Act 2010**, per s.124 Remedies: general, 's.124(2), the tribunal may – (b) order the respondent to pay compensation to the complainant'… '(6) The amount of compensation which may be awarded under subsection (2)(b) corresponds to the amount which could be awarded by a county court or the sheriff under s.119.' (Section 119 refers to civil court remedies such as proceedings in tort for compensation for unlawful discrimination and for injury to feelings.)

Unlike compensation for **unfair dismissal**, a compensation award for **disability discrimination** is not subject to any capped upper limit. Such awards can be high: £278,800 awarded in **Newsome v The Council of the City of Sunderland,** ET Case No.6403592/99.

An even higher award of compensation for disability discrimination was reported by the British Medical Journal on the 28 April 2010 - **'Doctor is awarded £500,000 after her employer refused to take account of back pain'** – which was that a former consultant in geriatrics and general medicine was awarded a near record £500,000 for disability discrimination after she felt forced to leave her job four years before retirement when her employers cut her pay and refused to make reasonable adjustments for her back problems. London North Employment Tribunal ruled last year that claims by Gwen Sayers, who worked at Northwick Park Hospital in north London, for constructive unfair dismissal, direct disability discrimination, failure to make reasonable adjustments, and unauthorised deduction from wages were all "well founded." The tribunal awarded her £550,000, one of the highest awards ever made under the Disability Discrimination Act. Her employers, Harrow Primary Care Trust, and her line manager, David Cohen, appealed but in a compromise agreement have now agreed to drop the appeal and pay her £500,000.'

Because discrimination on the grounds of disability is a statutory tort, the amount of compensation is calculated in the same way as damages in tort - per s.8(3) DDA 1995. The purpose of tort damages - so far as money can do so - is to put the applicant back into the position he or she would have been in had not the unlawful conduct happened. The foreseeable criteria applies similar to that in negligence (see the Negligence heading in this series) in that (a) the loss must be caused by the discrimination; (b) the loss must not be too remote a consequence of the discrimination; and (c) a complainant is under a duty to mitigate his or her loss.

Compensation for unlawful discrimination - be it on the grounds of age, disability, gender reassignment, marriage and civil partnerships, pregnancy and maternity, race, religion or belief, sex, sexual orientation - generally comes under two heads: financial loss and non-financial loss. Financial loss covers things such as loss of earnings (past, present and future - note: compensation for loss of future earnings to be paid gross if above £30,000, not net of tax: **Williams v Ferrosan Ltd (2004)** EAT, IRLR 607) plus fringe benefits. Non-financial loss covers things such as 'injury to feelings' per s.8(4) and aggravated damages. An injury to feelings award (to compensate the claimant for the worry, anxiety and upset of being subjected to a statutory tort such as discrimination) is now stated in s.119(4), Equality Act 2010. An 'injury to feelings' award is not taxable where the statutory tort occurred during the course of the employment contract and prior to, and unconnected to, the dismissal. But where the statutory tort occurred during or as a result of the termination of the contract of employment then the injury to feelings award is taxable (i.e. such a payment comes within s.401, Income Tax (Earnings and Pensions) Act 2003 but not within s.406 of the same Act) to the extent that it exceeds £30,000: **Moorthy v HMRC (2010)** UKUT (TCC) (judgment 14 January 2016). See Taxation of Termination Payments book in this series: ISBN 978-1-326-34306- 4.

Compensation for 'injury to feelings' is a head of claim that is available to those who have suffered **discriminatory treatment** including disability discrimination. The Court of Appeal gave guidance to tribunals for assessing compensation for injury to feelings in the case of **Vento v Chief Constable of West Yorkshire (No 2) (2003)** ICR 318, CA **- 'the**

Vento guidelines.' The Court of Appeal set out three broad bands of compensation:

(1) the top band should normally be between £15,000 - £25,000 and apply only to the most serious cases such as where there has been a lengthy campaign of discriminatory harassment on the grounds of sex, race, or disability. Only in very exceptional cases should an award of compensation for injury to feelings exceed £25,000;

(2) the middle band of £5,000 - £15,000 should be used for serious cases which do not merit an award in the highest band; and

(3) awards of between £500 - £5,000 are appropriate for less serious cases such as where the act of discrimination is an isolated or one-off occurrence. In general, awards of less than £500 should be avoided as they risk being regarded as being so low as not to be a proper recognition of injury to feelings.

Note: these bands are based on the money value figures of 2002. In September 2009, after adjusting for inflation of 20%, the uplifted upper figures are –

- top band: £30,000;
- middle band: £18,000;
- lower band: £6,000: per **Da'Bell v National Society for the Prevention of Cruelty to Children (2009)** EAT, 28.09.09 (Case No.0227/09).

On the 13 March 2014, Judge David J. Latham, the President of Employment Tribunals for England and Wales, issued Presidential Guidance, paragraph 14 of which stated the three bands of the Vento guidelines were now:

- top band: £19,800-£33,000;
- middle band: £6,600-£19,800;
- lower band: £660-£6,660.

Injury to feelings - a case in which the complainant was awarded the then suggested maximum of £25,000 for injury to feelings was that of **Gilbank v Miles (2006)** IRLR 538; (2006) EWCA Civ 543, CA 11 May 2006. The award was made joint and severally against the company and the majority shareholder/employee, the latter under s.42, Sex Discrimination Act 1975. Section 42 makes an individual liable for aiding the employer (via vicarious liability) to do a discriminatory act that the majority shareholder/employee did. Even though the company was subsequently dissolved, the Court of Appeal held that liability to pay compensation to the claimant still remained against the majority shareholder/employee for her part in encouraging a sustained campaign of bullying and discrimination by others against the claimant who was pregnant at the time.

Often the heads of compensation will overlap. If this happens, compensation for unfair dismissal and disability discrimination cannot be awarded twice: s.126, ERA 1996. In such circumstances, an applicant is advised to seek compensation under the discrimination legislation thereby avoiding the statutory maximum limit on the unfair dismissal compensatory award.

An uplift of 10% for non-financial loss in ETs from 04 July 2017:

In **Simmons v Castle (2012)** the Court of Appeal held that a 10% uplift shall apply to awards of damages for non-financial loss in discrimination cases the reason being that there had been a change in the civil litigation rules, the effect of which had reduced the amount that could be recovered by lawyers and their clients. So, to account for the rules' change, a recommendation was made that there be an increase in non-financial general damages which, subsequently, the Court of Appeal in **Simmons v Castle (2012)** EWCA Civ 1039, set at 10% and applies to all non-financial loss torts including the tort of unlawful discrimination. 'Non-financial loss' covers pain and suffering, loss of amenity, physical inconvenience and discomfort, social discredit, or mental distress. Although the Equality Act 2010, s.124(6), states that awards in employment tribunals correspond with those in civil courts there was uncertainty by some EAT judges about whether the 10% applied to compensation awarded by ETs for non-financial loss. In **de Souza v Vinci Construction (UK) Ltd (2017)** EWCA Civ 879 (04 July 2017) the Court of Appeal confirmed that it does. So unless that decision is appealed to and reversed by the Supreme Court, the existing Vento guidelines should be increased by 10% from the figures below:

- top band: £19,800-£33,000
- middle band: £6,600-£19,800
- lower band: £660-£6,600.

Stigma and future employment loss compensation:

Where a claimant suffers from stigma or diminished employment prospects as a result of being subjected to unlawful discrimination by his or her employer after maybe doing or suspected of doing a protected act or making a protected disclosure that his or her employer does not like and, thereafter, is subjected to detriment such as victimisation, harassment or dismissal and, if the latter, finds it difficult or impossible to obtain another comparable job may, if he or she makes a successful claim to an employment tribunal, be awarded compensation for 'stigma loss' and future loss of earnings (maybe to the end of his or her working life) to take account of the time it may take him or her to find alternative employment and the latter compensation can be awarded for a period that extends beyond the period in which the claimant might have ordinarily been employed by his or her employer: **Small v Shrewsbury and Telford Hospitals NHS Trust (2017)** EWCA Civ 882. See also: **Chagger v Abbey**

7.6 Disability discrimination questionnaire:

An individual who reasonably believed that he or she may have been subjected to an act of discrimination could submit a questionnaire to the alleged discriminator: s.56 DDA 1995. A similar procedure applies under the Equality Act 2010. The purpose of the questionnaire procedure was to assist him or her to ascertain whether he or she had reasonable grounds for taking action and a reasonable prospect of success. There was a statutory form of questionnaire together with a statutory form for replies. These statutory forms were set out in the Disability Discrimination (Questions and Replies) Order 1996 SI 1996/2793. If the questionnaire was served on the other party (usually an employer) within the statutory time limit, the questions and replies could then be used as evidence in tribunal proceedings: s.56(3)(a) DDA 1995. As mentioned, there is a similar procedure under the Equality Act 2010: s.138 'Obtaining information, etc.'

Under the Disability Discrimination Act 1995, the time limits stating when the questionnaire procedure was to be used was set out in Article 3, 1996 Order:

- where the questionnaire is served **before** an application to the tribunal, it must be served within **3 months** of the discriminatory act complained of;
- where the questionnaire is served **after** an application has

been lodged with the tribunal, it must be served within **21 days** of the application **unless** the tribunal gives leave for later service.

From 1st October 2004, the Regulations provided that an employer, on receipt of the statutory questionnaire, would have eight weeks within which to respond rather than 'a reasonable period' pre-1st October 2004: Reg.22 of the Disability Discrimination Act 1995 (Amendment) Regulations 2003.

The Equality Act 2010 states in s.138(4) that:' A court or tribunal may draw an inference from – (a) a failure by R to answer a question by P before the end of the period of 8 weeks beginning with the day on which the question is served; (b) an evasive or equivocal answer.'

Part 8

8.1 Sick pay:

In **O'Hanlon v Commissioners for HM Revenue & Customs (2007)** EWCA Civ 283 the Court of Appeal held that an employer was not obliged, as part of its duty to make reasonable adjustments, to ***extend*** the sick pay of an employee on disability-related sick leave. Further, on the assumption that the employee had been treated less favourably than non-disabled employees as a result of the employer's sick pay policy, the treatment was in any event justified. Compare with **Nottinghamshire County Council v Meikle (2004)** re sick pay - 6.2.

8.2 Holiday leave while on long-term sick leave:

Entitlement to statutory holiday leave while on long-term sick leave:

On the 20 January 2009, giving judgment in two joined cases, the Court of Justice of the European Union (CJEU) ruled that a worker who is on long-term sick leave ***is*** entitled to any holiday which accrues during his or her sickness absence (which the worker would take only after he or she has returned to work). In the event that the worker is dismissed, he or she is entitled to pay in lieu of any untaken leave that has accumulated during the sickness absence. The 'allowance in lieu' should be equivalent to normal pay.

In other words, the judgment of the CJEU is that under EU law (and under the Working Time Regulations which transpose this part of EU law into the domestic law of the UK) a worker does ***not*** lose his or her right to paid annual leave which he or she has been unable to take because of sickness. Further, the worker must be compensated for paid annual leave that he or she has not been able to take because of his or her long-term sickness absence, either in cash if he or she is dismissed or by paid holiday if he or she returns to work: **Stringer and others v Her Majesty's Revenue and Customs (2009) ECJ, 20.01.09, Cases C-350/06 and C-520/06.** Note that Stringer and others v HMRC (2009) was formerly Ainsworth and others v Commissioners of Inland Revenue (2005) ICR 1149. See too: HH Bean J. sitting alone - ***'Annual leave entitlement accrues during a period of sick leave:'*** **NHS Leeds v Larner (2011)** EAT 29 June 2011 (Case No.0088/11).

Summary of **NHS Leeds v Larner (2012)**: under Regulation 13 of the Working Time Regulations 1998 that implements Article 7 of the Working Time Directive 2003/88/EC, a worker/employee: (i) continues to build up an entitlement to at least four weeks' statutory annual paid leave (where working full-time or if working part-time, pro rata) during periods of sick leave; (ii) when on a period of sick leave, does not need to submit to the employer a request to take paid annual leave during or before the end of the relevant leave year; (iii) when unable to take annual paid leave during the leave year because he or she is on sick leave, has the right under Regulation 13 to have his or her leave entitlement carried over to the following leave year; (iv) on the termination of his or her employment, has the right to be paid an allowance in lieu by the employer for outstanding annual leave that he or she was unable to take because he or she was on sick leave.

The situation is different with regard to the entitlement to the period of additional leave of 1.6 weeks under Regulation 13A of the Working Time Regulations 1998. In **Neidel (2012)** [**Georg Neidel v Stadt Frankfurt am Main (Case C-337/10)**], the Court of Justice of the European Union held that an EU Member State could preclude, on the termination of a worker's employment, an allowance in lieu for untaken additional leave that was not taken by a worker because the worker was on sick leave. However, UK law states (Reg.13A(7)) that a worker can carry forward such untaken leave if a 'relevant agreement' so provides but only into the immediately following leave year. In other words, there is no absolute right to carry over untaken holiday leave or to be paid in lieu in the same way as under Reg.13; the right under Reg.13A is much more limited because, being UK State and not EU legislation, a Member State can lay down its own rules. On this latter point, Mummery LJ cautioned that, with regard to additional leave, ***'The unfolding law on paid annual leave is not in a complete state...'*** This was an issue that the Court of Appeal in **NHS Leeds v Larner (2012)** declined to rule on in the same way as it ruled on the requirements which now apply to the four weeks' period of paid annual leave. Instead, Mummery LJ suggested that ***'... the ETs and their users can derive assistance from the judgment in Neidel.'***

8.3 Further disability discrimination case authorities:

The following two cases are about claimants who presented complaints to employment tribunals claiming that they had been unlawfully discriminated against for the reason of having a **mental disability.** These two cases are interesting in that:

(1) the first case shows what is required to prove (a) unfair dismissal under the Employment Rights Act 1996 as well as (b) unlawful dismissal under the Disability Discrimination Act 1995;

(2) the second case shows what is required to prove that an impairment is likely to recur.

British Telecommunications plc v (Miss Lynn) Pelling (2004) EAT 25 May 2004 (Case No.0093/03) (at EAT Edinburgh). The appellant was BT plc who sought to appeal against the decision of an ET sitting in Glasgow, the decision of the ET being: (a) Miss Pelling had been unfairly dismissed by the respondent but (b) the respondent had not discriminated against her contrary to the Disability Discrimination Act 1995. The judgment of the Scottish EAT was delivered by Lord Johnston as follows:

(1) the employee suffered from a mental disability that, in part, manifested itself in agoraphobia (i.e. a manifestation of depression in which the sufferer experiences periods of irrational fear and panic when outside the perceived safety of the home) the condition of which caused her great difficulty when or if she left the house, thus preventing her going into work;

(2) the appeal was based on the simple submission that the ET had substituted its opinion for that of the employer which, it was submitted, was based on 'the reasonable response of a reasonable employer;'

(3) however, the EAT held that '***... the tribunal reached a decision they were entitled to reach upon the evidence and were not substituting their own view;***'

(4) the claimant, Miss Pelling (now the respondent in the appeal), cross-appealed the finding of the ET that she had not been unlawfully dismissed contrary to the provisions of the DDA 1995;

(5) reviewing the findings of the ET, Lord Johnston said that:

> *'... we consider that the tribunal has hopelessly misdirected itself... not least, by failing to appreciate the connection between the band of reasonable responses issue, in relation to unfair dismissal, and, the issue of reasonable adjustment in terms of sections 5(2) and 6 of the Disability Discrimination Act 1995;'*

(6) Lord Johnston continued:

'It seems to us that the less favourable treatment, being, of course, the dismissal, can only be justified if it can be shown that it was unconnected with the medical condition, or, unavoidable, (Jones v Post Office (2001) IRLR 384). It again, seems to us, that is very difficult to determine having regard to the fact that the reason for dismissal was the inability on the part of the respondent to go to her workplace because of her medical condition. Putting aside, however, for the moment the question of justification in that respect, what seems to us to be critical is that by being unable to leave the house to go to work, the respondent was plainly, in our opinion, at a disadvantaged state with regard to the requirement of the employer to work only at the workplace. Again, therefore, the case turns in this respect on the failure on the part of the employer to offer a reasonable adjustment, namely, investigation and possible offer of homework. The matter, therefore, turned on precisely the same issue that determined the question of unfair dismissal and must reach the same conclusion;'

(7) the appellant, BT plc, lost its appeal on the grounds that, (a) being the employer, it had failed to consider the possibility of home-working that would have constituted a reasonable adjustment under the DDA 1995; (b) it failed in its duty to consider adjustments and medical opinion; (c) it failed to obtain and consider suitably qualified and expert medical opinion before dismissing; (d) through lack of investigation of home-working, BT could not show whether the dismissal was justified (as the tribunal themselves agreed); (e) in contrast to the treatment of the respondent (Miss Pelling), the appellant (BT), allowed some 5,000 of its other employees to engage in home-working;

(8) in addition to BT losing its appeal, the cross-appeal by Miss Pelling was allowed and the question of remedy for disability discrimination was remitted back to the same

employment tribunal for consideration.

[See also: **Spencer v 02 UK (2004)** ET Case No.1805496/03, Leeds ET; date of decision was 29 March 2004; a disability discrimination and unfair dismissal case, the decision being (1) the decision to dismiss fell firmly outside the band of reasonable responses and the dismissal was therefore unfair; and (2) the dismissal amounted to unlawful disability discrimination].

Swift v Chief Constable of Wiltshire Constabulary (2004) EAT 18 February 2004 (Case No.0484/03) (at EAT London). The appellant was Mrs R. Swift who appealed against a decision of the employment tribunal regarding the application of paragraph 2(2) of Schedule 1 of the Disability Discrimination Act 1995. Schedule 1, paragraph 2(2) states: **'Where an impairment ceases to have a substantial adverse effect on a person's ability to carry out normal day-to-day activities, it is to be treated as continuing to have that effect if that effect is likely to recur.'**

Mrs Swift complained that her employer, Wiltshire Constabulary, had discriminated against her by failing to make adjustments in her workplace between **July 2002 and October 2002**. She submitted that during this period she remained a disabled person within the meaning of s.1 DDA 1995. The employment tribunal rejected her case, holding that she had **NOT** proved she was disabled **AFTER** the beginning of July 2002. It was this decision against which she appealed.

At the Employment Appeal Tribunal hearing:

(1) After being subjected to harassment and bullying by two colleagues at work, the appellant, Mrs Swift, was assessed by a consultant in adult psychiatry who said that she had a recognised psychiatric condition from approximately January 2001 to mid-2002;

(2) the consultant said that her memory and concentration were affected. He added that, between those dates, it appeared there were substantial and long-term adverse effects on her ability to carry out normal day-to-day activities. He said that after mid-2002, a formal psychiatric diagnosis was not appropriate;

(3) at the hearing her employer admitted that she became a **disabled person** within the meaning of s.1 DDA 1995 in January 2001. In turn, she conceded that the impairment

resulting from her illness had **ceased** to have a substantial adverse effect on her ability to carry out normal day-to-day activities in July 2002 when she returned to work;

(4) but Mrs Swift sought to establish that she was still a disabled person during the period between **July and October 2002** by reliance upon paragraph 2(2) of Schedule 1, DDA 1995. If she could show that she remained disabled then, potentially, her employer might have a duty to make adjustments in accordance with s.6 DDA 1995;

(5) pointedly, the EAT drew attention to the fact that her case **had not** been put on the basis of **past disability** (see s.2 DDA 1995 and the modifications to s.6 set out in **Schedule 2 of the Act). For clarity, the EAT said that it expressed no view as to whether the case could have been pursued successfully on the basis of past disability**;

(6) section 2 of the DDA 1995 states:

> '2(1) The provisions of this Part … apply in relation to a person who has had a disability as they apply in relation to a person who has that disability;
>
> (2) Those provisions are subject to the modifications made by Schedule 2;
>
> (3) Any regulations or order made under this Act … may include provision with respect to persons who have had a disability; paragraph 4(1) of Schedule 1 provides:
>
> '4(1) An impairment is to be taken to affect the ability of the person concerned to carry out normal day-to-day activities only if it affects one of the following- …
>
> (g) memory or ability to concentrate, learn or understand; …'

(7) s.3 of the DDA 1996 gives the Secretary of State the power to issue guidance to the Act. Accordingly, the Secretary of State issued guidance in July 1996. Part of the Guidance, namely, paragraph B3-5, deals with recurring effects. Paragraph B3 states:

> 'The Act states that if an impairment has had a substantial adverse effect on a person's ability to carry out normal day-to-day activities but that effect ceases, the substantial effect is treated as continuing if

it is likely to recur; that is, it is more likely than not that the effect will recur. In deciding whether a person has had a disability in the past, the question is whether a substantial adverse effect has in fact recurred. Conditions which recur only sporadically or for short periods (e.g. epilepsy) can still qualify.'
Paragraph B7 states that it is likely that an event will happen if it is more probable than not that it will happen. Paragraph B5 states that the likelihood of recurrence should be considered taking all the circumstances of the case into account;

(8) the EAT, after quoting the above sections of the Act and the Guidance, stated the steps and the tests to which tribunals should pay regard when considering the application of paragraph 2(2) of Schedule 1 of the DDA 1995 (the words of which are: '**Where an impairment ceases to have a substantial adverse effect on a person's ability to carry out normal day-to-day activities, it is to be treated as continuing to have that effect if that effect is likely to recur**);'

(9) STEP ONE: '**... was there at some stage an impairment which had a substantial adverse effect on the applicant's ability to carry out normal day-to-day activities?** An impairment will have such an effect only if it affects one or more of the functions listed in paragraph 4(1) of the Schedule. Even then, the effect must have been substantial and adverse. This is for the tribunal to assess, having regard to the Guidance. Where the impairment is said to have been a mental impairment resulting from or consisting of a mental illness, the illness must have been a clinically well-recognised illness. See, on the question of mental impairments, **Morgan v Staffordshire University (2002)** ICR 475;'

STEP TWO: '**... did the impairment cease to have a substantial adverse effect on the applicant's ability to carry out normal day-to-day activities, and if so when?** Asking and answering this question will ensure that paragraph 2(2) does not enter too early into the process of the tribunal's reasoning. Paragraph 2(2) deems an impairment to continue when, and only when, it has ceased to have a substantial adverse effect on an applicant's ability

> to carry out normal day-to-day activities. Until that point, the duration of an impairment's effect is assessed in accordance with paragraph 2(1) of the Schedule;'
> STEP THREE: **'... what was the substantial adverse effect?** This question needs to be answered with a degree of precision, for as we shall see, paragraph 2(2) requires the tribunal to consider whether THAT effect is likely to recur. The question should be answered by reference to the functions set out in paragraph 4(1) of the Schedule;'
> STEP FOUR: **'... is THAT substantial adverse effect likely to recur?** This is the question which must be answered if paragraph 2(2) is to come into play. The tribunal must be satisfied that the same effect is likely to recur and that it will again amount to a substantial adverse effect on the applicant's ability to carry out normal day-to-day activities. In this context, a substantial adverse effect is "likely to recur" if it is more probable than not that the effect will recur. See paragraph B7 of the Guidance and **Latchman v Reed Business Services (2002)** ICR 1453.'

The EAT continued: 'Whether a substantial adverse effect is "likely to recur" is by no means necessarily determined by the medical evidence, although medical evidence is of high importance. The medical evidence may point to circumstances in which the substantial adverse effect is likely to recur. If so, the tribunal will have to consider in practice how likely it is that those circumstances will occur. The tribunal will also take into account what is said in paragraph B5 of the Guidance.

Often in answering this question, the tribunal will be looking to the future. The relevant date will be the date when the tribunal is hearing the case. Sometimes, however, the date will be a date in the past, because the parties will pose for the tribunal the question whether an applicant continued to have a disability at a particular time. The present case is such a case. **Mrs Swift's argument was not that between July and October 2002 she had a past disability. Her case was that during that period she had a present disability.** In considering whether during a particular period in the past, a substantial adverse effect was likely to recur a tribunal is, of course, entitled to look at the evidence of what occurred during that period. In particular if it is said that an effect was likely to recur because certain circumstances would be likely to trigger it, a tribunal is entitled to consider whether those circumstances occurred during the period and whether the substantial adverse effect did recur. Such evidence is not necessarily conclusive. It is for the tribunal to assess.

Although the tribunal must be satisfied that the substantial adverse effect is likely to recur, it need not be satisfied that the recurrence is likely to last for at least twelve months. The effect of paragraph 2(2) is that the impairment is treated as continuing for as long as its substantial adverse effect is likely to recur. So, even if the impairment has ceased to have a substantial adverse effect, it "lasts" for the purpose of paragraph 2(1) for as long as its substantial adverse effect is likely to recur.'

In conclusion, the EAT said that the appellant, Mrs Swift,

> ***'... had to establish that there was likely to recur an impairment which affected memory or ability to concentrate to the extent that it had a substantial effect on her ability to carry out normal day-to-day activities.'***

But, because:

(1) of the fact that Dr Stevens' report expressly said that the substantial adverse effect on memory and concentration had continued only between January 2001 and mid-2002;
(2) the applicant had failed to prove that the substantial adverse effect (relating to or connected with her disability) was likely to recur (the latter of which is the statutory test per paragraph 2(2) of Schedule 1), the EAT concluded that the employment tribunal had applied the right test so that there was no error of law in the employment tribunal's decision.

For a hypothetical example of when a disability ceases but in law is deemed to be continuing, see the judgment of Underhill J. in **J v DLA Piper Ltd LLP (2010)** EAT (Case No.0263/09). See 2.7.

Guidance on the definition of disability – at A16 Equality Act 2010:

> 'The Act states that, except for the provisions in Part 12 (Transport) and s.190 (improvements to let dwelling houses), the provisions of the Act also apply in relation to a person who previously has had a disability as defined in paragraphs **A1 and A2 (S6(4) and Sch 1, Para 9)**. This means that someone who is no longer disabled, but who met the requirements of the definition in the past, will still be covered by the Act.'

Note: 'normal day-to-day activities' – meaning: although the approach of the Court of Justice of the European Union to disability was broadly the same as UK legislation, the main difference was that the CJEU focused on the effect of the impairment on an employee's professional life: **Chacón Navas v Eurest Colectividades SA (2006)** IRLR 706. Acknowledging that decision, the Employment Appeal Tribunal held that 'normal day-to-day activities' must be interpreted as including activities relevant to professional life: **Paterson v Commissioner of Police of the Metropolis (2007)** ICR 1522.

See **Banaszczyk v Bookers Limited (2016)** EAT (Case No.0132/15) for the meaning of 'day-to-day activities.' See paras.22 and 27 of the judgment for case authorities and Guidance.

Bullying:

When an employer or line manager or, indeed, colleagues, bully a worker what they are seeking to do is damage the mental health of the person whom they are bullying: that is their aim. Unlike physical bullying, there are no bruises, wounds or abrasions to be seen and therefore no visible evidence of an attack. But the effects on a person who is being bullied are often manifested in physical illnesses, the most common of which are stress, anxiety, insomnia, headaches, skin rashes, stomach upsets, as well as psychological disorders such as phobias, panic attack and depression, the latter of which can itself cause a variety of physical disorders. Unfortunately, what often happens thereafter is that the bullied person is subjected to further bullying and stress by the employer's HR department that puts pressure on the bullied person to return to the workplace where the bullying is likely to resume or be dismissed. Employment tribunals need to be aware that when they hear cases where the claimant states that they have been bullied while at work, what the claimants are saying is that they have been subjected to assaults which are akin to physical assaults and, where the bullying has continued for some while, maybe months or years, these assaults may actually have been more damaging and long lasting to claimants' mental health that physical assaults which tend to be sudden one-off attacks.

Remedies:

There are a range of civil and criminal provisions which prohibit conduct that constitutes bullying and which, if not effective in preventing such attacks, provide remedies by way of a civil claim for negligence or a criminal prosecution under the Protection from Harassment Act 1997. A successful prosecution under the latter Act can be followed by a civil claim for damages. If the police service and the Crown Prosecution

Service refuse to act, a private criminal prosecution can be instigated at a Magistrates' Court under s.6(1), Prosecution of Offences Act 1985. (Melinka Berridge is a partner specialising in private prosecutions at Kingsley Napley.)

Part 9

9.1 Comparative guide to the Disability Discrimination Act 1995 and the Equality Act 2010:

When the Equality Act 2010 came into effect on 01 October 2010, it repealed and replaced the Disability Discrimination Act 1995. An overview of the structure of the Equality Act 2010 is as follows -
Part 2 – Chapter 1 - defines The Protected Characteristics.
Part 2 – Chapter 2 – defines The Meaning of Discrimination.
Part 5 – Chapter 1 – define Discrimination at Work.
Part 9 – Chapter 3 – defines Actionable Discrimination.
This guide sets out some of the most important provisions in the Equality Act 2010 and compares them with the legislation in existence prior to that Act coming into force.

Equality Act 2010, section 4 – The Protected Characteristics:

s.4 - The protected characteristics

The following characteristics are protected characteristics –
Age;
Disability;
Gender reassignment;
Marriage and civil partnership;
Race;
Religion or belief;
Sex;
Sexual orientation.
(Pregnancy and maternity come under the protected characteristic of sex).

Disability Discrimination Act 1995 – there was no prior legislation.

Equality Act 2010, section 6 – Definition of Disability:

s.6 Disability

(1) A person (P) has a disability if:
P has a physical or mental impairment, and the impairment has a substantial and long term adverse effect on P's ability to carry out normal day to day activities.

(2) A reference to a disabled person is a reference to a person who has a disability.

(3) In relation to the protected characteristic of disability -

a) a reference to a person who has a particular protected characteristic is a reference to a person who has a particular disability;

b) a reference to persons who share a protected characteristic is a reference to persons who have the same disability.

(4) This Act (except Part 12 and section 190) applies in relation to a person who has had a disability as it applies in relation to a person who has the disability; accordingly (except in that Part and that section) -

a) a reference (however expressed) to a person who has a disability includes a reference to a person who has had the disability; and

b) a reference (however expressed) to a person who does not have a disability includes a reference to a person who has not had the disability…

(6) Schedule 1 (disability: supplementary provision) has effect.

Disability Discrimination Act 1995 -

s.1 –Meaning of "disability" and "disabled person"

(1) Subject to the provisions of Schedule 1, a person has a disability for the purpose of this Act if he has a physical or mental impairment which has a substantial long term adverse effect on his ability to carry out normal day to day activities.

(2) In this Act "disabled person" means a person who has a disability.

s.2 Past disabilities

(1) The provisions of this Part and Parts 11 [to 4] [and 5A] apply in relation to a person who has had a disability as they apply in relation to a person who has that disability.
(2) Those provisions are subject to the modifications made by Schedule 2.
(3) In any proceedings under Part [2,3,4, 5A] of the Act, the question whether a person had a disability at a particular time (the "relevant time") shall be determined… as if the provisions of… this Act in force when the act complained of was done had been in force at the relevant time.
(4) The relevant time may be a time before the passing of this Act.

Schedule 1 Provisions Supplementary Section 1

s.4 Normal Day to Day Activities –

(1) An impairment is to be taken to affect the ability of the person concerned to carry out normal day to day activities only if it affects one of the following:

a) mobility;
b) manual dexterity;
c) physical co-ordination;
d) continence;
e) ability to lift, carry or otherwise move everyday objects;
f) speech, hearing or eyesight;
g) memory or ability to concentrate, learn or understand;
h) perception or risk of physical danger.

Equality Act 2010, section 13 – Direct discrimination:

s.13 Direct discrimination

(1) A person (A) discriminates against another (B) if, because of a protected characteristic, A treats B less favourably than

A treats or would treat others.

(3) If the protected characteristic is disability, and B is not a disabled person, A does not discriminate against B only because A treats or would treat disabled persons more favourably than A treats B.

Equality Act 2010, section 15 – Discrimination arising from Disability:

s.15 Discrimination arising from disability

(1) A person (A) discriminates against a disabled person (B) if -

a) A treats B unfavourably because of something arising in consequence of B's disability, and
b) A cannot show that the treatment is a proportionate means of a achieving a legitimate aim.

(2) Subsection (1) does not apply if A shows that A did not know, and could not reasonably have been expected to know, that B had the disability.

Disability Discrimination Act 1995, s.3A - Meaning of Disability:

s.3A Meaning of disability (originally s.5, DDA 1995)

(1) For the purposes of this Part, a person discriminates against a disabled person if -

a) for a reason which relates to the disabled person's disability, he treats him less favourably than he treats or would treat others to whom that reason does not or would not apply; and
b) he cannot show that the treatment in question is justified.

(2) For the purposes of this Part, an employer also discriminates against a disabled person if -

a) he fails to comply with a section 6 duty imposed on him in relation to the disabled person; and
b) he cannot show that his failure to comply with that

duty is justified.

(3) Subject to subsection (5), for the purposes of subsection (1) treatment is justified if, but only if, the reason for it is both material to the circumstances of the particular case and substantial.

(4) For the purposes of subsection (2), failure to comply with a section 6 duty is justified if, but only if, the reason for the failure is both material to the circumstances of the particular case and substantial.

(5) If, in a case falling within subsection (1), the employer is under a section 6 duty in relation to the disabled person but fails without justification to comply with that duty, his treatment of that person cannot be justified under subsection (3) unless it would have been justified even if he had complied with the section 6 duty.

Equality Act 2010, s.19 – Indirect Discrimination:

s.19 Indirect discrimination

(1) A person (A) discriminates against another (B) if A applies to B a provision, criterion or practice which is discriminatory in relation to a relevant protected characteristic of B's.

(2) For the purposes of subsection (1), a provision, criterion or practice is discriminatory in relation to a relevant protected characteristic of B's if -

a) A applies, or would apply, it to persons with whom B does not share the characteristic,
b) it puts, or would put, persons with whom B shares the characteristic at a particular disadvantage when compared with persons with whom B does not share it,
c) it puts, or would put, B at that disadvantage, and
d) A cannot show it to be a proportionate means of achieving a legitimate aim.

Sex Discrimination Act 1975, section 1 – Indirect Discrimination against Women:

s.1 Indirect discrimination against women

s.1(2) In any circumstances relevant for the purposes of a provision to which this subsection applies, a person discriminates against a woman if - (b) he applies to her a provision, criterion or practice which he applies or would apply equally to a man, but:

i) which puts or would put women at a particular disadvantage when compared with men;
ii) which puts her at that disadvantage; and
iii) which he cannot show to be a proportionate means of achieving a legitimate aim.

(3) Subsection 2 applies to -

a) any provision of Part 11 [employment]…

Equality Act 2010, section 20 – Duty to make Adjustments:

s.20 Duty to make adjustments

(1) Where this Act imposes a duty to make reasonable adjustments on a person, this section, sections 21 and 22 and the applicable Schedule apply; and for those purposes, a person on whom the duty is imposed is referred to as A.
(2) The duty comprises the following three requirements.
(3) The first requirement is a requirement, where a provision, criterion or practice of A's puts a disabled person at a substantial disadvantage in relation to a relevant matter in comparison with persons who are not disabled, to take such steps as it is reasonable to have to take to avoid the disadvantage.
(4) The second requirement is a requirement, where a physical feature puts a disabled person at a substantial disadvantage in relation to a relevant matter in comparison with persons who are not disabled, to take such steps as it is reasonable to have to take to avoid the disadvantage.
(5) The third requirement is a requirement, where a disabled

person would, but for the provision of an auxiliary aid, be put at a substantial disadvantage in relation to a relevant matter in comparison with persons who are not disabled, to take such steps as it is reasonable to have to take to provide the auxiliary aid.

(6) Where the first or third requirement relates to the provision of information, the steps which it is reasonable for A to have to take include steps for ensuring that in the circumstances concerned the information is provided in an accessible format.

(7) A person (A) who is subject to a duty to make reasonable adjustments is not (subject to express provision to the contrary) entitled to request a disabled person, in relation to whom A is required to comply with the duty, to pay to any extent A's costs of complying with the duty.

(8) A reference in section 21 or 22 or an applicable Schedule to the first, second or third requirement is to be construed in accordance with this section.

(9) In relation to the second requirement, a reference in this section or an applicable Schedule to avoiding a substantial disadvantage includes a reference to -

a) removing the physical feature in question,
b) altering it, or
c) providing a reasonable means of avoiding it.

(10) A reference in this section, section 21 or 22 or an applicable Schedule (apart from paragraphs 2 to 4 of Schedule 4) to a physical feature is a reference to -

a) a feature arising from the design or construction of a building,
b) a feature of an approach to, exit from or access to a building,
c) a fixture or fitting, or furniture, furnishings, materials, equipment or other chattels, in or on premises, or
d) any other physical element or quality.

(11) A reference in this section, section 21 or 22 or an applicable Schedule to an auxiliary aid includes a reference to an auxiliary service.

(13) The applicable Schedule is, in relation to the Part of this Act

specified in the first column of the Table, the Schedule specified in the second column.

Part of this Act	Applicable Schedule
Part 3 (services and public functions)	Schedule 2
Part 4 (premises)	Schedule 4
Part 5 (work)	Schedule 8
Part 6 (education)	Schedule 13
Part 7 (associations)	Schedule 15
Each of the Parts mentioned above	Schedule 21

Disability Discrimination Act 1995, section 4A – Employers: duty to make adjustments:

s.4A Employers: duty to make adjustments

(1)Where:

a) a provision, criterion or practice applied by or on behalf of an employer, or
b) any physical feature of premises occupied by the employer, place the disabled person concerned at a substantial disadvantage in comparison with persons who are not disabled, it is the duty of the employer to take such steps as it is reasonable, in all the circumstances of the case, for him to have to take in order to prevent the provision, criterion or practice, or feature, having that effect.

(6) Nothing in this section imposes any duty on an employer in relation to a disabled person if the employer does not know, and could not reasonably be expected to know -

a) in the case of an applicant or potential applicant, that the disabled person concerned is, or may be, an applicant for the employment; or
b) in any case, that that person has a disability and is likely to be affected in the way mentioned in subsection (1).

Equality Act 2010, section 21 – Failure to comply with Duty:

s.21 Failure to comply with duty

(1) A failure to comply with the first, second or third requirement is a failure to comply with a duty to make reasonable adjustments.

(2) A discriminates against a disabled person if A fails to comply with that duty in relation to that person.

(3) A provision of an applicable Schedule which imposes a duty to comply with the first, second or third requirement applies only for the purpose of establishing whether A has contravened this Act by virtue of subsection (2); a failure to comply is, accordingly, not actionable by virtue of another provision of this Act or otherwise.

Equality Act 2010, section 23 – Comparison by reference to Circumstances:

s.23 Comparison by reference to circumstances

(1) On a comparison of cases for the purposes of section 13, 14, or 19 there must be no material difference between the circumstances relating to each case.

(2) The circumstances relating to a case include a person's abilities if

a) on a comparison for the purposes of section 13, the protected characteristic is disability;

b) on a comparison for the purposes of section 14, one of the protected characteristics in the combination is disability.

Disability Discrimination Act 1995, section 3A – Meaning of Discrimination:

s.3A Meaning of discrimination (originally s.5, DDA 1995)

(5) A person directly discriminates against a disabled person if, on the ground of the disabled person's disability, he treats the disabled person less favourably than he treats or would treat a person not having that particular disability whose

relevant circumstances, including his abilities, are the same as, or not materially different from, those of the disabled person.

Equality Act 2010, section 25 – Reference to particular strands of Discrimination:

s.25 Reference to particular strands of discrimination

(2) Disability discrimination is -

a) discrimination within section 13 because of disability;
b) discrimination within section 15;
c) discrimination within section 19 where the relevant protected characteristic is disability;
d) discrimination within section 21.

Disability Discrimination Act 1995 – there were no equivalent provisions. The provision in the Equality Act 2010 is really just an aide memoire/quick reference.

Equality Act 2010, section 26 – Harassment:

s.26 Harassment

(1) A person (A) harasses another (B) if -

(a) A engages in unwanted conduct related to a relevant protected characteristic, and
(b) the conduct has the purpose or effect of -

i) violating B's dignity, or
ii) creating an intimidating, hostile, degrading, humiliating or offensive environment for B.

(2) A also harasses B if -

a) A engages in unwanted conduct of a sexual nature, and
b) the conduct has the purpose or effect referred to in subsection (1)(b).

(3) A also harasses B if -

a) A or another person engages in unwanted conduct of a sexual nature or that is related to gender reassignment or sex,
b) the conduct has the purpose or effect referred to in subsection (1)(b), and
c) because of B's rejection of or submission to the conduct, A treats B less favourably than A would treat B if B had not rejected or submitted to the conduct.

(4) In deciding whether conduct has the effect referred to in subsection (1)(b), each of the following must be taken into account -

a) the perception of B;
b) the other circumstances of the case;
c) whether it is reasonable for the conduct to have that effect.

(5) The relevant protected characteristics are -

a) age;
b) disability;
c) gender reassignment;
d) race;
e) religion or belief;
f) sex;
g) sexual orientation.

[Note that marriage, civil partnership, pregnancy and maternity are not included. Harassment for any of these reasons would be actionable under the direct discrimination provisions.]

Disability Discrimination Act 1995, section 3B – Meaning of "Harassment:"

s.3B Meaning of harassment

(1) For the purposes of this Part, a person subjects a disabled person to harassment where, for a reason which relates to

the disabled person's disability, he engages in unwanted conduct which has the purpose or effect of -

a) violating the disabled person's dignity, or
b) creating an intimidating, hostile degrading, humiliating or offensive environment for him.

(2) Conduct shall be regarded as having the effect referred to in paragraph (a) or (b) of subsection (1) only if, having regard to all the circumstances, including in particular the perception of the disabled person, it should reasonably be considered as having that effect.

Equality Act 2010, section 27 – Victimisation:

s.27 Victimisation

(1) A person (A) victimises another person (B) if A subjects B to a detriment because:

a) B does a protected act, or
b) A believes that B has done, or may do, a protected act.

(2) Each of the following is a protected act –

a) bringing proceedings under this Act;
b) giving evidence or information in connection with proceedings under this Act;
c) doing any other thing for the purposes of or in connection with this Act;
d) making an allegation (whether or not express) that A or another person has contravened this Act;

(3) Giving false evidence or information, or making a false allegation, is not a protected act if the evidence or information is given, or the allegation is made, in bad faith.
(4) This section applies only where the person subjected to a detriment is an individual.
(5) The reference to contravening this Act includes a reference to committing a breach of the equality clause or rule.

PART 9

Disability Discrimination Act 1995, section 55 – Victimisation:

s.55 Victimisation

(1) For the purposes of Part 2 [work]... a person ("A") discriminates against another person ("B") if -

a) he treats B less favourably than he treats or would treat other persons whose circumstances are the same as B's; and
b) he does so for a reason mentioned in subsection (2).

(2) The reasons are that -

a) B has:

i) brought proceedings against A or any other person under this Act; or
ii) given evidence or information in connection with such proceedings brought by any person; or
iii) otherwise done anything under or by reference to this Act in relation to A or any other person; or
iv) alleged that A or any other person has (whether or not the allegation so states) contravened this Act; or

b) A believes or suspects that B has done or intends to do any of those things.

(3) Where B is a disabled person, or a person who has had a disability, the disability in question shall be disregarded in comparing his circumstances with those of any other person for the purposes of subsection 1(a)...

(4) Subsection (1) does not apply to treatment of a person because of an allegation made by him if the allegation was false and not made in good faith.

(5) In the case of an act which constitutes discrimination by virtue of this section, sections 4, 4B, 4D, 4G, 6A, 7A, 7C, 13, 14A, 14C, 15B, and 16A also apply to discrimination against a person who is not disabled.

Equality Act 2010, section 40 – Employee and Applicants: Harassment:

s.40 Employees and applicants: harassment

(1) An employer (A) must not, in relation to employment by A, harass a person (B) -

a) who is an employee of A's;
b) who has applied to A for employment.

(2) The circumstances in which A is to be treated as harassing B under subsection (1) include those where -

a) a third party harasses B in the course of B's employment, and
b) A failed to take such steps as would have been reasonably practicable to prevent the third party from doing so.

(3) Subsection (2) does not apply unless A knows that B has been harassed in the course of B's employment on at least two other occasions by a third party; and it does not matter whether the third party is the same or a different person on each occasion.

(4) A third party is a person other than -

a) A, or
b) an employee of A's.

[If the harassment is done by another employee, being a colleague of the person harassed, then s.26, Equality Act 2010 would apply.]

Disability Discrimination Act 1995, section 3B – Meaning of "Harassment:"

s.3B Meaning of "Harassment"

(1) For the purposes of this Part, a person subjects a disabled person to harassment where, for a reason which relates to the disabled person's disability, he engages in unwanted conduct which has the purpose or effect of -

a) violating the disabled person's dignity, or
b) creating an intimidating, hostile, degrading, humiliating or offensive environment for him.

(2) Conduct shall be regarded as having the effect referred to in paragraph (a) or (b) of subsection (1) only if, having regard to all the circumstances, including in particular the perception of the disabled person, it should reasonably be considered as having that effect.

Equality Act 2010 – Occupational Requirement Defence:

Schedule 9, Part 1, section 1 – Occupational Requirement Defence

Paragraph 1 General

(1) A person (A) does not contravene a provision mentioned in sub-paragraph (2) by applying in relation to work a requirement to have a particular protected characteristic, if A shows that, having regard to the nature or context of the work -

a) it is an occupational requirement,
b) the application of the requirement is a proportionate means of achieving a legitimate aim, and
c) the person to whom A applies the requirement does not meet it (or A has reasonable grounds for not being satisfied that the person meets it).

(3) The references in sub-paragraph (1) to a requirement to have a protected characteristic are to be read -

a) in the case of gender reassignment, as references to a requirement not to be a transsexual person (and section 7(3) is accordingly to be ignored);
b) in the case of marriage and civil partnership, as references to a requirement not to be married or a civil partner (and section 8(2) is accordingly to be ignored).

(4) In the case of a requirement to be of a particular sex, sub-paragraph (1) has effect as if in paragraph (c), the words

from "(or" to the end were omitted.

[Note that:

(1) the new test under the Equality Act 2010 requires the application of the requirement to be a proportionate means of achieving a legitimate aim.

(2) The old test under previous legislation required the occupation requirement to be a 'genuine' and 'determining' occupational requirement.

(3) The new test applies to disability whereas the previous one did not.

(4) Employers may provide childcare facilities to children of a particular age (this provision is designed to protect employers from associative age discrimination).

(5) The reference to specific occupations (i.e. drama, entertainment and modelling) in the Sex Discrimination Act 1975 and the Race Relations Act 1976 are removed)].

Disabled employees and workers can obtain advice and help, including the possibility of direct financial and other support for employment case appeals, from the Disability Rights Commission - see: www.drc.gov.uk

****

EMPLOYMENT TRIBUNAL AWARDS

There is no statutory cap on compensation that is awarded to a claimant because he or she has been subjected to unlawful discrimination because of one or more protected characteristics he or she has or is perceived to have or someone with whom the claimant associates has or is perceived to have. The characteristics which are protected in law and for which compensation is awarded for unlawful discrimination are: age, disability, gender reassignment, marriage and civil partnership, pregnancy and maternity, race, religion or belief, sex or sexual orientation. In addition to compensation for loss of earnings, etcetera, where unlawful discrimination has been found to have occurred, an award of compensation may be made for injury to feelings. There is also no limit on compensatory awards where the employee was dismissed for carrying out health and safety activities (s.100, ERA 1996); for making a protected disclosure (s.103A, ERA 1996); was selected for redundancy for one of the above reasons (ss.105(3),105(6)(a), Employment Rights Act 1996).

Statutory Instrument: **The Employment Rights (Increase of Limits) Order 2017; Statutory Instrument: 2017 No.175;**

Made: 18 February 2017;

Laid before Parliament: 22 February 2017;

Coming into force: **06 April 2017.**

Type of payments	Minimum from 06 April 2017 to 05 April 2018	Maximum from 06 April 2017 to 05 April 2018	Statutory reference
Limit on a week's pay (gross) for certain purposes (see 1)	No minimum	£489	Section 227(1), ERA 1996
Unfair dismissal basic award	No minimum	£14,670	Section 119, ERA 1996
Unfair dismissal compensatory award (see 2)	No minimum	£80,541 or gross annual pay, whichever is the smaller.	Section 124(1), ERA 1996
Unfair dismissal additional award (see 3)	Lower of 26 weeks' pay or £12,714	52 weeks' pay (up to £25,428)	Section 117(3), ERA 1996
Statutory redundancy payment	No minimum	£14,670	Sections 155, 162, 163,ERA 1996
Guarantee pay limit for a day's pay during short-time or temporary lay off	No minimum	£27 a day (subject to a maximum of 5 days or £135 in any three months)	Section 31(1), ERA 1996

Type of payments	Minimum from 06 April 2017 to 05 April 2018	Maximum from 06 April 2017 to 05 April 2018	Statutory reference
Basic award where the principal reason for dismissal is for trade union membership or activities (see 4)	£5,970 (minimum basic award for automatic unfair dismissal)	£14,670	Sections 152(1) & 153; TULR(C)A 1992
Basic award where the principal reason for dismissal is for carrying out activities as a health and safety representative	£5,970 (minimum basic award for automatic unfair dismissal)	£14,670	Section 100(1)(a) & (b), 101A(d), 102(1) or 103, ERA 1996
Basic award where the principal reason for dismissal is for carrying out duties as an occupational pension scheme trustee	£5,970 (minimum basic award for automatic unfair dismissal)	£14,670	Section 102(1), ERA 1996
Basic award where the principal reason for dismissal is for carrying out functions or activities as an employee representative or candidate	£5,970 (minimum basic award for automatic unfair dismissal)	£14,670	Section 103, ERA 1996

Type of payments	Minimum from 06 April 2017 to 05 April 2018	Maximum from 06 April 2017 to 05 April 2018	Statutory reference
Basic award where the principal reason for dismissal is based on working time grounds	£5,970 (minimum basic award for automatically unfair dismissal)	£14,670	Section 120, ERA 1996
Award for employees excluded or expelled from a trade union (EAT cases only)	£9,118	£95,211	Section 176(6A), TULRCA
Unjustifiable discipline by a trade union	no minimum	£95,211	Section 67(8), TULRCA
Unfair refusal of employment or services of employment agency on union membership grounds	No minimum	£80,541	Section 140(1)(a) and 2, TULR(C)A 1992
Consultation with union on training	No minimum	2 weeks' pay (up to £978)	Section 70C, TULR(C)A 1992
Breach of right to be accompanied (see 5)	No minimum	2 weeks' pay (up to £978)	Section 11(3), Employment Relations Act 1999

Type of payments	Minimum from 06 April 2017 to 05 April 2018	Maximum from 06 April 2017 to 05 April 2018	Statutory reference
Breach of contract cases heard in the employment tribunal	No minimum	£25,000	Employment Tribunal's Extension of Jurisdiction (England and Wales) Order 1994, Art. 10
Failure to inform or consult over collective redundancy	No minimum	90 days' actual pay (gross)	Section 188, TULR(C)A 1992
Failure to inform or consult over a TUPE transfer (see 6)	No minimum	13 weeks' actual pay (gross)	Regulation 16(3), TUPE Regs
Failure to give statement of employment particulars	2 weeks' pay (up to £978)	4 weeks' pay (up to £1,956)	Section 38, Employment Act 2002
Breach of flexible working regulations (see 7)	No minimum	8 weeks' pay (up to £3,912)	Regulation 7, Flexible Working (Eligibility, Complaints and Remedies) Regulations 2002
Blacklisting (see 8)	£5,000	£14,670	s.104F, ERA 1996

1 For the purposes of calculating the basic or additional award for unfair dismissal (and a redundancy payment), a 'week's pay' is limited to a statutory maximum of £489 where the effective date of dismissal falls on or after 06 April 2017. (Prior to 06 April 2014, the date when increases of employment tribunal awards took effect was 01 February each year).

2 Compensatory award: there is no limit on the amount of a week's pay for the purposes of calculating financial loss although the statutory maximum limit (for the year from 06 April 2017) is £80,541 or no more than the claimant's gross yearly pay, whichever sum is the lowest. This sum can be exceeded if an additional award is made. There is no limit on the compensatory award where the employee is dismissed unfairly because of unlawful discrimination; or is dismissed unfairly or selected for redundancy for carrying out health and safety activities or for making a protected disclosure. From 29 July 2013, the compensatory award for unfair dismissal is capped at the lower of one year's (gross) pay or £80,541. If the employee's annual earnings are more than £80,541, then the £80,541 statutory limit will apply.

3 An 'additional award' is made to an employee where the employer has failed to comply with a reinstatement or re-employment order made by an employment tribunal. The minimum and maximum amounts which can be ordered are calculated with reference to a week's pay, subject to statutory limits. An additional award is a penal and deterrent remedy.

4 TULR(C)A, 1992 is the Trade Union and Labour Relations (Consolidation) Act 1992.

5 s.11(3), ERA, 1999 is the Employment Relations Act 1999.

6 TUPE Regs. These are the Transfer of Undertakings (Protection of Employment) Regulations 2006, SI.2006/246.

7 FW(E,C&R) Regs.2002 are the Flexible Working (Eligibility, Complaints and Remedies) Regulations 2002, SI.2002/3236.

8 Blacklisting of employees and workers usually for trade union participation or as a means of victimising them is an automatically unfair statutory tort. These awards (minimum and maximum) were introduced in 2010 and are not up-rated by the compulsory annual RPI-linked increase under

s.34, Employment Relations Act 1999.

Increases are based on the increase in the retail prices index of 1.0% from September 2015 to September 2016. Statutory authority: section 34(2), Employment Relations Act 1999.

The increases apply where the event giving rise to the entitlement to compensation or other payments occurred on or after 06 April 2017. Note that the date for the annual index-linked increase in the compensatory award changed from 01 February to 06 April each year starting from 2014: s.22, Enterprise and Regulatory Reform Act 2013. The Secretary of State now has the discretionary power to reduce the cap on the compensatory award, e.g. from the year's maximum of (from 06 April 2017) £80,541 to the lower of a year's earnings or the national annual median wage and has exercised that power in that the cap on the compensatory award is reduced as from 29 July 2013: s.15, Enterprise and Regulatory Reform Act 2013. See the Progress on Reform document of March 2013 issued by the Department for Business, Innovation and Skills which indicated that the BIS intended to implement the one-year cap initially (but was silent on the median wage cap). From 06 April 2017, if the employee's annual earnings are more than £80,541, then the £80,541 cap will apply.

Calculation dates and limits – how to calculate different claims based on weekly pay, limits and the calculation dates:

Some heads of loss, such as the Basic Award, must have a week's pay calculated according to ss.220-227 of ERA 1996. In some cases the weekly pay is capped (it is capped at £489 for the year from 06 April 2017) and in other cases different limits apply. It can be difficult to remember whether or not the definition of a week's pay applies and, if so, whether there is any limit.

In addition, it is important to calculate the weekly pay as at a particular date (called the calculation date). The table below: (i) lists all the claims to which ss.220-227 apply; (ii) the calculation date; (iii) and whether a weekly limit is applicable. It can be assumed that other claims or heads of loss, such as the compensatory award, are not subject to these provisions.

Claim	Calculation date	Limit on week's pay
Additional award.	Date on which employee is given notice or the 'Effective Date of Termination' (EDT).	£489.
Basic Award.	If the employee is summarily dismissed or dismissed with less than the statutory notice, the calculation date is the date on which the employment ended. If the employee was dismissed with notice equal to or more than the statutory notice, the calculation date is found by subtracting the statutory notice period from the actual notice given. This means that if statutory notice is given, the calculation date is the date that notice was given. For example, if statutory notice is 3 weeks and actual notice given is 4 weeks, the calculation date is the day after the end of the first week of notice.	£489.
Guarantee pay.	The day when the guarantee pay is due.	No limit, but see separate limits.
Insolvency.	For arrears of pay and holiday, the date on which the employer became insolvent; for the basic award the latest of: (i) the date on which the employer became insolvent; (ii) the date of the termination of the employee's employment; and, (iii) the date on which the award was made; and in relation to any other debt	£489.

Claim	Calculation date	Limit on week's pay
	whichever is the later of (i) the date on which the employer became insolvent; and, (ii) the date of the termination of the employee's employment.	
Protective award.	The date on which the protective award was made or, in the case of an employee who was dismissed before the date on which the protective award was made, the calculation date for the purpose of computing the amount of a redundancy payment.	No limit.
Remuneration while suspended on medical grounds.	The day before suspension began.	No limit.
Right for union member not to be unjustifiably disciplined/expelled and blacklisting claims.	Date the application was made, although the statute does not make this clear.	£489 for the basic award element.
Time off to look for work or arrange training after being dismissed for the reason of redundancy.	The day on which the employer's notice was given.	Actual gross weekly pay is used but limited to 40% of a week's pay.
Time off for antenatal care.	Day of ante-natal appointment.	No limit.
Time off for employee representatives (including ICE and	Date on which time off was taken or should have been permitted.	No limit except for study or training

Claim	Calculation date	Limit on week's pay
OPPS); Pension trustees; Union duties; Activities and union learning reps; Study or training; Young person for study or training; Members of a European Works Council.		where the limit is £489. Note: not young person study or training).
TUPE claims.	In the case of an employee who is dismissed by reason of redundancy, the date which is the calculation date for the purposes of any entitlement of his to a redundancy payment; in the case of an employee who is dismissed for any other reason, the effective date of termination; in any other case, the date of the relevant transfer.	No limit.
Right to be accompanied at a disciplinary or grievance meeting.	Date of dismissal/Effective Date of Termination or if no dismissal the date of the hearing.	£489
Right to request flexible working.	Date on which the application was made.	£489
Written reasons for dismissal.	Date notice was given or if no notice, the Effective Date of Termination.	No limit.
Written statement of particulars.	If the employee was employed by the employer on the date the proceedings were begun, that date. If he was not, the effective date of termination.	£489

Claim	Calculation date	Limit on week's pay
Paid annual leave under the Working Time Regulations.	Payment based on a normal week's pay on the first day of the period of leave in question.	No limit.
Redundancy payments.	Depends on the circumstances. The relevant date as defined by sections 145 or 153 of the Employment Rights Act 1996.	Statutory redundancy weekly limit is £489.

INSOLVENCY

Type of payment	Maximum from 06 April 2015	Statutory reference
Insolvency: limit on recoverable debts, calculated using the limit on a week's pay being (for the year from 06 April 2017) £489.	Arrears of pay: 8 weeks' pay, up to £3,912 Statutory notice pay: 12 weeks' pay, up to £5,868 Holiday pay: 6 weeks' pay, up to £2,934 Basic award or statutory redundancy pay: £14,670	ss.184(1)(a) and 186, ERA 1996 ss.184(1)(b) and 186, ERA 1996 ss.184(1)(c) and 186, ERA 1996 ss.119-122, 162, ERA 1996

FAMILIES AND PREGNANCY

The rates from 05 April 2015 were prescribed by the Welfare Benefits Up-rating Order 2015, SI.2015/30. Although working benefits are subject to a 4-year freeze from 2015 to 2019/2020 (announced in the summer Budget 08 July 2015), maternity pay and disability benefits are excluded from the freeze.

Social Security Benefit and Pension Up-rating 2017-18

The Parliamentary Under Secretary of State for Welfare Delivery, Caroline Nokes MP, made the following Written Statement in the House of Commons on 28 November 2016.

'Today I am announcing the proposed social security benefit and pension rates for 2017-18. I have attached the table of rates to this statement and I will place a copy of the proposed benefit and pension rates 2017-18 in the House library. The annual up-rating of benefits will take place for state pensions and most other benefits in the first full week of the tax year. In 2017, this will be the week beginning 10 April. A corresponding provision will be made in Northern Ireland.

The annual up-rating process takes into account a variety of measures:

- The basic and new State Pension will be increased by the Government's 'triple lock' manifesto commitment, meaning that they will be up-rated in line with the highest of prices, earnings or 2.5%.
- The Pension Credit Standard Minimum Guarantee will be up-rated in line with the annual rise in earnings, as reflected in Average Weekly Earnings (AWE).

Benefits linked to the additional costs of disability, and for carers, are increased by the annual rise in prices, as reflected in the Consumer Price Index (CPI). A number of other elements – including Non-Dependant Deductions (NDDs) – will also be up-rated in line with prices. The majority of working-age benefits have been frozen at their 2015-16 levels for four years under the Welfare Reform and Work Act 2016.

The list of proposed benefit and pension rates also includes a change to the Carer's Allowance Earnings Rule, which will be increased for 2017-18 from £110 to £116 a week.'

Type of payments	**From 02 April 2017 - 01 April 2018**	**Maximum period**	**Statutory reference**
Statutory maternity pay (SMP) (earnings-related rate)	90% of employee's average weekly gross pay	Six weeks	Section 166(1)(a), Social Security Contributions and Benefits Act 1992 (SSCBA 1992)
Statutory maternity pay (prescribed rate).	£140.98 a week or 90% of average gross weekly earnings, whichever is the lower	20 weeks, or 33 weeks for those whose expected week of childbirth (EWC) falls on or after 1 April 2007	Reg.6, Statutory Maternity Pay (General) Regs.1986.
Maternity allowance (For those either low-paid or self-employed.)	£140.98 a week or 90% of average gross weekly earnings, whichever is the lower	26 weeks, or 39 weeks for those whose EWC falls on or after 1 April 2007	Schedule 4, s.35A, SSCBA 1992
Statutory paternity pay (SPP)	£140.98 a week or 90% of average gross weekly earnings, whichever is lower	Two weeks	Section 171ZE, SSCBA 1992

Type of payments	**From 02 April 2017 - 01 April 2018**	**Maximum period**	**Statutory reference**
Additional Statutory Paternity Pay (Additional paternity leave and pay will remain in place for parents of children with an EWC before 05 April 2015, and for children placed for adoption before that date, thus additional paternity leave and pay will remain until mid-April 2016)	£140.98 or 90% of average gross weekly earnings whichever is lower	26 weeks' additional paternity pay (that comes after 2 weeks of ordinary paternity pay.)	Additional Paternity Leave Regulations 2010; Work and Family Act 2006; 125, Children and Families Act 2014.
Shared parental pay. (This replaces Additional Statutory Paternity Pay from 05 April 2015.)	£140.98 or 90% of the normal weekly earnings of the person claiming ShPP	39 weeks, less any weeks spent by the child's mother or adopter in receipt of SMP, MA or SAP	The Statutory Shared Parental Pay (General) Regulations 2014, SI.2014/3051.
Statutory adoption pay	90% of employee's average gross weekly pay.	For 6 weeks	Section 124, Children and Families Act 2014

Type of payments	From 02 April 2017 - 01 April 2018	Maximum period	Statutory reference
Statutory adoption pay (prescribed rate). Applies where the adoption pay period begins on or after 05 April 2015.	£140.98 a week or 90% of average gross weekly earnings, whichever is the lower.	For remaining 33 weeks from 05 April 2015.	Section 171ZN, SSCBA 1992. Welfare Benefits Up-rating Order 2015, SI.2015/30.

STATUTORY SICK PAY

Weekly rates	Sick days on or after 06 April 2017 - 05 April 2018	Maximum period	Statutory reference
Statutory sick pay (standard rate).	£89.35 a week.	28 weeks in any period of incapacity for work (PIW) or any linked series of PIWs spanning a maximum of three years.	s.157, Social Security Contributions and Benefits Act 1992.

INCAPACITY/EMPLOYMENT AND SUPPORT ALLOWANCE;

INCOME SUPPORT & INCOME-BASED JOBSEEKER'S ALLOWANCE;

PERSONAL ALLOWANCES.

Since October 2008, there have been no new claims for Incapacity Benefit. Instead, new claimants who cannot work due to ill-health or disability are able to claim Employment and Support Allowance (ESA). This benefit was previously increased yearly by the higher index of inflation. However, from 2011, the Government announced that the ESA will be increased in line with the lower inflation index that is the Consumer Prices Index.

Type	From 10 April 2017
Single person 25 or over	£73.10
Single person under 25	£57.90
Single person under 18	£57.90
Lone parent 18 or over	£73.10
Lone parent under 18	£57.90
Couple, both under 18	£57.90
Couple, both under 18 with a child	£87.50
Couple, both under 18 (main phase)	£73.10
Couple, both under 18 with a child (main phase)	£114.85
Couple, one 18+, one under 18 (conditions apply)	£114.85
Couple where both are 18+	£114.85
Claimant under 25, partner under 18	£57.90
Claimant 25+, partner under 18	£73.10
Claimant (main phase), partner under 18	£73.10
Premiums, enhanced disability: single person	£15.90
Premiums, enhanced disability: couple	£22.85
Severe disability: single person	£62.45
Severe disability: couple (lower rate)	£62.45
Severe disability: couple (higher rate)	£124.90

UNIVERSAL CREDIT

In 2013, Universal Credit began to replace a range of means-tested benefits and tax credits for working-age families (income-based Jobseeker's Allowance, income-related Employment and Support Allowance, Income Support, Child and Working Tax Credits, Housing Benefit). Universal Credit is means-tested and payable to both in-work and out-of-work recipients. The main regulations for Universal Credit came into force on 29 April 2013 (Universal Credit Regulations, SI.2013/376.) It was intended that this scheme would be fully in effect from early 2015 onwards.

Universal Credit awards consist of the following elements:

- Standard Allowance: based on the personal allowances in JSA/ESA/Income Support;
- Child Element: set at the same level as Child Tax Credit family and child elements;
- Housing cost element: the equivalent of Housing Benefit;
- Childcare cost element: the equivalent of Working Tax Credit childcare element;
- Work Allowance: for those with earnings or other income, a single taper applies such that as earnings rise, Universal Credit is withdrawn at a constant rate of 65 pence for each Pound of net earnings above the family's monthly earnings disregard (or 'work allowance.')

Note that although Work Allowances are set to increase in line with CPI inflation, Work Allowances are being kept frozen at their initial 2013-14 cash levels until 2017-18 inclusive.

UNIVERSAL CREDIT - RATES

Standard allowances	10 April 2017
Single, over 25+	£317.82 (monthly)
Single, under 25	£251.77 (monthly)
Couple, one or both aged 25+	£498.89 (monthly)
Couple, both under 25	£395.20 (monthly)
Child element, first child	£277.08 (monthly)
Second/subsequent child	£231.67 (monthly)
Disabled child addition, lower rate addition	£126.11 (monthly)
Disabled child addition, higher rate addition	£372.30 (monthly)
Limited capability for work element	£126.11 (monthly)
Limited capability for work and work-related activity	£318.76 (monthly)
Carer element	£151.89 (monthly)
Childcare costs element	
Maximum for one child	£646.35 (monthly)
Maximum for two or more children	£1108.04 (monthly)

INCAPACITY BENEFIT

Type	From 10 April 2017
Short-term Incapacity Benefit (under state pension age)	
Lower rate	£80.25
Higher rate	£95.00
Short-term Incapacity Benefit (over state pension age)	
Lower rate	£102.10
Higher rate	£106.40

PERSONAL INDEPENDENCE PAYMENT

Type	From 10 April 2017
Daily living component standard rate	£55.65
Enhanced rate	£83.10
Mobility component standard rate	£22.00
Enhanced rate	£58.00

SEVERE DISABLEMENT ALLOWANCE

Type	From 10 April 2017
Severe disablement allowance, basic rate	£75.40
Higher rate (age-related addition)	£11.25
Middle rate	£6.25
Lower rate	£6.25

HOUSING BENEFIT –PERSONAL ALLOWANCES

Type	From 10 April 2017
Personal allowances	
Single claimant 25+	£73.10
Single claimant under 25	£57.90
Entitlement to main phase ESA	£73.10
Lone parent 18+	£73.10
Lone parent under 18	£57.90
Lone parent, entitlement to main phase ESA	£73.10
Couple, one or both 18+	£114.85
Couple, both under 18	£87.50
Dependent children	£66.90

NATIONAL MINIMUM WAGE

NATIONAL LIVING WAGE

In his summer Budget of 08 July 2015, the then Chancellor of the Exchequor, George Osborne, MP., announced that from the start of the tax and benefit year from April 2016, all employers will have to pay their workers who are aged over 25 a new living wage of no less than £7.20 an hour. He said that this will rise to £9 an hour by 2020. Effectively, the 'new living wage' is a renamed national minimum wage for workers and employees who are aged 25 and above.

The National Minimum Wage (Amendment) Regulations 2016 - in force on 01 April 2016.

These are the five age-related minimum hourly rates from 01 April 2017:

age 25+ £7.50 per hour (the National Living Wage)
age 21-24 £7.05 per hour
age 18-20 £5.60 per hour
age 16-17 £4.05 per hour
apprentices £3.50 per hour.
accommodation offset (maximum daily allowance deduction from NMW) £6.40.

UNITED KINGDOM STATE PENSION

For the year, 2012/13, there was an increase in the basic State Retirement Pension of 5.20% in line with the September 2011 Retail Prices Index resulting in the single rate rising by £5.30 per week and the married rate by £7.20 per week. The single weekly pension rate increased from £102.15 to £107.45 and the couple rate from £163.35 to £171.85. For the year 2013/14, increases were based on an inflation rate of 2.2%. For 2015-16 up-rating, the basic state pension increased by 2.5%, that was above both the inflation rate of earnings or CPI price inflation. Because of the triple lock, the State retirement pension was increased by 2.5%. However, the UK State retirement pension is still one of the lowest of the leading industrial nations. In the Republic of Ireland, for example, the State retirement pension is £190 per week.

PENSION CREDIT MINIMUM GUARANTEE

From April 2013, the weekly rate for Pension Credit Minimum Guarantee was £145.40 (single person) and £222.05 (couple). Pensioners aged 80 and over are awarded an age-related Addition Supplement of 25 pence a week. From 06 April 2014, the Pension Credit Minimum Guarantee was £148.35 (single person) and £226.50 (couple). From 06 April 2015, the Pension Credit Minimum Guarantee was £151.20 (single person) and £230.85 (couple) an increase that equates to 1.9%. From 11 April 2016, the weekly rate for Pension Credit Minimum Guarantee was £155.60 (single person) and £237.55 (couple). From 10 April 2017, the weekly rate for Pension Credit Minimum Guarantee is £159.35 (single person) and £243.25 (couple).

STATE RETIREMENT PENSION WEEKLY RATE

Basic State Pension	10 April 2017 - 08 April 2018	11 April 2016	06 April 2015/16	2014/15
Single person	£122.30	£119.30	£115.95	£113.10
Married couple	£195.60	£190.80	£185.45	£180.90

State pension 2017-2018

category A or B £122.30 (single person);
category B (lower) spouse or civil partner's insurance £73.30;
category C or D - non-contributory £73.30.

Note that there is not, in actual fact, a State retirement pension for a married couple in the sense that a single person is entitled to one rate and a married couple to a different rate that is less than two single pensions. Both partners in a marriage may each be entitled in their own right to the single rate. Broadly speaking, the Basic State Pension (Category A pension, was £107.45 in 2012/13) is that for which people qualify on the basis of their own contribution record and can claim from State Pension Age. Therefore, if each spouse individually qualifies for the Category A pension, then they will both receive the full amount. The Category B pension payable to some married men and women, widows and widowers was £64.40 a week in 2012/13. Married individuals with insufficient contribution records to qualify for a full Basic State Pension in their own right may qualify for a Category B pension based on their spouse's contributions. This is paid at 60% of the BSP (£66.00 in 2013/14). This means that the rate for a married couple who fall into the latter Category B (lower or Category C or D non-contributory) for 2013-2014 is £176.15. This is made up of the single rate of the State Pension (Category A or B) of £110.15 plus 60% of that rate being £66.00 thereby giving a total amount for a married couple of £176.15 for the year April 2013-2014.

Links:

DWP table for all benefits before and after the 2017 up-rating –

https://www.gov.uk/government/uploads/system/uploads/attachment_data /file/572844/proposed-benefit-and-pensions-rates-2017-to-2018.pdf

INDEX

LINKS

Directgov A-Z of Central Government
http://www.direct.gov.uk/en/Dl1/Directories/A-ZOfCentralGovernment/index.htm

Some Departments and Agencies involved with Employment:

ACAS (Advisory, Conciliation and Arbitration Service)
http://www.acas.org.uk

ACAS: for free employment law advice – telephone 0845-7474747.

Appeals Service
http://www.appeals-service.gov.uk

Attorney General's Office
http://www.attorneygeneral.gov.uk

Department for Business, Innovation and Skills (BIS) **and the Department for Innovation, Universities and Skills** (DIUS)
http://www.bis.gov.uk

Courts Service
http://www.hmcourts-service.gov.uk/

Department for Work and Pensions (DWP)
http://www.dwp.gov.uk

Disability Rights Commission
http://www.equalityhumanrights.com

Employment Tribunals
http://www.employmenttribunals.gov.uk

Equality and Human Rights Commission
http://www.equalityhumanrights.com
Equality and Human Rights Commission: telephone 0845-6046610.

Department for Work and Pensions
http://www.dwp.gov.uk

Other useful links:

The Law Society of England and Wales
http://www.lawsociety.org.uk/home.law

The Law Society of Scotland
http://www.lawscot.org.uk/

The Law Society of Northern Ireland
http://www.lawsoc-ni.org/

Helplines
A helpline that combines five previous helplines was set up by the government in September 2009 to answer queries and give advice about: the National Minimum Wage; the Agricultural Minimum Wage; and the Working Time Regulations: **telephone 0800-917-2368**.

Whistleblowers:
The charity 'Public Concern at Work' has set up a national helpline for workers to report fraud, abuse or unfair practices in their workplaces: **telephone 020-7404-6609**.

Mediation:
A National Mediation local rate telephone helpline was launched in March 2005 to help settle small claims (£50,000 maximum limit) fees from £250 to £750: **telephone: 0845-6030809**.

Business Link for employers:
http://www.businesslink.gov.uk

NOTES

Printed in Dunstable, United Kingdom

77227110R00154